PRIMARY EDUCATION: A SOURCEBOOK FOR TEACHERS

edited by
Alan Cohen
Durham University
and
Louis Cohen
Loughborough University of Technology

P·C·P

Paul Chapman
Publishing Ltd

First published 1986
by Harper & Row Ltd, London

Reprinted 1988
by Paul Chapman Publishing Ltd
London

British Library Cataloguing in Publication Data

Primary education: A sourcebook for teachers.
  1. Education, Elementary—Great Britain
  I. Cohen, Alan   II. Cohen, Louis
  372.941   LA633

  ISBN 1 85396 016 0

Typeset by Inforum Ltd, Portsmouth
Printed and bound by Butler & Tanner Ltd, Frome and
London

CONTENTS

Introduction: Rhetoric or reality?   vii
Section 1   DEVELOPMENTS IN PRIMARY EDUCATION   1
  1 The primary school revolution: myth or reality?
     B. Simon   2
  2 Primary education: the multicultural context
     B. Woodroffe   22

Section 2   CHILD GROWTH AND DEVELOPMENT IN
THE PRIMARY YEARS   31
  3 Individuality and its origins: patterns of growth in the early
     years of childhood: growth patterns of the middle years
     J. Brierley   32
  4 Sex role differentiation in social development
     C. Hutt   47

Section 3   CHILDHOOD THINKING AND LEARNING IN
THE PRIMARY YEARS   55
  5 Introduction to Piaget's theory: a psychological critique
     G. Brown and C. Desforges   56
     and
     Piaget's research into the minds of children
     K. Sylva and I. Lunt   57
  6 Why children find school learning difficult
     M. Donaldson   82

Section 4   ORGANIZATION IN PRIMARY SCHOOLS   91
  7 Open plan primary schools: rhetoric and reality
     M. Brogden   92
  8 Primary school organization: some rhetoric and some reason
     K. Ridley and D. Trembath   107

Section 5   CLASSROOM PRACTICE IN PRIMARY SCHOOLS   117
  9 Junior school teachers: their methods and practices
     J. Barker-Lunn   118
 10 From *The quality of pupil learning experiences*
     N. Bennett, C. Desforges, A. Cockburn and B. Wilkinson   135

Section 6   THE PRIMARY SCHOOL CURRICULUM:
PROBLEMS AND PERSPECTIVES   141
11   The curriculum and curriculum change
     D. Lawton   142
12   Learning how to learn and learning by discovery
     R.F. Dearden   155

Section 7   THE PRIMARY SCHOOL CURRICULUM:
POLICY STATEMENTS   171
13   The curriculum in primary schools
     Schools Council   172
14   The curriculum
     Department of Education and Science   179

Section 8   THE PRIMARY SCHOOL CURRICULUM IN
ACTION   187
15   Personal and social development
     Schools Council   188
16   The place of mathematics in primary schools: planning
     the mathematics programme
     Department of Education and Science   203
17   How can children's progress in science be monitored,
     recorded and evaluated?
     B. Davis   218
18   The growth of language and reading
     D.M.R. Hutchcroft   232
19   Aesthetic Development
     Assessment of Performance Unit   250
20   Assessing children with learning difficulties
     G. Lowden   260
21   Towards more effective record-keeping
     W.R. Porter   272
22   The primary school and the microcomputer: some policy
     issues
     R. Garland   284
23   The integration of children with special educational needs
     into ordinary schools
     K. Pocklington   293
Bibliography   301
Index   311

Introduction • Rhetoric or reality?

During the period after 1950 educational growth in this country increased at a pace hitherto unknown since the Education Act of 1870. One of the most pervasive demands from millions of parents in the immediate post-war years was to have more and better education for their children than they themselves had received. In consequence, more schools were built, more teachers trained and more children enrolled in classes. Concomitant claims were made for better resources and equipment, new technology products and up-to-date textbooks. These self-same requirements not only raised the costs of education but 'established a pattern of expectation, the political and social costs of which are likely to be among the most troublesome features of the slower growth and, in some respects, actual decline that will characterise the eighties' (Taylor 1981, p. 17. See also Briault 1982, pp. 209–19).

A considerable proportion of the capital expenditure on education during this expansionist period was directed towards the primary sector with tenfold increases in money terms occurring between 1960 and 1974 and total expenditure on primary education increasing in real terms by 54 per cent between 1964 and 1974 (Richards 1982, p.8). Growing interest in primary education was shown in three-year inquiries by the Central Advisory Council for Education culminating in the Plowden Report in 1967 (CACE 1967), rapid expansion in teacher training and nursery education, and massive building programmes initiated during the period. A golden age of primary education seemed imminent. It proved to be a false dawn. Present-day contractions in terms of falling rolls,[1] cuts in government expenditure[2] and decline in political, public and professional expectations of schooling[3] have to be examined against a backcloth of demographic, economic and political changes that have taken place in this country since the heady days of the early 70s.

The period following the publication of the Plowden Report was marked by a gathering force of virulent criticism of child-centred ideology and progressive approaches to teaching and learning. Inevitably the primary curriculum itself became an area of controversy as demands increased for the investigation of its range, structure, appropriateness, consistency and continuity. Richards (1982, p. 12; 1979, pp. 39–55) has identified four major ideologies as areas of conflict:[4]

(1) *liberal romanticism* — which celebrates the supremacy of the child in the teaching-learning situation and regards the curriculum as the sum total of learning experiences both offered to them and created by them as they interact with their surroundings.

(2) *educational conservatism* — which stresses the importance of continuity with the past and the curriculum as the repository of worthwhile cultural elements which need transmitting from one generation to another.

(3) *liberal pragmatism* — which views the curriculum as a set of learning experiences largely but not entirely structured by the teacher, but respecting to some degree both the individuality of the child and the importance of cultural transmission.

(4) *social democracy* — which views the curriculum as a means of realizing social justice and focuses around the social experience of pupils (Midwinter 1972).

Until the mid-1970s, when criticism and controversy over primary pedagogy and curriculum reached a peak, no detailed investigation of either teaching methods (*formal* or *progressive*) or curriculum (*range, structure, appropriateness, consistency, continuity*) had been attempted. There was neither evidence of their extent nor their effectiveness in terms of pupil performance. The continuing controversy was conducted on neither a sound conceptual nor an empirical base. By 1976, however, several attempts were under way to examine aspects of pedagogical and curriculum dissension more rigorously.[5] Ensuing evidence has served to illuminate the gulf that exists in primary education between rhetoric and reality.

The Plowden Report (1967) had claimed to recognize a number of quickening trends leading to more progressive approaches. Many thousands of teachers hailed the Report as an inspirational document which gave the stamp of approval to their progressive aspirations. Yet the evidence is that Plowden judged only 10 per cent of primary schools to be *good* or even *outstanding*, and two-thirds of them to be *adequate, mediocre* or *bad* (Simon 1981). It might be expected that ten years later, given the purported trends towards more progressive approaches, a considerable change in these proportions would be identified. The HMI Primary Survey (1978a) found no such evidence. Alexander (1984, p. 11) comments that the Primary Survey 'was one of several rather sobering empirical studies . . . which contribute to a now fairly comprehensive picture of primary practice as occasionally exciting, usually competent in the so-called "basics" at least, but not infrequently mediocre or inadequate', and further, that the basics have received consistently high priority — often to the detriment of the rest of the curriculum.[6]

The gulf between rhetoric and reality, between the ways in which primary ideology and primary professional practice contradict each other has been a common theme in several research studies. Their evidence highlights the paradox of progressive rhetoric voiced across practically the whole range of primary organization and practice, and the actuality of day-to-day events in most primary classrooms. Both the HMI Primary Survey (1978) and the ORACLE studies of Galton and his associates (Galton and Simon 1980), for example, demonstrate that progressive commitment to informality, discovery, exploration, group work and individualization is not strongly reflected in the ways in which teachers work.[7] Similarly, with regard to primary school organization, Barker-Lunn, surveying 732 junior schools involving some 5,000 third and fourth year children found that although organizationally streamed classes (streaming by ability) had more or less disappeared, children were none the less regrouped by ability or attainment for those parts of the curriculum which teachers regarded as being both sequential and important (Barker Lunn 1982, pp. 250–61). Such selective teaching groups, she asserted, could be described as a refined form of streaming.

Barker-Lunn's most recent survey (see Reading 9 in this volume) suggests that the overall picture is remarkably similar to that in 1965 when the NFER conducted comparable research. She doubts that in the intervening years there ever was a large scale swing away from the traditional curriculum and traditional methods.

Alexander (1984, p. 14) writes that the picture that emerges is of 'routine teaching dominated by the basics coupled with a progressive rhetoric which argues strenuously that primary education is so much more than this'.

It is certainly the case that present-day rhetoric and reality are influenced by a deep-rooted elementary school tradition from which today's schools have emerged, a tradition which, with typical nineteenth-century administrative thoroughness and efficiency, produced a pedagogical system of class teaching allied to a curriculum geared largely to a utilitarian preoccupation with the skills of literacy and numeracy — the 'basics'. The tradition has persisted as shown by the high priority accorded to the basic skills of reading, writing and mathematics in our schools today and, in contrast, the relatively low precedence given to creative and expressive arts, social and environmental studies, moral and religious education and science. Nor is this preoccupation with the basics confined to primary teachers. The HMI Primary Survey (1978a) made its assessment of children's progress solely on the basis of tests in reading and mathematics (see Alexander, 1984, chapters 1 and 3). Clearly, as Alexander wryly comments, 'if one wishes to evaluate the quality of the education provided for children between the ages of five and eleven one should use test score gains in reading, written English and mathematics'! (Op.cit. p. 62.)

Our discussion has been largely concerned with an examination of what is seen as the most pervasive and continuing paradox in primary education — that of discrepancies which surface at every level of examination between the claims that are made for child-centredness and the 'whole' curriculum, and the manifest qualitative inconsistencies that appear to abound in *practice*. Yet this is not to deny that considerable change *has* taken place in primary schools since Plowden. It is nevertheless somewhat of a sad commentary that a number of innovations and developments have had patchy and uneven impact on the primary school curriculum. This is clearly seen when contrasting curriculum areas which have an established, historically high priority — mathematics for example — with the aesthetic areas of the curriculum.[8] It suggests that empirical evidence on primary practice which has been accumulating during recent years confirms three related hypotheses posited by Alexander (op. cit. p. 73).

What teachers do not adequately understand they are unlikely to teach well.
What teachers do not value they are unlikely to teach well.
What teachers do not understand they are unlikely to value.

To no small extent, the selection of readings in this volume is influenced by the need to examine how fundamental claims and assumptions which underpin the arguments of child-centred ideology are translated into classroom practice and to consider their effects upon children's learning.

Section 1 contains two papers that relate directly to current changes and developments in primary education in Britain. The central focus of Simon's scholarly account of the emergence of contemporary primary schools is his questioning of the tag of progressivism with which they are commonly labelled. Woodroffe highlights the multicultural nature of contemporary society and points to the need for a shift in policies and practices that will permeate the whole of the primary curriculum.

Section 2 consists of two readings in the field of Child Growth and Development. Brierley's contribution outlines landmarks in human growth from birth to adolescence and draws attention to the uniqueness of the individual. Sex roles and sex stereotypes are the specific concern of Hutt's paper, which traces the process of gender identification.

Section 3. The seminal influence of Piaget on our understanding of childhood thinking guides the selection of papers contained in this section of the Sourcebook. Brown and Desforges' short introduction to Piaget's ideas sets the scene for the lucid account of cognitive development in the growing child by Sylva and Lunt. Donaldson's discussion of childhood language and thinking and her report of recent experiments echo the point made in the introductory paper that the conception of a problem necessarily informs the choice of data selected as pertinent to its resolution.

Section 4 examines aspects of organizational practice in primary schools. Brogden outlines the rationale of the open plan school, describing the organizational strategies that underpin it and questioning the *rhetoric* which links open plan with child-centred practices. Ridley and Trembath concern themselves with the quality of the school environment and its crucial importance to the process of significant learning. They question the nature of skills which many children are expected to acquire, the priority which is granted to them and the use to which they are put.

The intention of *Section 5* is to present an account of current classroom practice. In the first of the two readings, Barker-Lunn describes teaching methods as revealed in her recent survey of some 2,500 primary teachers. In the second article, Bennett and his associates explore classroom learning in terms of the matching of task allocation with pupil attainment.

Section 6 is the first of three parts of the Sourcebook that focus in their entirety on the primary school curriculum. Lawton identifies two general issues that dominate current discussion about the curriculum — its *content* and its *control.* He shows how two different approaches to the curriculum, the *behavioural objectives* model and the *cultural analysis* model, underpin the broad issues of content and control. Dearden's closely argued paper is a systematic examination of 'learning how to learn' and 'learning by discovery'. Learning by discovery, Dearden insists, characteristically aims to engender intrinsic interest both in what is learned and in the process of learning it. At the same time, however, to the extent that the skills of learning how to learn have themselves to be taught, there is still a place for learning how to learn in 'the more traditional uncelebrated sense.'

Section 7 is concerned with two policy statements on the primary curriculum. Reading 13, from Schools Council Working Paper 75, provides an account of activities and skills that all children in primary schools need to engage in. At the same time, the document is concerned to identify necessary differences of programme in light of individual aptitudes and needs. Reading 14 reports the findings of a survey of primary schools carried out by Her Majesty's Inspectorate. *Inter alia*, it raises questions to do with the teaching of basic skills, the range of the curriculum, differences among children within a class, and the expectations that teachers have for many children in inner city schools.

The nine readings included in *Section 8* reflect the wide range of the primary curriculum. Working Paper 75 is concerned with children's personal and moral development. It contains examples of syllabuses of religious education from the Schools Council Religious Education in Primary Schools Project. The DES discussion document on Mathematics 5–11 sets out a coherent statement of the main objectives of mathematics teaching and offers advice on planning and assessing programmes of work. Davis's account of children's progress in science suggests what ought to be looked for in terms of attitudes and skills, and identifies scientific concepts that can be explored successfully at the primary stage of education. Hutchcroft's detailed discussion of language work in the primary years provides guidelines in the form of flowcharts for beginning reading with a new class and for selecting schemes in early phonic work. The APU document argues the case for objective assessment of artistic development, not least on the grounds that unless the student has learned the objective criteria of an art form he will be unable to develop his own creative potential. Lowden's paper on the assessment of children with learning difficulties focuses upon questions of *who, what* and *when*, in relation to assessment procedures and decisions. Porter provides a refreshingly down-to-earth account of the development of record keeping in his own primary school. In his discussion of the microcomputer, Garland argues that compared with other technological innovations that have been incorporated in the primary curriculum, microcomputers are qualitatively different in their enormous scope, their motivational potential, and their interactive nature. Finally, a timely contribution by Pocklington sets out essential requirements for the integration of children with special educational needs into ordinary schools and puts plainly before teachers just what these demands will mean for the day-to-day work of the classroom.

Notes

1. Within the period 1950–1975 the total school population grew rapidly, reaching some 9 million by 1977. By 1990 total enrolments will probably be not much more than 7 million. Primary totals reached 6.3 million in 1973. By 1987 they may very well be down to 4.5 million (W. Taylor 1981, p. 18).

2. For example, in 1976 a package of £6000 million public expenditure cuts was introduced. Capital expenditure for nursery education peaked at £46 million in 1975/76 and fell to less than £15 million in succeeding years. What did contract during this period was *planned* expenditure for the expansion of the education service (C. Richards 1982, p. 10).

3. In the mid 1970s politicians had become increasingly disillusioned with the proposition that economic growth could be stimulated by educational investment. Furthermore, many educationists were coming to realize the limitations of their influence on individual and social development and to appreciate that their belief that the extension of educational provision would produce socially equalizing effects and fulfil democratic ideals had not happened on anything like the scale they had originally envisaged (Alexander, 1984, pp. 13, 65).

4. Alexander (1984 p. 13) suggests that the uneven impact which the developmental, or child-centred tradition has enjoyed can be accounted for by the fact that it is but one of three to some extent competing traditions in primary education: the developmental (particularly strong in infant and first schools), the elementary (particularly in junior schools) and the secondary (subject) tradition with the arrival in middle schools of ex-secondary subject specialists. He notes that the latter produces a tension which is often reflected in the transition from *class* to *subject* teaching in the third or fourth year and that the situation may well be exacerbated by HMI's (DES 1983) recommendation that middle-school *subject* teaching should be strengthened and extended.

   For an account of how the current psychological emphasis in 'developmental' or 'child-centred' education overlays an earlier philosophical tradition, exemplified, for example, in the writings of Rousseau and Dewey, see G.M. Blenkin and A.V. Kelly *The Primary Curriculum*. London: Harper and Row 1981.

5. In 1976 Bennett's study of the relationship between 'informal' and 'formal' teaching styles and their supposed effects on pupil attainment was published: N. Bennet *Teaching Styles and Pupil Progress*. London: Open Books 1976. In 1974 a feasibility study was begun which resulted in the Department of Education and Science (1978) *Primary Education in England: A Survey by HM Inspectors of Schools*. London: HMSO. In 1975 the Bullock Report was published. Department of Education and Science (1975) *A Language for Life* (The Bullock Report) London: HMSO. It was not until the late 1970s that the APU became part of the educational scene, monitoring the performance of primary school children in mathematics, language and science.

   The DES announced the establishment of the Assessment of Performance Unit, designed to assess and monitor pupils' achievements in school, in 1974.

6. Examples of other studies include: Ashton et al. (1975); Sharp and Green (1975); Bennett (1976); King (1978); Bassey (1978); DES (1982).

7. Only one fifth of ORACLE's teachers (of junior school children) used a heavily individualized teaching approach.

8. The immediate impact for example of the Cockcroft Report, Department of Education and Science (1982), as compared with the relative indifference towards the publication of *The Arts in Schools: Principles, Practice and Provision*. London: Gulbenkian Foundation 1982.

Acknowledgement

We are grateful to the sources named at the beginning of each extract, for permission to reprint the material. *Topics for discussion* and *Suggestions for further reading* have been added by the editors.

SECTION ONE
DEVELOPMENTS IN PRIMARY EDUCATION

READING ONE • The primary school revolution: myth or reality?
B. Simon

I want to attempt a cool, historical appraisal of primary school developments in the 1960s. In particular to answer the question: was there a primary school revolution, and, if so, how do we assess it?

There is no doubt that some thought there was, that anarchy and disorder were becoming the rule, leading to chaos and dark night. Nor is there any doubt that, as what many call the 'educational backlash' got under way in the 1970s, the brunt of the attack fell for a time at least on the primary schools. This campaign, taken up and propagated by the mass media (including both the popular press and the minority press) reached a climax in October 1976 with *The Times's* notorious leader on the 'wild men of the classroom' (equating these with trade union disrupters) who must be brought to heel, implicitly labelling all primary school teachers in this way. The leader was sparked by the Tyndale affair, and was one of the features paving the way for Callaghan's Ruskin speech, which warned against 'modern methods' in the primary school.

We may first remind ourselves of the main stages in the build-up of this image of the primary school – as undergoing a 'revolution' where anything goes, all forms of activity are legitimate.

I

Black Paper I 'Fight for Education' was published in 1969. Generally it received a bad press and in particular was slammed by Ted Short, Secretary of State for Education, who referred to the authors as 'thugs'. Nevertheless it is now clear that this publication marked an important new phase in terms of a new type of populist educational ideology — having as its purpose

B. Simon, 'The Primary School Revolution: Myth or Reality?' in, B. Simon and J. Willcocks (Eds), *Research and Practice in the Primary School*. London: Routledge and Kegan Paul, 1981, pp. 7–25.

halting, and if possible turning back, those developments in the 1960s which tended to open up the system, rendering it more egalitarian and less hierarchic. Here the word 'revolution' makes its appearance. I quote from the Letter to MPs:

> Since the war revolutionary changes have taken place in English education — the introduction of free play methods in primary schools [this comes first — BS], comprehensive schemes, the expansion of higher education, the experimental courses at new universities . . .
> At primary school some teachers are taking to an extreme the belief that children must not be told anything, but must find out for themselves . . . at the post-eleven stage there is a strong impetus to abolish streaming, and the grammar school concepts of discipline and hard work are treated with contempt . . . the new fashionable anarchy flies in the face of human nature [*sic* — BS], for it holds that children and students will work from natural inclination rather than the desire for reward.

1969, of course, saw the climax of the movement of student unrest in universities and colleges, including the Hornsey College of Art affair where the students successfully took control of their own education for several months in the summer and autumn of 1968, radically changing its character (The Hornsey Affair, 1969). Black Paper I linked student unrest to the primary school, referring to an article by Timothy Raison, now Minister of State at the Home Office, but then editor of *New Society*, published in the *Evening Standard* earlier. The roots of student unrest, Raison is quoted as saying, are to be found as early as the primary school. Referring to the 'anarchistic beliefs' of the Hornsey students, Raison wrote: 'I sometimes wonder whether this philosophy . . . does not owe at least something to *the revolution in our primary schools*' (my italics — BS). So there the seed of the idea was planted. And of course Raison should know. He was, after all, a member of the Plowden Committee and a signatory to its report.

On Timothy Raison's hypothesis a few points may be made which may help to clear the air. If the student unrest or revolt of 1968–9 was partly due to the primary school 'revolution', that revolution must be dated back at least ten to fifteen years, that is, to 1958 and earlier, when the students at Hornsey and elsewhere would have been in primary schools being inducted into their anarchistic attitudes. The Black Paper I Letter to MPs in fact claims the 'introduction of free play methods' was one of the revolutionary changes that had taken place 'since the war' — that is, from 1945.

But this seems historically inaccurate. Of course it is the case that the Hadow reports of 1931 and 1933 (on the primary school and infant and nursery schools respectively) had both stressed a 'child-centred' approach with the famous phrase on 'activity and experience' central to each of them. Indeed Professor R.J.W. Selleck, has argued that a kind of watered-down progressivism had become the 'intellectual orthodoxy' among training college lecturers, HMIs, etc. by 1939 (Selleck 1972), but the reality, as opposed to the rhetoric, appears to have been rather different.

It is quite true that there was a move towards 'free activity', or modern methods, in the late 1940s, epitomized by M.V. Daniel's 'Activity in the Primary School' (1947), and this may have had a permanent impact on practice as Alec Ross argued in 1960 even if, as he says, 'the time was not a propitious one for experiment' (Ross 1960, p.33). But at that time the 11-plus examination was still the rule throughout the country, Leicestershire's reorganization was only just beginning, only 150 comprehensive schools were in existence; the move to abolish streaming in the primary schools was in its first stages. The students of 1968 were, in fact, the products of the streamed, divided, hierarchical system from which we only began to emerge in a significant way in the mid 1960s — products of the system which the Black Paper writers look back to with such cloying nostalgia. In *Inside the Primary School* (1967) Blackie, a senior HMI, confirms this. Asked by foreign visitors to arrange visits to 'activity' schools, HMIs, to whom the request was referred, 'found great difficulty in discovering any'. Change was taking place in the period 1947 to 1953, but 'slowly, cautiously', and, as he puts it, 'sensibly' (p. 11).

To interpret Raison's argument and that of the Black Paperites charitably, we should remind ourselves that the Plowden Report, basing itself on theories relating to the inherent curiosity of children and their innate desire to learn, on the need for individualization of the teaching/learning process, on the pedagogical value of discovery methods, with the teacher leading from behind, had been published only two years earlier in 1967. At that time, this report appeared to represent a wide consensus as to the ideal nature of primary education, and, indeed, to reflect what was going on in the schools — or, at least, the main trends or tendencies. The fact that the publication of the report coincided fairly closely with the student unrest (an international phenomenon, incidentally) may have led Raison to speculate on the relationship between the two, a speculation taken up for their own purposes by the Black Paper editors. In this way the myth was perpetrated that the one was responsible for the other when, of course, that could not be the case.

Nevertheless, the idea that primary school methods, or teachers, were getting out of hand, a point of view that was presented in a sustained critique in the whole series of Black Papers (five or six in all), caught on, and, of course, exploded in the mass media with the Tyndale affair covering the years 1974 to 1976. Though this is outside our period, it bears closely on developments in the 1960s, so it is as well to remind ourselves of the way these rather dramatic events unfolded, especially around 1975–6.

The Tyndale affair broke in the press first in 1974. Though the key issue at stake was who, in the last resort, controls the schools, the extreme version of 'progressive' teaching methods espoused by the leading teachers under-lay the conflicts. Given that, following the Jencks and Coleman Reports which, briefly, reached the conclusion that schools made no difference, as well as the massive cut-backs in educational plans and spending in the late 1960s, the early 1970s marked a period of disenchantment with education as a panacea for social ills. In this situation the Tyndale affair provided a focus for public discontent and frustration on much wider issues than education alone. This was the context of the rise of the populist agitator, Rhodes Boyson, now a Minister of State, and of the politicization of the whole critique of the educational advances of the 1960s, including in particular comprehensive schooling. Just after the Tyndale affair had drawn to its close, and in the atmosphere thus created, in May 1976, Neville Bennett's small-scale research project (Bennett 1976), which appeared to show that formal teaching was more effective than informal, received a highly unusual degree of mass media coverage. In October that year, as mentioned at the start, the high point of near hysteria was reached with *The Times* leader. There followed the HMI's so-called 'Yellow Paper' which also (characteris-tically, and in contrast to earlier strong HMI support for such methods) now appeared to challenge the spread of new methods in the primary school, drawn up to brief the Prime Minister, and Callaghan's Ruskin College speech, in which he specifically warned against the way some teachers used these methods in the classroom (*Education*, 22 October 1976). From this developed the Green Paper (July 1977), the Great Debate, the Assessment of Performance Unit (although this had been set up earlier), the imposition of mass testing by several local authorities, and new HMI/DES initiatives relating to the curriculum and school organization. Primary education, to say the least, had come under a cloud — or rather had now been forced into the limelight, as a national political issue.

II

The question we have to resolve is what the basis was of all this? What had, in fact, being going on? Had there been a fundamental change in practice and procedures in primary schools? Was the child-centred, 'discovery' approach widely implemented? Were children being left on their own to determine their own curricula and activities? Was there a neglect of 'the basics' — of the skills of numeracy and literacy — and a more central focus on other areas embodying different objectives — creativity, self-expression?

First, there is no doubt that some people perceived this to be the case. I refer here in particular to a whole series of more or less distinguished American educationists who visited this country, toured the key areas of the break-out, if one may use the term (Oxfordshire, Leicestershire, the West Riding, Bristol and London in particular), and then wrote about their experiences, generally focusing on the concepts and practices of advanced British schools as a model from which Americans could learn with advantage. This phenomenon is, in my view, more part of the American history of education than the British, for, in the late 1960s and early 1970s, the crisis in schooling in the United States was at its height. The British primary school, it was thought by many, while not necessarily copyable, was linked with the move towards what the Americans call 'open' education, and could provide insights of value.

So we have Joseph Featherstone's famous series of 'New Republic' articles printed under the heading: The Primary School Revolution in Britain, in 1967 — and there we have that word again. These were reprinted with other articles in a book entitled *Schools Where Children Learn* (1971a). Featherstone also wrote the introductory volume to the series entitled *British Primary Schools Today* (1971b), a cooperative endeavour by American and British educators aiming to publicize modern procedures across both sides of the Atlantic. 1970 saw the publication of Charles Silberman's *Crisis in the Classroom: the Remaking of American Education*, a project massively funded by the Carnegie Corporation. Over 100,000 copies of the hardback edition were sold together with 240,000 copies of the paper-back edition; the book was also awarded seven prizes. This drew greatly on the author's British experience, even if of a subjective, episodic character. He followed this up by publishing, in 1973, the *Open Classroom Reader*, another massive compilation drawing heavily on British writers. The same year (1970) saw the publication of Vincent Rogers's *Teaching in the British*

Primary School, again produced for American readers but contributed, in a series of articles, by the leading British educators with experience of the primary school, with a strongly adulatory introduction by Rogers, Professor of Education at the University of Connecticut and a convinced proponent of new forms of education. 1971 saw the publication of Lisa and Casey Murrow's *Children Come First*, subtitled 'The Inspired Work of English Primary Schools', also based on descriptions of activities in selected British primary schools, while in the same year Lilien Weber's useful and comprehensive *The English Infant School and Informal Education* was also published in England. This, actually worked on in 1965–6, differs from the others in that it focused very specifically on the infant school which Lilien Weber saw as the centre of the thrust towards what she describes as 'informal' education.

It is certainly the case that some of these writings were propagandist in character and tended, therefore, to convey what was, perhaps, a rose-hued version of developments in British primary schools in general; the common tendency of these authors, who visited many schools predominantly in the areas already mentioned, was to identify with these developments and processes and to persuade fellow Americans of their viability. 'I visited these two schools in Oxfordshire,' writes Vincent Rogers, 'and I have not been quite the same since' (Rogers 1970). Silberman's influential book is built up largely of vignettes of teacher and pupil interaction, or activities, derived from visits again to selected, or recommended schools. He claimed that: 'In every formal classroom that I went to visit in England, children were restless, were whispering to one another when the teacher was not looking, were ignoring the lesson or baiting the teacher or annoying other children', while in the schools organized on the basis of informal schooling 'the joyfulness is pervasive; in almost every classroom visited, virtually every child appears happy and engaged. One simply does not see bored or restless or unhappy youngsters, or youngsters with the glazed look' (Silberman 1970, pp. 228–9). Featherstone, although he used the term 'revolution' in the primary schools, is careful to underline that it is Plowden's 10 per cent 'best' ('outstanding') schools that he is talking about, and, as far as junior schools are concerned, makes clear that many of these are as arid, poverty-stricken, and dull as he perceives most American education to be. For him, however, as with Vincent Rogers and, of course, Plowden, it is the 'best' schools that represent the trend, to which other schools are likely to approximate. Thus, although the American literature does provide welcome evidence, largely in the form of descriptive material of an unsystematic character, as to processes and procedures in what may be called the most advanced primary schools, we need to be aware of its provenance before accepting it at face value.

Suppose we turn now (before attempting an examination of such 'hard' evidence as we can find) to British educationists and writers — what can we learn from them of relevance to our theme? How did they perceive, describe and define changes in primary education in these years? In 1971 Sir Alec Clegg wrote a booklet for the National Association of Elementary School Principals (NEA) in the United States. It was entitled *Revolution in the British Primary School*, which seems to settle the matter at least as far as Sir Alec was concerned. The paper is reproduced in Silberman's Reader, which states that Sir Alec 'is widely acknowledged as one of the giants of British education', and 'one of the leaders of the quiet revolution that has transformed British primary education since World War II'. Many would agree with this evaluation, and, in this paper, Clegg outlines what he sees as the central changes in attitudes and approach that have taken place. Children no longer sit in rows facing the blackboard; the teacher gives formal lessons less frequently; learning is based on experiences rather than subjects; children work at their own pace on topics they choose from 'a range carefully prepared by the teacher' so that the 'integrated day has superseded the day cut up into subject times'; spelling lists and mechanical sums are now rarely used; the teacher encourages pupils to seek knowledge themselves rather than telling everything; there are few set books and more individual books and resources. In spite of indications to the contrary, Clegg continues, 'there is no doubt that the change in English primary schools is a momentous one.' 'Our primary schools, at their best, are models of the kind of social communities in which we would all wish to live.' (It is interesting to note that, in a section entitled 'What have we gained from the revolution in our primary schools', Clegg states baldly that these developments have nothing to do with 'educational philosophers' — Caldwell Cook and Dewey are cited — and owe nothing to the progressive school movement of the 1920s and 1930s (Silberman 1973, pp. 71, 82).)

Evidently, then, Clegg perceived that an educational revolution had already taken place in our primary schools, and of course the West Riding achieved a national reputation as one of the main centres of this break-out.[1] We now turn briefly to another such centre, Leicestershire. According, once again, to its then Director of Education, Stewart Mason, the abolition of the 11-plus in the experimental areas where the Leicestershire Plan was first tried out had its immediate and most direct effect on the primary schools. Mason linked new developments in the primary schools directly with the abolition of streaming consequent on the elimination of the 11-plus. The increased flexibility which resulted, he says, has led to the inclusion of a second language, greater concern with creative writing, the arts, music and drama, while 'the most striking change of all is taking place in the teaching of mathematics'. 'The ozone of enthusiasm and tang of enquiry are in the air,' he concluded, 'and one cannot help breathing them in ' (Mason 1960, p. 29). This, it is worth noting, was written as early as 1960; but Leicestershire was ahead of most other areas in the country in its comprehensive plan implemented systematically in succeeding areas in the county from the late 1950s onwards.

These, then, are the impressions, or perceptions, of two directors of education in areas where the revolution in the primary school has generally been considered to have been taken furthest. It may be relevant here to quote from Maurice Kogan, commenting on the way educational policy is sometimes formed through the interaction between teachers, local authority administrators, inspectors and advisers and even councillors. 'No-one who has witnessed the powerful cultural and social networks established within some local education authorities where, for example, primary education was changing its ways in the 1940s and 1950s can fail to have seen how policy was being made by the sanctioning and encouragement of progressive educational practices' (Kogan 1978, pp. 128–9).

One of the most authoritative, and probably influential, writers assessing British primary schools in the 1960s was the then Chief Inspector for Primary Education, John Blackie, who also acted as an assessor to the Plowden Committee. His book, *Inside the Primary School*, written officially and published by HMSO in 1967 (the Plowden Report was published in January that year) popularized the Plowden message (and was shot through with its ideology, of which more later). In a later book, entitled *Changing the Primary School: an Integrated Approach* (1974), the author states that 'this little book' (*Inside the Primary School*), reprinted in 1968, 1969, 1972, 'has sold 70,000 copies in the U.K. and U.S.A.' (and that an American edition was also published in 1971). The book was intended, he said, for parents and the general public, 'but has proved popular among teachers'. In *Inside the Primary School*, Blackie paints a picture of the ideal type primary school and discusses present trends. There is a chapter on 'Exploring the World' focusing on discovery methods and first-hand experience; another on creating ('the creative instinct, the desire to make something new for oneself, is unique in man'); another on a foreign language. In his later book,

Changing the Primary School, Blackie makes clear his own position at the start. The first chapter opens with the remark that 'the assumption on which this book is written is that primary schools ought to be changed', while the second chapter follows this up by saying that 'anyone who recommends a revolutionary change in an educational system might be expected to do two things', and proceeds to do them.

The whole question of the role of HMIs in supporting and propagating the 'primary school revolution' is an interesting one that deserves serious consideration. Important here, for instance, must be the role of Christian Schiller, who appears (to the outside observer) as a kind of prophet. Many of his carefully worked out but apparently spontaneous talks are given in the privately printed book, *Christian Schiller in his Own Words* (edited by Christopher Griffin-Beale, 1979). Here is an example:

> The most important thing that has happened as far as the children are concerned is that we treat them differently. We have come to think of them differently — we no longer think of them as objects into which you push something called knowledge, and if it doesn't go easily, give it a knock. We think of them as individuals growing, learning, and learning as part of growing. We have come to think of them differently and so we have come to act towards them differently. And in turn they have come to act differently towards us. For centuries, boys and girls crept like snails unwillingly to school. In many, many primary schools now the children not only come willingly, they want to come and when they are there they enjoy what they do — and they do so much. For one thing, they learn and even like learning.

And here are the last words of his closing lecture at the annual Plowden Conference of 1975:

> We have pioneers now. It is very difficult to see ahead. It will be difficult without any doubt. We've got a long long way to go — a very long way to go. All sorts of new problems will come. I have been voyaging a long time, but I never thought that I could live to see the voyage get so far forward as it has. So may it be with you. Not farewell, fareforward, voyagers!

And if Christian Schiller, with his stress on human potential, appears evangelical, there is also the influence of such HMIs as Edith Biggs who certainly had her feet firmly planted on the ground. Her 'Mathematics in Primary Schools' (Schools Council Curriculum Bulletin No. 1), published in 1965, sold 165,000 copies in four years. Her activities are generally regarded as highly influential in bringing about methodological and organizational change in the primary schools — specifically in the area of mathematics or number on which, as we shall see, primary school pupils spend a lot of their time.

Material has now been presented on how some directors of education and HMIs, both influential groups, assessed the situation. And here is a benevolently inclined summary of these developments made in 1978 by Maurice Kogan, one-time secretary to the Plowden Committee (Kogan 1978, pp. 55–6):

> There had been perhaps twenty or thirty years of triumphant progress by the primary schools in which it seemed that all that was good was happening through them. A powerful humanitarianism seemed to suffuse the best of the primary schools. To the visitor they seemed unbelievably good in their relationships between adults and children, able to elicit powerful interest on the part of the pupils, and yet still be highly productive in work that was both creative and skilful. Successive reading surveys since 1948 had shown that 11 year olds in 1964 were reaching the standards that children 17 months older in 1948 had attained. Against evidence such as this it was difficult for attacks on the primary schools to be sustained. The new mathematics in the primary schools seemed exciting and impressively difficult to those brought up in traditional maths.

The Plowden Committee's Report, Kogan goes on, celebrated the achievement of the primary schools in several hundred pages. So let us now turn to that Committee and its Report, a very characteristic product of the 1960s.

The Plowden Committee, of course, was sitting at a particular moment in time. Appointed in August 1963 by Lord Boyle, then, as Sir Edward, Minister of Education, it got to work just a month or two before the Robbins Committee reported with its great expansionist programme, immediately and enthusiastically accepted in full by Sir Alec Douglas-Home, then Conservative Prime Minister. The Plowden Committee reported in January 1967, that is, just before the Labour government ran into really severe economic difficulties, and began to cut education as well as other public expenditure, postponing the raising of the school leaving age. It is clearly evident from their Report that the Committee's general perspective was one of continuous economic growth, full employment, enhanced affluence and the more or less inevitable emergence of a more egalitarian sociey, where human potential, which they saw as unlimited, would find realization. 'Unemployment has been almost non-existent since the war, except in some areas and for a small minority of workers,' they write. 'Incomes have risen, nutrition has improved, housing is better, the health service and the rest of the social services have brought help where it is needed' (Plowden Report, 1, p. 29). Most of the children, they add, 'are now physically healthy, vigorous, curious and alert'. This was, perhaps, the last point in time

(1965–6) when such a general optimism expressed something of a consensus. This is the context of the committee's deliberations, and it is, perhaps, reflected in what might be called the educational optimism of the committee's theoretical outlook, and of the practical proposals concerning the role of both teachers and pupils, and of classroom procedures generally. It is on this aspect that I want to concentrate, as most relevant to the present topic.

The committee specifically identify with what they called, and so, presumably, perceived, as a number of trends already extant in the schools, and to some degree claim to base their proposals on these; however, their theoretical standpoint is also, and perhaps more particularly, grounded on the concept of the unique make-up of each individual child, as set out in detail in the first chapter of their report. Not only is each child unique in his rate of development across three dimensions, physical, intellectual, emotional, but also children generally have an innate, enquiring, discovery-oriented, searching character or 'nature'. This is central to their reasoning, as Richard Peters has pointed out (Peters 1969). From this is derived the immense stress on the need to individualize the work and activities of the children, and so of the teachers' involvement with the children. Class teaching should be reduced, work should be individualized, grouping should be used if only as an economy of teacher time. Education is a process of discovery or enquiry, and this is what is central to learning. The teacher must lead from behind, stimulating, encouraging, unobtrusively guiding. Each child's activities must be appropriate for that particular child, having these particular rates of development, at this particular moment in time. Such was the blueprint of the role of the ideal-type teacher, and of the pupil, as set out by Plowden.

It can hardly be denied that this was a highly 'progressive' picture or syndrome, one that was built on, developed, and took further the 'child-centred' ideology of the past, and, it was claimed, one which reflected what was actually happening in the schools themselves — or at least the main trends there. I suggest, given the context of the time, it was this picture of the schools that made a major impact. No one was in a position to know what actually went on in the schools, or ever will be presumably. Plowden stated what should happen; how many mistook the rhetoric for the reality?

III

We come now to the most difficult part of this chapter. What was really happening in the primary schools in the 1960s? I have just said that no one can really know. And that is clearly true. But can we attempt a reconstruction?

First, what can be culled from the Plowden Report itself? There is first the survey the HMIs undertook on behalf of the committee. This categorizes the 20,000 plus primary schools in the country under nine mutually exclusive categories. Characteristically, no explanation is given as to how the HMIs set about this job, and little information on what they were actually asked to do.

What transpires is that the HMIs held that 10 per cent of schools were good and even outstanding. And that in all about one-third of the schools were good in terms of the general, but rather vague, criteria used. The bulk of these, 23 per cent, are defined as schools that are 'good . . . in most respects without any special distinction'. Of the remaining two-thirds (that is, the large majority) 16 per cent were in Category 4, that is, there was hope they might improve, 28 per cent were in Category 6, defined as 'decent . . . run of the mill' schools (a description that sounds intentionally derogatory), 6 per cent (Category 5) were good on personal relations but were poverty stricken or swamped by 'immigrants', while 9 per cent were defined as 'curate's egg schools' (Category 7), a definition that is difficult to make much sense of, containing both 'good and bad features'. These latter categories cover about 60 per cent of all primary schools of all types.

Presumably, or perhaps, the 10 per cent best schools can be equated with schools in which the primary school 'revolution' had taken place — or should the 23 per cent in Category 3 also be included? It may be best to confine this assessment to Categories 1 and 2, to regard schools in Category 3 as half-way there, and those in Category 4 as hopefully (according to Plowden) also going the same way.

However this may be, it would seem that, in 1964 or 1965, when the survey was made, only a minority of primary schools had been transformed along 'modern lines', though an uncertain proportion of others was perceived as following in that way. The report gives a description of three schools at this stage 'run successfully on modern lines', which, it is said, might fall into any of Categories 1, 2 and 3. These are an infant, a junior mixed, and a junior mixed and infants' (JMI) school. These descriptions might prove useful, but they give little indication, for instance, relating to teaching styles or what goes on inside the classroom. It is the feel or tone of the school or classroom as a whole that they describe, and seem most interested in, rather than the teaching/learning process going on within them (Plowden Report 1, pp. 103–6).

Further information, though also of a rather imprecise character, can be gleaned from some of the surveys carried through for the Plowden Committee in 1964, reported in volume 2. In a sample survey, for instance, HMIs were asked to rate schools on a five-point scale on the extent to which they were 'in line with modern educational trends'. Three per cent of the sample were rated as 'very good' as far as acceptance of these trends was concerned, 18 per cent as 'good', 47 per cent as 'average', 29 per cent as 'below average', and 3 per cent as 'poor'.[2] Summing the first two categories together gives 21 per cent in either the 'very good' or 'good' categories. The 'modern educational trends' which the HMIs were specifically asked to take into consideration were four: (i) 'Permissive discipline?' (ii) 'Provision for individual rates of progress?' (iii) 'Readiness to reconsider the content of education?' (iv) 'Awareness of the unity of knowledge?' While this gives an interesting indication of the Plowden Committee's perceptions as to what in fact were the most significant modern educational trends, it is difficult to know what to make of the quantitative evidence provided. HMIs were instructed, in answering this and similar questions involving five-point scales, to 'allow for a national distribution of (i) 5 per cent (ii) 20 per cent (iii) 50 per cent (iv) 20 per cent (v) 5 per cent.' This seems fairly effectively to prejudge the situation. Perhaps the most significant figure, taking this instruction into account, is the 29 per cent 'below average' schools, since this is significantly greater than the recommended statistical pattern of 20 per cent only.

The same survey also reported that 55 per cent of this sample of schools classified children by 'age and achievement', that is, used streaming, while 43 per cent classified children by age only, which implies non-streaming; the remaining 2 per cent classifying children by 'other means'.[3] Further information gained shows that, in the words of the report, 'junior schools were much more likely than the others to be streamed', that 'three-fifths of J.M.I. schools were also streamed', and that the larger the schools were the more likely they were to be streamed (for instance, 70 per cent of schools with 500 or more pupils were streamed, compared with 56 per cent of schools with from 351 to 500 pupils).

Since the move to non-streaming is a specific feature of the mid-late 1960s, and since it has important implications for the methodology and ethos of the school and classroom in terms of teaching procedures, it is worth pursuing this topic in greater detail.

Volume 2 contains an appendix (11) giving an abridged version of two reports submitted to the Plowden Committee by the National Foundation for Educational Research, which had been commissioned by the DES to carry through a study of the organization of junior schools and effects of streaming with the aim of reporting to the Committee. The full report was, of course, only finally published in 1970, but this is not here referred to.

The data in this appendix derive from a general survey of current practice conducted by questionnaire in 1963, sent to 2,290 schools (there was an 82 per cent response). From the figures presented it is concluded 'that a junior school pupil in 1963 was much more likely to be in a school using a form of homogeneous rather than heterogeneous ability grouping — in fact at least 56 per cent of all pupils were in schools using homogeneous ability grouping', though a note states that the figure is probably nearer 70 per cent. Once again, it is the large schools which are shown to use streaming most consistently — 65 per cent of them were streamed, only 6 per cent entirely unstreamed, and 5 per cent unstreamed except for one year group. Nevertheless a later statement says that '19 per cent of schools at present using homogeneous streaming intended to introduce non-streaming or to extend it beyond the first year'; this statement occurs in a section headed New Trends in Junior School Organisation. Similarly 36 per cent of schools using non-streaming 'streamed' their fourth year pupils, but 24 per cent intended to change this and unstream them (Plowden Report, 2, pp. 550ff.).

In a section entitled The Characteristics and Attitudes of Teachers in Streamed and Non-Streamed Schools, it is stated that 'the climate in the unstreamed school — if we are to judge by what its teachers say about themselves, their methods and their attitudes — is more permissive and tolerant, less structured and places less emphasis on the more traditional methods of class teaching than its streamed counterpart'. An attempt was made to dichotomize teachers answering the questionnaire according to the types of lessons they gave, into those giving 'traditional lessons' and those giving 'progressive lessons'. Item analysis yielded versions containing the following items:

'Traditional' — writing class-prepared compositions; learning lists of spellings; formal grammar — understanding parts of speech; saying and learning tables by rote.

'Progressive' — projects — in which the child does his own 'research'; pupils working or helping each other in groups; practical arithmetic, e.g. measuring, apparatus work; free activity.

It seems that these two types, or styles of teaching, related to whether the school was streamed or unstreamed. Generally it was also found that the younger teachers tended to have more 'progressive' opinions, particularly in their rejection of 11-plus selection, their 'permissiveness' and their 'tolerance of noise'. Those with two years' experience or less were the most hostile to the 11-plus. On teaching methods it is said that teachers in streamed schools, on average, tended to make more frequent use of 'traditional lessons' and less frequent use of 'progressive lessons' than teachers in non-streamed schools. Again it was in the streamed schools that significantly more use was made of tests of various kinds to check progress and diagnose difficulties. However, analysis of the 'traditional and progressive scores' of teachers in streamed and non-streamed schools shows that *'teachers in both types of school are fairly "traditional"'* ' (my italics — BS); the differences between them, it is said, would seem to be 'nuances rather than marked divergences of opinion'. This, I think, is an important and significant finding. Analysis relating to the degree of permissiveness, attitudes to physical punishment, etc., are used to support this statement. As already indicated, the 'most discriminative statement between the two sets of teachers (streamed and non-streamed) is "the 11 plus examination is an entirely fair method of assessing a child's abilities" '. 69 per cent of non-streamed teachers disagreed with this, while 56 per cent of streamed teachers agreed. However, as is then pointed out, this indicates that 'substantial proportions of teachers in both groups are opposed to the system' (Plowden Report, 2, pp. 557–65).

This interim report concludes with a short section on attitudes of teachers to streaming and non-streaming. The conclusions given are that 'substantial proportions of teachers are in favour of streaming' and that 'since of all junior schools in the country which are large enough to do so, at least 65 per cent stream and only 11 per cent clearly do not, it seems reasonable to suppose that the majority of junior school teachers in England and Wales are in favour of the practice, that a substantial proportion are undecided, and that only relatively few are firmly committed to the opposing view', that is, to non-streaming. The researchers continue, rather rashly, as things worked out, that 'this finding must be stressed at a time when some writers suggest that the death knell of streaming has already sounded'. They add that, coupled with the finding concerning parents' views (parents generally preferred streaming) the evidence suggests that 'any universal change recommended may meet with considerable opposition — particularly since the attitudes for or against streaming seem to form part of a whole syndrome of views, practices and beliefs' (Plowden Report, 2, p. 571).

I have placed considerable emphasis on the data concerning the move to unstreaming in primary schools because, in spite of the researchers' predictions, in fact non-streaming took off with astonishing rapidity during the mid to late 1960s, having the expressed support of the Plowden Committee itself, which stated its views moderately but firmly on this issue. We do have further hard data which makes this clear beyond doubt. For instance, Deanne Bealing, in a survey of two local authorities in the Midlands carried through in 1971, to which we will return shortly, found that the vast majority of primary schools were, in fact, unstreamed (Bealing 1972). Neville Bennett found much the same thing in his survey of all primary schools in Lancashire and Cumbria in 1975 — only 13 per cent of the schools which replied to his questionnaire were streamed (Bennett 1976, p. 58). Finally the HMI primary survey of 1978 found that only 4 per cent of children in 9-year-old classes in the survey were streamed (HMI Survey 1978, p. 28). Within fifteen years, then, the position found in 1963 was totally reversed. While it can, of course, be argued that fine streaming may have continued within the non-streamed class, the swing to unstreaming as a principle of school organization appears to be one chief characteristic of the so-called 'primary school revolution' which cannot be gainsaid. Its implications will be discussed later.

IV

The first systematic study of the actual organization of junior school classrooms was that undertaken by Deanne Bealing in 1970, and published in 1972 (Bealing 1972). This was a questionnaire survey of a 10 per cent sample of teachers in two local authority areas in the Midlands, one of which organized its secondary education on a comprehensive basis, the other on a selective basis. An 89 per cent response was achieved from 189 teachers in a carefully drawn representative sample of classes. The survey results reflected, as the author puts it, the 'new ideas and trends in primary education [which] have resulted in the erosion of the traditional classroom layout with its rows of desks and static children'. It was found that 'the overwhelming majority of classrooms contained children of mixed abilities and attainments. With the exception of remedial classes, streaming was totally absent in the comprehensive authority schools and even under the selective authority less than one in five teachers had streamed classes.' It was also found that the system of grouping was widely popular. About four teachers in five adopted a group layout for their classrooms although only a small proportion were equipped with modern tables or table units. Again 'only about one fifth of the teachers reported that their desk was in the traditional centre front position', and about two-thirds of teachers split their time about equally between sitting at their desk and circulating amongst the children — the other one-third 'circulated most of the time'. The prevalance of group layout, teacher mobility and opportunities for pupils to work independently outside the classroom 'all suggest an informal approach to organisation'.

While the survey found that a considerable amount of mobility was permitted to pupils, it was also found 'that teachers still reserve a relatively tight measure of control'. Further about two-thirds of the teachers streamed within the class in terms of their grouping strategy, though grouping was also widely based on friendship patterns. Finally, as regards the organization of children's work, it appeared that class teaching was still quite widely used for all subjects except reading, but that the most striking feature relating to teaching methods was 'the predominance of individual work' — an outcome to which the whole thrust of the Plowden Report was directed. The evidence on the nature of group work was difficult to interpret, though this also was popular in all subjects, especially mathematics and art and craft. Bealing concludes as follows:

> Some of the results, if substantiated in follow-up work, question widely held beliefs about the 'primary school revolution'. Despite the relatively informal classroom layouts adopted by the vast majority of teachers there was so much evidence of tight teacher control over such matters as where children sit and move that it seems highly doubtful that there is much opportunity for children to choose or organise their own activities in most classrooms. There was widespread use of groupings based on similar abilities and attainments although the overwhelming majority of teachers were working with un-streamed classes (Bealing 1972, p. 235).

These conclusions are supported by another survey of a different character carried through by Moran a year earlier, and published in 1971. In this study, also carried through by questionnaire, Moran gained information about how teachers who specifically operated 'the integrated day' organized their classes. The subjects were members of a conference run on the topic a year or two earlier. It is interesting to note that a main point which emerged was similar to Bealing's; that is, that the bulk of teachers organizing their classes in this way in fact normally maintained a tight control over the children's activities. This is worth bringing out here, because 'the integrated day' is generally regarded as the most 'way-out' method of organizing children's learning activities, though it should be quite evident that complex organizations of this kind, if they are to be carried through successfully, do specifically require a high degree of teacher control.

The next survey, which can claim to have a systematic character, was that carried through by Neville Bennett at the University of Lancaster, as a preliminary to his controversial study published as *Teaching Styles and Pupil Progress* (1976). This was also a questionnaire survey, directed specifically to class teachers in primary schools. It covered both teaching methods adopted by the teachers (e.g. seating arrangements, classroom organization, curriculum organization, discipline problems, etc.) and elicited teachers' opinions about education, relating, for instance, to aims, educational issues, and teaching methods. On the basis of responses to this questionnaire, Bennett, using cluster analysis, classified his teachers into twelve teacher types or what he called teaching 'styles'. Only one of these styles, comprising just 9 per cent of the population studied (468 teachers) was categorized as 'progressive' in the Plowden sense; that is, met the Plowden criteria relating to progressive education. The rest are described as either 'mixed' in their styles, or largely 'traditional'. Although the data on which Bennett's categorization was made can be criticized, nevertheless it is legitimate to draw the conclusion that the 'primary school revolution' had only marginally penetrated the north-west, and this, indeed, is one of Bennett's own conclusions (1976, pp. 37ff). Incidentally, Bennett found that 83 per cent of his teachers held that 'pupils should be told what to do and how to do it.'

Finally there is the evidence from the first large-scale observational study in primary schools, that carried through as part of the ORACLE research programme, based at Leicester. This focused on close observation both of pupils and teachers in over 100 primary school classrooms in three local authority areas in the Midlands; the results of the first year's observation, carried through in 1975–6, has recently been published (Galton et al. 1980). Briefly, it was found that the vast majority of these classes were what is best called 'informally' organized, in Bealing's sense. Perhaps the most striking finding was the extent of individualization both of work and of attention in the primary classrooms. However, for our purposes, an important outcome was the extent to which the teaching was found to be largely didactic in character. The promotion of enquiry or discovery learning appeared almost non-existent. Since this was a main prescription of the Plowden Report, this finding is significant. Collaborative group work or enquiry was also found to be seldom realized — many teachers never used collaborative group work at all for any subject. Further, as regards the content of education, a major emphasis on 'the basics' was also found. One-third of normal teaching sessions was devoted to number work, or mathematics, one-third to language (the great bulk of which time was spent on writing), and one-third to general subjects, topic and project work, art and craft, and science (which hardly featured, as the HMIs survey also found.)[4] These findings concerning the curriculum confirm Bassey's study (in Nottinghamshire), and the HMI Primary Survey of 1978 (Bassey 1978; HMI Survey 1978). Certainly there was little evidence there of any fundamental shift either in the content of education or in the procedures of teaching and learning, in the sense that didacticism still largely prevails.

V

What can we conclude about all this? Perhaps it is too early, yet, to conclude anything, but one general point may be made. It seems that there has been a rather fundamental change in primary schools (perhaps more in infant than in junior schools) in terms of their internal structure, organization, and perhaps particularly in relationships. But whether it ever amounted to anything which might be called a 'revolution' seems extremely doubtful. Within the general change to non-streaming, which is symptomatic of a transformation in attitudes and approach (and in objectives) within the classroom, didacticism is the most general mode, or at least so it appears from the evidence to hand. While pupils are now given much greater responsibility in the organization of their work, it does not seem that they have much opportunity to control its content and direction, except, perhaps, in marginal cases. In other words, the image of the way-out, 'progressive' teacher, propagated by the media as a result of the Tyndale events, seems very far indeed from actuality. If this is true, we are left with a problem. Why did it all happen? What is it all about? How was it that primary school methods became a national political issue around 1975–6?

It may, perhaps, be argued, that, as the Plowden Committee reported and hoped, there was a definite 'trend' taking place within the primary schools in the late 1950s and early 1960s which had the potential of carrying all before it. Such concepts as enhanced pupil responsibility for their own studies, the promotion of enquiry and of independent initiative on the part of pupils, flexibility of organization which is a keynote of the report, allied with wider contemporary phenomena or 'happenings', may have been seen as a threat of a breakout developing also within secondary schools and higher education implying that the so-called control function of education was at risk. It was not only the primary schools, of course, that were subjected to criticism at the time of Callaghan's speech at Ruskin College in 1976. Wider issues were also raised, especially about the relations of education to industry. In fact the whole 'relatively autonomous' area of education was under attack, and a mobilization taking place of those elements in society that wished to see a strong reimposition of control. Such a tactic may have underlain the exaggeration of the rhetoric about primary education in a deliberate attempt to provide a rational basis for the reimposition of control. No one who visited a number of primary schools in an industrial area on the day after the publication of Bennett's book, as I had the opportunity of doing, can doubt its immediate deflationary effect on teachers in the schools. They saw it, or rather, its presentation by the media, as a denial of all the values they cherished. And this, of course, was only one of the elements in the situation.

Perhaps the explanation is simpler than that. As suggested earlier, the mid 1960s were the last expansionist period both in the economy and in education. Some kind of 'revolution' in education was then seen as appropriate by almost everyone. By the end of the 1960s this situation had changed radically, and was to change further for the worse in the early 1970s. An educational revolution was no longer seen as appropriate. Any such tendency, therefore, was no longer to be encouraged. The primary school revolution, perhaps it may be concluded, if it took place at all, was premature.

Notes

1. See Gosden and Sharp (1978), pp. 197–200, for a description of Clegg's part in these developments.
2. This survey related to a sample of 171 schools, see Plowden Report, 2, Table 6, pp. 225, 278.
3. Plowden Report, 2, Table 7, pp. 226. The actual Table, as printed, gives 35 per cent and 45 per cent in the first two categories, but these statistical errors (repeated in the text, p. 225) must have evaded the proof readers.
4. Observations on which this analysis is based relate to 'normal teaching sessions', i.e. those taking place in the classroom. They exclude physical education, dancing, singing, games, etc.

Topics for discussion

1. Discuss some of the major factors which contributed towards the virulent criticism of so-called *informal* or *progressive* methods following the Plowden Report.
2. What evidence is there to suggest that *progressivism* as defined by Plowden was hardly to be found in practice?
3. What are some of the most important changes that *have* taken place in primary education since the Plowden Report?

Suggestions for further reading

1. Richards, C. (ed.) (1980) *Primary Education: Issues for the Eighties*. London: A. and C. Black.
2. Bloomer, M. and Shaw, K.W. (eds) (1979) *The Challenge of Educational Change: Limitations and Potentialities*. Oxford: Pergamon Press.
3. Simon, B. and Taylor, W. (eds) (1981) *Education in the Eighties: The Central Issues*. London: Batsford Academic and Educational.

READING TWO • Primary education: the multicultural context   *B. Woodroffe*

Awareness

Many of us find it difficult to make any real sense of the idea that Britain is a multicultural society. It is certainly easier for us to grasp that Britain has problems of race relations. It is easier, too, to understand that our future in relation to world politics demands both knowledge and understanding of not only the 'first' and 'second' worlds but also the 'third world'. The increasing impact of Islam and the centrality of Africa in current political events are pointers to the new awareness that is demanded. The importance of such issues obliges us to look at how the educational system is preparing young people for this new awareness. It obliges us, also, to question the

B. Woodroffe, 'Primary Education: the multicultural context', in, C. Richards (Ed), *Primary Education: Issues for the Eighties*. London; A & C Black (Publishers) Ltd. 1980. pp 73–82

educational arrangements we make for young people of different races, ethnic and cultural groups to learn and work alongside one another. We need to direct our attention not only to the inner cities which are multi-ethnic and multicultural but also throughout Britain.

It is possible, and easy, to assert the need for this approach but it is necessary to return to the question of why we find it so difficult to make sense of the idea of a multicultural society. We need to look at our own formal education and the formative experiences that have shaped our attitudes, awareness (or lack of it) and our understanding. Whatever our age, we almost certainly followed a formal curriculum that was ethnocentric and European-based; the hidden curriculum for those of us over thirty either ignored much of the rest of the world or subtly placed low value or ridicule upon it. Remember the messages of books, comics, jokes and fantastic tales of 'fuzzy-wuzzies' or exotic but inefficient 'Asiatics'. More recently the hidden curriculum has dwelt upon the problems, disadvantages and dangers of being from the 'third world' — a black teacher told me recently of his amazement on being asked at an interview what he thought of Idi Amin. The issue that we have to confront is how do we, within the educational system, prepare young people to understand, make sense of, and develop a multicultural society in a shrinking world. Crucially we need to develop a positive approach to the strengths of difference: difference in culture, in experience, in perception and in values which our former experience of imperialism and colonialism has eroded and distorted.

That distortion has led to racism becoming embedded in our society. It is impossible, and would be wrong, to try to divorce emotion from the question of racism, the main plank of which is an assumption of one's own race, whatever we mean by that, being in nearly all ways superior to others. Yet if we are to develop education within a multicultural context, we have to be objective, logical *and* imaginative. We must recognize that we are products of a certain sort of society and that those of us with British backgrounds share a history with those whose backgrounds lie in what was once the British Empire. Unless we start from this point, our responses in education are likely to contain the same distortions as in the past.

It is essential also to be quite clear of our response up to the present time, for though we have responded at times effectively, more often we have not, and where our response has been ill-judged it has still become built into our educational arrangements. The Plowden Report (1967) contains a chapter entitled 'Children of Immigrants' whose essential focus of concern can best be understood by its recommendations:

(i) Colleges, institutes of education and local education authorities should expand opportunities through initial and in-service courses for some teachers to train in teaching English to immigrants and to increase their knowledge of the background from which children come.

(ii) Work already started on the development of suitable materials and methods for teaching English to immigrants should continue and be expanded.

(iii) Dispersal may be necessary but language and other difficulties should be the criteria employed.

(iv) There should be an expansion of remedial courses in spoken English for immigrant teachers.

(v) Schools with special language problems . . . should be generously staffed: further experiments might be made in the use of student volunteers.

This focus on special needs is consistent with current thinking and shows a proper concern with *one* aspect within the multicultural context. What is significant, though, are the statements in the report that 'the purposes of the various measures we have discussed should be to eliminate, not perpetuate, the need for them' and 'special measures inevitably identify children as "different" and their duration should be as brief as possible'. The report hopes that immigrant children will be quickly 'absorbed into the native population'. I find it interesting that elsewhere in the same report suggestions are made both about broadening the curriculum and checking books for bias and distortion through stereotypes. The lack of consistent thinking and true understanding of the multicultural context and its implications throws up inconsistent responses but more worryingly suggests by the term absorption the idea that a process of assimilation will make us all 'British' and thus wipe away the differences for which special measures are inconveniently required.

The years between the Plowden Report and the HMI primary survey may be characterized by, on the one hand, a growing number of specialist reports by bodies such as the Parliamentary Select Committee on Immigration and Race Relations and by organizations representing minority group opinion, which continually to a greater or lesser degree question the approach as expressed in Plowden, and on the other hand the partial reference which is allowed to appear in major educational documents such as the Bullock Report. *Primary Education in England* (DES1978a) attaches importance to the arrangements and approaches to second language learners and notes some expansion of the curriculum in relation to the multicultural context. Amongst the recommendations is stated: 'More might be done to make all children aware of other beliefs and to extend their understanding of the multi-cultural nature of contemporary society. In the course of work on these and other matters, children acquire information and learn to respond imaginatively to what they see, hear and otherwise experience'. Close scrutiny of the report does indicate a proper shift in thinking, yet, as I believe the extract shows, there is no *clear* intention to place the issue centrally into the debate concerning primary education nor therefore to give firm leadership. 'More *might* be done'!

Aims and issues

What can be done? What needs to be done? First and foremost, we need to recognize the centrality of the issues presented by the multicultural context. They are central because they add a dimension to all aspects of the thinking of those engaged in primary education. We need to spell out the aims of multi-ethnic education along the lines of those outlined by the Inner London Education Authority in a recent report:

a   to prepare all pupils and students to live and work harmoniously and with equality of opportunity in that society;
b   to build upon the strengths of cultural diversity in that society;
c   to define and combat racism and the discriminatory practices to which it gives rise; and
d   to meet appropriately and effectively the particular needs of all people, having regard to their ethnic, cultural, linguistic or historical attachment.

In order to respond effectively to aims such as these we need to follow a process of identification, review of our policies and practices, development and consolidation. For example, racism affects the young child both in Harwich and in Handsworth, yet our detailed response will need to take in the difference of experience of these two areas. To put it as succinctly as I can, we need two sorts of checklist. One will be addressed to the issues to which primary education should respond; the other will be addressed to the aspects of primary education where the responses can be most appropriately developed.

In discussion of multicultural education these issues have been somewhat confused because of the settlement patterns of ethnic minorities in the inner city areas. Multicultural education has become synonymous with education in the inner cities, itself heavily overlaid with ideas of disadvantage. There is no doubt that the initial difficulties that follow immigration have been compounded by discrimination tabulated, for example, in PEP reports and recognized by Parliament with the resultant 1976 Race Relations Act. Such discrimination, allied to a widespread belief that we should 'treat all children alike' (usually meaning like a stereotype of white indigenous children) has led to inappropriate pragmatic responses. It is essential, if we are to formulate appropriate policies, that this confusion is untangled. The issues to isolate are these:

(a) assisting children to a self-identity in a multicultural society; this is of equal importance to indigenous white British children as to others;
(b) creating the basis of a wider world understanding through broader cultural and historical sources and experience;
(c) combating racist ideas which are often supported in education by a narrow approach to values and by the development of stereotypes;
(d) fostering the development of inter-group relations through the ethos of the school, curriculum and other activities;
(e) introducing the idea of linguistic diversity, in the world, in Europe, in this country.

As I have indicated earlier, these issues are national issues and, we must remember, European ones. If we could only respond effectively, we would destroy many of the disadvantages placed upon learners from minority ethnic groups and so be able to identify the particular needs that relate to a learner's 'ethnic, cultural, linguistic or historical attachment'.

Policies

Policy implications exist at three levels: national, local authority and school. At national level there has been an indication of such policy in the Green Paper, *Education in Schools* (DES1977):

> Our society is a multicultural, multiracial one, and the curriculum should reflect a sympathetic understanding of the different cultures and races that now make up our society. We also live in a complex, interdependent world, and many of our problems in Britain require international solutions. The curriculum should therefore reflect our need to know about and understand other countries.

It is important that such 'signals', as the Minister of Education in the Netherlands, Dr Pias, recently put it, be made regularly and consistently by the government and the DES and that these signals permeate thinking, presentation and day-to-day work. There is a need to place emphasis more widely through national surveys, curriculum guidance and reports. It is necessary to continue this emphasis within the work of the Schools Council, in the development of policies in relation to initial and in-service training and in the production of resources for teaching and learning. A more coherent approach to research and development drawing upon the resources of institutions of higher education, the NFER and funding bodies, such as the SSRC, needs to be developed.

At local authority level there needs equally to be a signalling of the centrality of multi-ethnic issues. An overall policy strategy should concentrate upon development with clear administrative implications. A key factor is the creation of time for teachers, with advisers, to plan, develop, test and evaluate methods and approaches; successful development then requires proper means for dissemination. One possible model is exemplified in the development of the 'Reading through Understanding' project within the ILEA. Here an initial hypothesis that dialect used at home interfered with the young child's acquisition of literacy was found not to be valid. Through research and observation of children in the classroom it became apparent that children of Caribbean origin were adversely affected by the overwhelmingly 'White English' content of materials and by the lower expectation and attitude of teachers towards them as learners and readers. Strongly concentrating on cooperation with classroom teachers, the project team developed materials at initial reading level, top infant and lower junior, top junior and lower secondary, which were set in a multicultural British locality, drew upon folk tales from other cultures especially African and Caribbean, and included stories of people with fine qualities who came from different parts of the world. These materials, and most importantly the approach and method, have now become the central point for an in-service training programme for primary teachers. It needs to be stressed that a key part of the development was the central involvement in the team of a teacher of Caribbean origin whose knowledge and experience were essential. At local authority level, then, in addition to a clear administrative policy, advisers should develop in-service training, methods of guidance and the support and dissemination of good practice, drawing into this process at all levels people with the necessary background, experience and, where possible, training.

At school level the headteacher has a most positive rôle to play in bringing the issues into the whole life of the school. A policy and an approach to its development need to be made, if a genuine shift in the learning experiences offered all children is to be achieved. In many schools at the moment one or more teachers are developing their own approaches which could be translated into a constant factor throughout the school.

There are many opportunities which could be taken by teachers, given the support and coordination provided by a policy. For example, stories could be used to open up the multicultural world for young children. By choosing stories with varied settings teachers could begin to open up for the child similar experiences shaped in different settings — universal themes in varying contexts. By their selection of stories to be told, looked at and, in time, read by the child, and their implicit acceptance of values in other societies, teachers could lay the foundation of important attitudes. They could destroy for the next generation the penetratingly harmful stereotypes that shaped their own attitudes and values. Allied to this could be an introduction to the vitally important theme of man's adaptation to his physical, social and economic environment. Very simply, the location and structure of a house in a tropical country in relation to the demands of the climate could be understood and enjoyed by a young child and could thereby provide a sensible base for the more complex learning of later years. This approach could be extended so young children are introduced to the variety of family structures, social customs, social organization, faiths and, indeed, to the bases on which Jerome Bruner built his middle years curriculum, *Man: A Course of Study.*

Of course, I am advocating a policy of permeation throughout the primary curriculum, a permeation which could have marked effects on both teacher and taught. One more example: just think of the idea that those of us whose families have lived in Britain for generations share a history with the countries of the Commonwealth, and that that shared history involves the influence of both the coloniser and the colonized. This could lead teachers to question the interpretation of the history they were given and to seek out the 'hidden' history. After that, could they continue an approach which gave a special value to the technological achievements, the artistic expression and indeed the ethos of Western society, whilst by subtle implication it devalued that of other societies? It is by teasing out meaningful reference points for young children in primary classrooms that teachers could begin to prepare the ground upon which new awareness is forged.

Relocation

In conclusion, it is perhaps appropriate to recognize that a major national acceptance of the multicultural dimension in education may not be forthcoming, though hopefully the government enquiry into multicultural education might take on significance. Whether such an acceptance and a corresponding shift of policy and practice occur or not, the relocation of individuals' perspectives can occur, will occur and is occurring all the time. It is not an exaggeration to say that a person achieves a real release by becoming free of misconceptions and the results of racism and ethnocentrism. The primary teacher, the adviser, the inspector, the administrator and the curriculum developer can and need to share the same perspective. As I have stressed earlier, education in and for a multicultural society needs at all levels the full participation of members of all ethnic and cultural groups.

Topics for discussion

1. 'The whites have a problem and we're landed with it' (A West Indian mother). Discuss *institutional racism* in light of this comment.
2. What are the main differences between policies of *assimilation* and policies of *pluralism?*
3. What is the author suggesting in his call for 'a policy of permeation throughout the primary curriculum? (p. 28)

Suggestions for further reading

1. Cohen, L. and Manion, L. (1983) *Multicultural Classrooms.* London: Croom Helm.
2. Tomlinson, S. (1984) *Home and School in Multicultural Britain.* London: Batsford.
3. Jeffcoate, R. (1984) *Ethnic Minorities and Education.* London: Harper & Row.

SECTION TWO
CHILD GROWTH AND DEVELOPMENT IN THE PRIMARY YEARS

READING THREE ● Individuality and its origins: patterns of growth in the early years: growth patterns of the middle years
J. Brierley

Individuality and its origins

Individuality (and therefore variety) is one of the major characteristics of people — in shape, walk, thoughts, intelligence, emotions, actions and so on. It is of course a truism that *likenesses* in looks or character, for instance, are passed on in families, sometimes skipping a generation. 'He has his father's eyes' or 'his mother's good temper' or 'his grandfather's quickness at figures' are common enough sayings in families but even so each child is 'himself', not exactly like his brothers and sisters or his parents.

Likenesses and differences

Similarities are easy enough to understand but it is not quite so easy to understand the *differences*, slight or large, between family members. A child often has the 'family face' but his own version of it. Sometimes he bears little resemblance to his brothers and sisters. He may be exceptionally bright or, sadly, handicapped in some way or perhaps he may be a startling red-head. Variety among children in a family is commonplace. Every teacher with a class of children in front of him bears witness to it daily. In a group of 14 year old boys puberty has started in one but not in another: one is a man in body already, the rest still boys. Amongst five year olds, one has excellent hand control and uses scissors to cut out skilfully, another is clumsy; one has a large vocabulary on entering school but another of the same age a meagre one. One child starts school at five and on her first day stands and watches shyly while another goes to play at once.

The explanation of these likenesses and differences between people in

J. Brierley, *Children's Well Being: Growth, Development and Learning from Conception to Adolescence.* Slough: N.F.E.R. 1980
'Individuality and its origins' pp 24–29
'Patterns of growth in the early years of childhood' pp 50–55
'Growth patterns of the middle years' pp 124–129

character and intelligence, whether they are related or not, is not an easy one. Broadly speaking characteristics are divided into those that are hereditary or genetic on the one hand and those that are due to the environment on the other. This is not a simple, clear-cut matter because heredity and environment interact in the production of each and every character and we cannot say how much has been contributed by each to most human characteristics. A few characters are unaffected by the environment: the blood group or finger-print pattern for instance. The most important human attributes and all those that are the concern of this book — height, weight, skin-fold thickness, 'intelligence', indices of mental stability, emotion — are the product of the heredity/environment interaction. The proportion of the inherited to the environmental component is unique to each individual. Put in another and more practical way, the family and school environments are crucial in determining which and how much of the potential inherited from parents is fulfilled.

Just how difficult it is to unravel which characteristics are due to heredity and which to environment is shown by a study of the causes of weight variation in babies at birth. Thirty per cent of the variation is due to unknown causes — perhaps the position of the foetus. The rest have been categorized thus: the influence of the hereditary constitution of the mother (20 per cent); of the child (16 per cent); the sex of the child (2 per cent). Environmental influences: 24 per cent of the weight variation is due to the mother's health and nutrition; 7 per cent to the order of the baby's birth; 1 per cent to the mother's age.

Heredity

Basic information on the working of heredity is now well known (. . .) The bringing together of hereditary material is ensured by having two different kinds of reproductive cells (gametes), a relatively large passive egg and a small active sperm which fuse at fertilization. The human egg can just be seen by the naked eye and is slightly smaller than the stop at the end of this sentence (140 µm in diameter). The sperm is scarcely 10 µm across and 100 µm long. After fertilization the zygote (fertilized egg) weighs about 34 thousandths of a gram.

The normal human sperm and egg each contain 23 chromosomes and these form the genetic dowry of the child. The chromosomes themselves are microscopic, threadlike bodies each of which carries a code for the future development of the individual. The code is contained in units (genes) which are too small to be detected by the microscope. These remarkable gene units which number probably 10^4 or 10^5 on the 23 pairs of chromosomes contain the chemical instructions for the design and development of the foetus provided the right 'environment' is present in the uterus in the shape of proper food and oxygen for growth.

The fertilized egg (zygote), then, has 46 chromosomes in 23 pairs. One of each pair has been obtained from the father through the sperm and the other from the mother through the egg. Forty-four of these chromosomes can be seen under the microscope to be in matching pairs. In a boy there is a discrepancy in the twenty-third pair. One chromosome of this pair is much smaller than the other and is known as the Y or male sex chromosome. It is in fact the male determiner. On its presence or absence depends whether a boy or girl baby is born. The Y's partner is the X chromosome. A boy baby has 22 matching pairs of chromosomes and an odd pair XY. A girl has no such odd pair and has 23 pairs of matching chromosomes of which one pair is the XX pair.

The sex of the child is settled in the first half-hour of life. There is nothing mysterious about this for gender is determined by the father's sperm. Half a man's sperm cells carry a Y chromosome and half an X. If a Y-carrying sperm fuses with an egg, an XY zygote is formed which eventually develops into a boy. The XX zygote develops into a girl.

The boy/girl difference is perhaps the most basic kind of human variety. Other variations within a family come about because the genetic blueprint of the child is often slightly different from that of each parent because the egg and sperm from which a child is formed each carries a different arrangement of genes from each of the parental sets. This is because the units of heredity, the genes, can be combined and recombined in different ways during egg and sperm formation so that, although all the genes in a child may well be identical to those of his parents, they may as indicated be shuffled into a slightly different order on the chromosomes and so have a slightly different effect in the offspring.

Rarely, a gene may be quite different from that of the parent because its chemical nature has changed through mutation. A mutation can help to make us differ from our parents, however slightly. Sometimes an extra chromosome gets caught up in the fertilized egg to make a package of 47 rather than the normal 46. In some cases this causes Down's syndrome (. . .)

It is an amazing thought that a child with all its attributes develops from the tiny fertilized egg weighing only a fraction of a milligram.

When the fertilized egg in the uterus begins to divide into two, four, eight, sixteen cells, each cell contains the set of 46 chromosomes. From the time of fertilization up to the end of the eighth week the mass of cells which will become the baby is technically called the embryo; from the ninth week to birth it is called a foetus.

When a baby is born it has about 25 million million cells all of which are identical in chromosome number, exactly duplicating the genetic information in the original fertilized egg.

The uniqueness of the individual

One might ask why the maintenance of human variety is essential. Variety of people in a society not only adds delight and interest to the human scene but is of great importance since it makes the human species more adaptable to change. The hereditary machinery as explained makes variety possible by dealing out different packages of genes to each individual. It has been estimated that each human parent is potentially capable of producing over eight million genetically unique types of gamete.

The unique character of each child can sometimes make it very hard for parents to value and love him for himself whatever his attributes. Children need more than anything to be accepted and rejoiced over, whoever and whatever they are. For teachers it can be equally hard because some children are downright nasty and unlikeable even at five. But for each and every one, success needs to be found and praise and encouragement need to be given — 'we get interested in what we get good at' — to quote Jerome Bruner's simple truth (Bruner 1960). Human variety suggests an important principle for education: equal treatment for all is not fair treatment for all. 'Discovery' methods for instance thoughtlessly applied to all children in a class may put some at grave disadvantage since some shy, introverted children like rules to work to while extroverted children do better by having explanations of 'rules' after practical, discovery methods.

On a more general plane, to make the most of individual abilities each child because of his or her different (not 'better') hereditary endowment needs a different environment to develop his or her talents to the utmost. This is a far-off goal but it is one worth striving for. Many primary schools adopt a variety of types of organization in arranging the work of the classes. The report on *Primary Education in England* (DES 1978) states that in the mass of schools the organization is designed 'to provide satisfactorily for children of different attainments and abilities, to accommodate various types of work, including practical work, and to take advantage of the resources and teaching strength available within a particular school'. Most secondary schools attempt to give educational justice to children; some by streaming, grouping or setting in groups of roughly similar abilities, others by 'mixed ability' teaching. Whatever system is used it follows from a knowledge of human variation that it is just to treat different children differently so long as each is treated as well as possible.

Patterns of growth in the early years of childhood

Eighty to a hundred years ago infant mortality was very great; parents then had large families but did not expect all their children to live. New-born babies and infants have always been frail and vulnerable but in the relatively short space of time since the reader's father or grandfather was born, childbirth has become much safer. Now birth and the first years of life are less hazardous than they were, at least in developed parts of the world. There are fewer children in families and greater expectations for their health and education. This optimism has solid foundations. Besides safer birth, improvements in housing, cleanliness, nutrition and immunization have almost wiped out diseases that killed babies and young children in their thousands. All the same there are, as indicated earlier, many remaining black spots in the health and life chances of many children as recorded in infant and perinatal mortality rates.

Early growth patterns

Patterns of growth in children are complicated and fairly well defined. No prediction can be made at birth about a child's ultimate height because the size of a new born baby reflects the environment in the mother's uterus and not its future pattern of growth. A boy may be born small but grow large because of his genetic endowment. Not all genes are active at birth and some begin to act only after a period of time. Perhaps this phased effect of genes lends support to the common observation that children grow to resemble their parents increasingly as they grow older.

The average boy at four is 58 per cent and at five 62 per cent of his adult height, so comparisons can be made. An average girl, always more advanced in her growing than a boy, is already 62 per cent of her adult height at four; 66 per cent at five. The 'girls-first' rule is shown by the fact that she reaches 50 per cent of her adult height at 1.75 years compared with two years in a boy. There is so much variation among normal children however that this information cannot be used to work out how tall a child will become when he or she is grown up.

After birth a child grows faster than at any other time in life (but not as fast as before birth) usually doubling its birth weight in the first six months and reaching about three times its birth weight by a year. Even so from birth onwards the speed of growth declines compared with before birth. Just as a car may speed up or slow down within an hour or so the speed of growth may change from one part of a year to another, but this is not to say that growth takes place in fits and starts — it is a smooth process.

Up to about the age of four or five the speed of growth falls dramatically and from then up to the start of the adolescent spurt, at about 11 on average in girls and 13 in boys (the maximum speed is on average 12 in girls and 14 in boys) come the years of unspectacular growth when the rate remains practically constant with a height gain of about one centimetre per year. During the period of rapid growth in infancy a sufficient supply of Vitamin D is important for the calcification of bone, and the supplement of this vitamin may be necessary in the winter months up to the age of five and in children where there is a risk of malnutrition with either inadequate or imbalanced diets.

Boys and girls

The growth curves of boys and girls from birth to about five differ slightly. At birth the average boy is growing a bit faster than a girl but the velocity equalizes at about seven months. After this the boys' rate of growth falls off more than the girls' until aged four, and from then on there is no difference until adolescence.

A fat layer begins to be laid down 10 to 14 weeks before birth (26–30 weeks after conception) and infants born at the normal time have about 12 per cent of body weight as fat. Fat increases greatly in the first year of life. Girls are already a bit plumper than boys at birth, a trait that becomes more marked during childhood. But from about a year to around seven, both slim down and become sturdier; muscle replaces fat as infants turn their attention from eating and growing to walking and playing. In the arm, for example, the circumference remains the same from four to seven but the muscle/fat ratio changes in favour of muscle. In other words the pre-school and infant years are those in which the chunky physique of the newborn changes into the more elongated build of the child.

A number of sex differences in growth patterns quite apart from the reproductive organs, are present before puberty. Boys have longer and thicker forearms, relative to upper arms and as we shall see in a later chapter a boy's legs grow faster than the trunk just before puberty to give him relatively longer legs than a girl. This latter feature is mainly due to the longer period of pre-adolescent growth in boys.

Children of five or six are well aware of sex differences: 'boys are rougher, they fight'; 'men don't have babies — boys have different bodies'; but 'you get tom-boys and tom-girls'; 'they (boys) don't speak the same, some girls talk quietly, boys' voices are rougher and deeper'.

The description of growth in height given a moment ago is a coarse one and there are finer periods of growth which underlie the general growth rate. Within a year's space, as parents must have noticed, children of between five and nine do not grow at the same speed. For some the slowest growth takes place during autumn and winter, the fastest between January and July. For others there are comparable changes in growth rate but apparently independent of season. Before about five, when the speed of growth is decelerating rapidly, and during the adolescent spurt, seasonal changes in growth rate are masked by the speed of the overall change. Growth in weight is usually fastest in the autumn.

There is some slight evidence that day length, which varies during the seasons, may affect growth perhaps by influencing the glands controlling growth, through the eyes. In totally blind children the rate of growth does not vary as much with the seasons as it does with children of normal sight. This is not to say that blind children grow at a constant rate but their fastest and slowest growth may take place in any season. This fact however applies to many children with normal sight.

Early growth of the brain and head

Change in height is normally taken as an overall measure of growth but in man this masks a remarkable pattern of differential growth, particularly marked in the early years of life. Up to puberty the brain and head, including the sense organs, are growing faster than the body and it is only during and after the adolescent growth spurt at about 18 or 20, that the body catches up. Thus at the age of five the brain and head are about 80 per cent grown, the body only about 40 per cent. At around seven, the brain and head are 90 per cent grown, the body not quite at the half-way mark.

Like all products of evolution this pattern of growth is a highly efficient one for learning because up to puberty children are adapted for passing through a long period when they are relatively small, weak and dependent — in a physical sense. Yet the brain and sense organs are well developed and rapidly absorb and use experience from the environment. During the early years of life, in fact right up to puberty, a child is under 'tuition'; he can be kept in order and taught and can play with others without them hurting each other much. Because in the long past the human life span was short, evolution time-tabled these dozen or so years from birth to puberty as critical ones for learning. The growth spurt of puberty changes children into adults, themselves capable (in evolutionary terms) of dominating the young and caring for them.

Evolution has seen to it, therefore, that the brain at birth is poised ready to learn and to go on learning fast during the long childhood up to puberty. The brain itself is finely tuned and is in a two-way dynamic relationship with the environment and seems to strengthen its powers by practice. During these early years a child needs plenty of stimulus, play and language experience and good models to imitate if he is to develop well. If a child is socially and culturally deprived or underestimated at school by his teachers he is likely to make poor progress. The development of his mind could be hampered, not necessarily by physical damage to the brain by altering nerve pathways — though this is quite possible — but by creating an unsatisfactory state of mind by poor motivation and by learning to have a poor expectation of life. In this context *Primary Education in England* (DES 1978) indicated that children in inner city schools were more likely than others to be underestimated by their teachers and least likely to be given work which extended their capabilities. The evidence suggested that further improvement in the children's performance was possible.

Some factors affecting growth

Apart from some abnormalities, growth rates at any stage of development can be hampered by bad feeding, disease and unhappiness. When health and well-being improve a return to normal height is achieved by a big catch-up growth to a normal pattern. How this catch-up growth is regulated is not understood but its machinery is so sensitive and effective that it allows growth to return almost completely to its previous pattern after a set-back. This is a sensible arrangement for in bad times the child stops growing, saves his energy and waits for better times.

Happiness, as we all know, is essential to good health and growth in children but it is hard to pin down exactly how it operates. Commonsense tells us that good food, warmth, comfort, cleanliness, love and a ready ear to worries are all important to health and growth and 'good' homes are not necessarily dependent upon plenty of money or property. There is one classical case which 'proves' that good growth is linked with love and happiness. It happened in Germany just after the last war. Extra food was given to childen but it did not result in the expected growth. This was because it was given by a disagreeable, harsh and repressive sister-in-charge who frightened the children. She had favourites, however, who benefited from the extra food by gain in weight (. . .)

There is some evidence too that some children do not grow so well in term-time as in school holidays no matter whether they are day pupils or at boarding school.

The effect of stress on happiness, appetite and consequently nutrition and growth is clearly complex, certainly involves the body glands, and needs further investigation. The Bible sums up human wisdom on the matter: 'Better a dinner of herbs where love is than a stalled ox and hatred therewith'. This is the simple message that needs to be taken seriously and acted upon.

What has been written about growth in general terms should not conceal the important fact that each child will have its own pattern of growth. Some children are fast, some slow growers, something that will be considered further in the chapter on adolescence. To treat all as equal is to follow a programme which is suitable for the few who happen to fit the mean course of growth.

Growth patterns of the middle years

During this middle year period of growth big changes take place in children — in body size, in physiology and in social behaviour. At the age of seven boys and girls in a top infant class are much the same in build, though boys are a shade taller, less plump and more muscular. By contrast at 12 most boys are only on the threshold of puberty but many girls are in the middle of it as judged by their growth spurts. These statements are of course about averages and need qualification. A boy reaches the great spurt of growth (one characteristic of puberty) at about 14 but it can take place between 9 and 15. Girls grow fastest at about 12 but the spurt can happen at any age between 10 and 15. Girls are much more advanced sexually than boys at 12 and, from about 10½ to around 13, on average a shade taller, rather more muscular and heavier than boys. This does not mean of course that all girls are bigger than all boys at 12. There is a range but it is true that the tallest girls are appreciably taller than the biggest boys while the shortest girls are taller than the smallest boys.

In a class of 12 year olds in a middle or secondary school, therefore, the sex differences have opened up and there is a big variation in body size, strength, shape, degree of sexual maturity and in behaviour. These variations may be hard for the individual pupil to cope with and it is important for the teacher to understand these differences.

Details of body composition

This is a rather bare description of physical development, and some detail can be illuminating. From the age of seven in girls there is a gradual increase in body fat which continues through puberty. In boys there is an interesting pre-adolescent spurt in fat growth at about ten and then a loss of fat from limbs during puberty. But the gap in total body fat between girls and boys is considerable and persists, girls continuing to put on fat as adolescence proceeds while in boys the gain stops and reverses. The proportion of muscle tissue remains more constant in both sexes, contributing more weight in boys than in girls at all ages. One set of data gives the percentage of fat in girls of nine as around 16 per cent and in boys, 12 per cent; for muscle, the figures are, for girls 42 per cent, for boys 46 per cent. At 12 girls are about 22 per cent fat and 44 per cent muscle while boys are 18 per cent and 46 per cent respectively. At 15 girls still have around a fifth of their body weight as fat and this proportion continues at least in the young adult. Boys have shed some fat by about 15 and are down to about 15 per cent body weight. The proportion then drops to about 10 per cent in young adults. The puppy fat about which some girls are often embarrassed in adolescence gives them feminine curves and even at twelve increases their sexual attractiveness before they are mature enough to be interested in the opposite sex.

Apparently these broad trends in body composition mask a cyclical accumulation of fat and muscle during childhood but as stated, fat accumulation predominates in early childhood and puberty. In many children the rate of accumulation is greater than it should be and they become obese. Indeed obesity is a common condition with an incidence of at least 6 per cent in the early and middle school years; it may approach 20–30 per cent in adolescence, especially in girls, and is often accompanied by emotional and physical disability. Such children are often teased at home but more at school. They may become isolated because they are morose and difficult as well as physically sluggish. To be fat and happy (. . .) is not the lot of the fat child. Prevention of obesity is easier than cure. Treatment consists of a balanced diet containing fewer calories than the energy requirements of the child, supported and accompanied by considerable psychotherapy.

School tuck shops can be a pitfall for the obese and potentially obese. Too often they sell chocolate and biscuits easy to stock and undeniably popular, rather than fruit which can be stored for a limited period of time only.

Coordination

Regarding the coordination and physical capabilities of children in these years there appears to be little difference in strength, agility and balance between boys and girls before adolescence. Arm thrust and pull is similar, strength of leg muscles is no different but there is a marked difference in strength of hand grip, boys having the stronger grip from about nine or ten.

After the growth spurt boys catch up and overtake the girls and finish some 10 per cent greater in weight and most external measurements, and a good deal stronger.

Coordination of hand and eye improves steadily through the primary years. Children of five often have difficulty in catching or hitting a ball; at ten or eleven they are much more dextrous.

After adolescence too the coordination skills, strength and speed of boys increase. There is no shred of evidence that clumsiness is a characteristic of adolescence; a clumsy twelve or thirteen year old is likely to have been a clumsy eight year old and will grow up into a clumsy man or woman.

The Primary Survey (DES 1978a) makes it clear that, as children grow in physical strength and capabilities, team games are played with considerable enthusiasm and a great deal of skill is achieved by many. In addition, many schools encourage experience of body movement through dance, drama and large physical movements such as climbing, balancing and swimming. During the primary school years, the proportions of children change; legs become longer, bodies comparatively compact. The ability to run and leap increases from five to eleven. Children of ten and eleven outgrow the typical primary school hall and much of the apparatus provided in it. To cope with the growing powers of coordination and skill children of ten to thirteen need facilities that allow the development of football, cricket, hockey, netball and tennis. In these later years separation of boys and girls for some aspects of PE may be considered necessary. Boys' and girls' interests in games and athletics often run in different directions or, where they are similar, the greater speed and increasing strength of boys may indicate a need for separate teaching.

The importance of exercise

Perhaps something should be said at this point about the importance of regular exercise to the young and the need for parents to encourage individual, non-competitive sporting pleasures. The message is already getting across to adults that they may be able to stave off heart disease by preventive measures. There is understandably much less consciousness of the need for these measures among children but childhood is a vital time to start good behaviour patterns to prevent later disease. Regular exercise helps to maintain a healthy weight and to keep blood pressure and cholesterol levels down. Children today do not walk much or take regular exercise in other forms. Besides the team games and physical education of school (which are unlikely to be continued when they leave) there is a need for parents to encourage walking and cycling for pleasure, also skating and perhaps, after twelve, golf, squash and tennis. The seeds sown in childhood may grow into pleasurable experiences later.

Girls and boys

Strength and toughness are important in the world of the small boy and advantage is given in this respect to the early maturer who at ten or eleven is likely to become top dog on the field, in the playground and in the street. At this age and in these circumstances, the small, immature boy is at a disadvantage. For most boys of eleven or twelve, however, the growth spurt and the manifestations of puberty are still to come. In girls on the other hand, the growth spurt starts at ten and reaches its maximum speed at twelve. The first sign of the changes of puberty in a girl is usually a slight growth of the central area of the breast — the 'bud'. This happens on average at about eleven and by twelve it has occurred in 75 per cent of girls. In more advanced girls the breasts may be fully mature by 12 but in others the process is not completed before 19.

Pubic hair growth appears in about half of girls at just over eleven, before the development of the breast bud and the adult distribution of hair in girls is usually attained between twelve and seventeen. In most boys, however, full adult hair is seldom reached until the mid-twenties. Hair first appears just after twelve but does not grow rapidly until the growth spurt at about fourteen.

Although the growth spurt happens earlier in girls than boys by about two years, other aspects of sexual development do not take place much later in boys than girls. Boys' reproductive organs start to develop about the same time as breasts in girls and complete sexual maturity is reached about the same average age in both sexes. Girls' looks at puberty — bigger than boys, with obvious breast development — make eleven and twelve year old boys look immature. But in boys the early development of the reproductive organs is concealed by clothes, and the obvious changes, the shooting up in height, deepening of the voice and the development of facial hair, do not happen until the reproductive organs are nearly mature.

Underlying the growth process and indeed the start of puberty is the control of hormones. No simple scheme is known for the hormonal control of growth in children but it is well understood that puberty is started by a nervous signal (about which nothing is known) from the hypothalamus at the base of the brain which triggers the pituitary gland into increasing the output of certain hormones. These in turn cause other hormones to be secreted in larger quantities from the ovaries or testes and adrenal glands and these hormones are the immediate causes of the changes of puberty — the growth spurt, changes in body fat/muscle and the appearance of the secondary sexual characteristics. In most girls the full spate of the hormone changes begins by twelve and in boys the activity of the adrenal glands is gradually increasing. As with the instruments of an orchestra, no hormone is more important than another in the process of growth and adolescence, and a deficiency of any will lead to impaired growth.

Developmental age

J.M. Tanner (1978) has been a steady and convincing advocate of the importance of developmental rather than chronological age in education. The facts are that children who are physically mature for their age score slightly higher in intelligence tests than those who are less mature but of the same chronological age. The difference is consistent and detectable as early as six and a half. Early maturers have been found to be significantly more successful in 11+ tests than late maturers though as far as it is known the difference in intelligence tests scores between early and late maturers vanishes as each completes his or her growth. It should be emphasized however that the demonstration of these relationships in large groups of children does not imply that all large or early-maturing children are more intelligent than all small or late maturing ones. Similarly in emotional development, few top classes of primary schools are without children who have started their growth spurt with an increase in self-consciousness. In the 11–13 years of middle and secondary schools most girls are 'mature', most boys not. As Tanner points out 'when boys and girls are educated together we must never lose sight of the fact that girls are physically and emotionally more advanced at all ages than boys'.

In girls, the early developer, conscious of her developing breasts, may slouch and find the public conditions of showers after games or PE an agony that needs great understanding from adults. In relation to the clumsiness mentioned earlier, the girl who slouches and wears a shapeless cardigan to hide her growing breasts appears clumsy to the beholder. The late maturer may have his or her problems too, wondering privately whether he or she will ever grow up into a sexually normal adult. In these respects and others it is most important that teachers should discuss the normality of human variation at this time, to reassure the girl, for example, one of whose breasts enlarges before the other, or the boy who is embarrassed by the temporary enlargement of his breasts. Time will put these worries right but they are hard to bear at the time. Indeed if children are not taught about the wide variance in normal growth and development, they perceive such variance as abnormal, to the detriment in some cases of their psychological development.

Throughout this paper the biological uniqueness of the individual has been stressed. Abilities and personalities differ from individual to individual and some children develop early and others late. All this is hard evidence for the importance of the notion of developmental age. However, for administrative purposes in education the convenient but very misleading criterion of chronological age has to be used: that is, the age from birth.

Developmental age is educationally a more sensible criterion because it is based on a flexible and dynamic and not an archaic, rigid view of growth and development. All would be straightforward if all children jumped their developmental hurdles at the same time, but the evidence tells us that they do not. Age of admission to school, age of transfer from one school to another, age of leaving, classification by IQ and examinations, the type of curriculum, are all mainly based on chronological age.

The basic aim of most schools is to develop the potentialities of the individual child, and to create the right sort of atmosphere in which he can learn and develop his abilities, both social and intellectual. Schools strive to do this and to 'know individuals' despite the differing rates of development of the children in their charge. The Newsom report (DES 1963) makes this relevant point about human individuality:

> There were well over two and three-quarter million boys and girls in maintained secondary schools in 1962, all of them individuals, all different. We must not lose sight of the differences in trying to discover what they have in common.

Topics for discussion

1. Outline the hereditary basis of individuality.
2. What major differences occur in the growth curves of boys and girls from birth to adolescence?
3. What use is the concept of *developmental age* to the classroom teacher?

Suggestions for further reading

1. Bower, T.G.R. (1979) *Human Development*. San Francisco: W.H. Freeman and Co.
2. Bruner, J. and Garton, A (eds) (1978) *Human Growth and Development*. Oxford: Clarendon Press.
3. Mussen, P.H., Conger, J.J. and Kagan, J. (1979) *Child Development and Personality*. New York: Harper and Row, 5th edition.

READING FOUR • Sex-role differentiation in social development   C. Hutt

Sex-roles or sex stereotypes?

Sex-roles constitute the sum of those interests, attitudes, behaviours and expectations which an individual, as a result of being man or woman, boy or girl, holds, enacts and fulfils.

Stereotypes are economical and convenient ways of categorizing and generalizing our knowledge. Stereotypes, therefore, embody our notions of what is typical, of what is characteristic of most of the members of any category. When categories are dichotomous, such as male and female, the stereotypes tend to be extreme, since traits are more readily regarded as sex-typical or not. What stereotypes ignore is the degree of overlap there is between the categories, but such an omission is inevitable in exclusive categorical generalizations. Moreover, the categories of male and female are more definitive than any other form of categorization of behaviour, traits or attitudes, since they are based on generally unambiguous physical characteristics.

Arising from these stereotypes are sex-role standards or expectations about the way members of each sex should behave. It is customary and fashionable to deplore these sex stereotypes and the consequent sex-role standards as a procrustean imposition of 'Society', thereby ascribing to an abstract social construct the properties of operators and manipulators. Society, however, consists of people, of agents, of institutions, of organizations, and the pressures that emanate from these sources and the manner in which they operate are by no means similar. Nothing is to be gained, in understanding or in argument, by the ascription of influences to an ephemeral and mythical agency. What is required is a close examination of how individuals — parents, teachers — institutions, the media, etc. convey their expectations and exert their influences. Furthermore, it is imperative to enquire as to the source of these expectations: why does 'society' expect

C. Hutt, 'Sex-role differentiation in social development', in, H. McGurk, *Issues in Childhood Social Development*, London: Methuen, 1978, pp 171–202

males to be aggressive and females to be affiliative, males to be achieving and competitive and females to be dependent?

Such examinations, however, often reveal that the bases for some of these expectations lie in differences in aptitudes or behaviour between the sexes. For example, Stein and Smithells (1969) looked at sex-role standards about achievement in certain academic areas. Their subjects were 7-year-olds, 11-year-olds and 16- to 19-year-olds. Altogether, social, artistic and reading skills were considered most feminine (and least masculine) whereas athletic, spatial and mechanical and arithmetic skills were considered most masculine. It may be seen that, in general, the subject-areas which are rated feminine are the areas in which girls perform better and vice versa.

Thus expectations, preferences and choices are to a large extent determined by differences in aptitude which in turn appear to have some biological basis.

Or consider again Haavio-Mannila's (1967) survey of sex-role expectations and performance in Finland which showed that women were expected to participate less in social activities outside the home than were men. In terms of their *actual* behaviour this difference was borne out, despite the fact that two-thirds of Finnish women work outside the home. Furthermore, women were more satisfied with their occupational positions, even though few of them occupied influential or prestigious ones — than with the division of household tasks. This example from a society which professes to hold egalitarian views of sex-role again illustrates that the stereotypes and expectations have some factual basis, however slight. Of course it could be argued that men or women behave in a particular way because they have been socialized to do so but this circular argument is both facile and sterile, and leaves unanswered the question of why socialization pressures are the way they are.

Sex-roles and sex stereotypes have their origins in the division of labour associated with reproductive roles. Only women menstruate, gestate and lactate. In primitive societies these three functions alone led to the differentiation of other associated activities as sex-typical behaviours. Broadly speaking women were concerned with those activities to do with the rearing of children and this function inevitably meant a focusing of attention on domestic functions, even if these sometimes entailed physically exacting activities like carrying heavy jars of water long distances to the home. Males, on the other hand, were traditionally concerned with the procurement of food and therefore predominantly with labours outside the house, and which eventually involved them in the decision-making processes associated with the apportionment of resources (. . .) The roles of men and women in the distribution of these resources still leaves the 'administrative' balance in favour of the males.

A number of aptitudes and characteristics were also associated with these traditional sex-roles and were clearly selected for in the process of evolution (. . .) Many of the characteristics have a neural or hormonal basis, suggesting that in the struggle for survival they did confer a selective advantage (. . .)

Such characteristics form the bases of sex differences like the spatial superiority of males and linguistic superiority of females. Many of these characteristic differences also constitute the bases of sex-roles. The aggression, competitiveness and assertiveness of the male and the nurturant, affiliative propensities of the female have some hormonal basis (. . .)

Consideration of the outcomes in those societies which have espoused an ideological commitment to the abolition of the sexual differentiation of labour is particularly instructive, since in every case the disparity between the ideology and the practice is considerable. The exploitation of women in the Soviet Union is explicitly proscribed but Lenin's exhortations have an ironic ring in the context of a system which determines that one job for the man means two for the wife. The statistics (. . .) present a gloomy picture indeed of the working mother's life and leisure.

The picture is far from rosy for Russian women: they are under-represented in the decision-making machinery and over-represented in the more menial jobs. In the People's Republic of China similar distinctions prevail (Tavris and Offir 1977):

> Some occupations are still regarded as 'women's work': almost all teachers in primary school, nurses, daycare attendants, and flight attendants are women. All visitors observe that fathers and grandfathers have a warm and tender relationship with their young relatives and spend much time with them, but there have been no efforts to get men to work professionally with children.

In Scandinavia, where protagonists of egalitarianism have been vociferous, no less than in many other countries, and irrespective of national policy or ideology, the traditional division of labour is maintained.

It is perhaps in the Kibbutz that the strongest endeavours have been made to eliminate sex-roles and to achieve complete equality of the sexes. After the initial period of ideological fervour, however, there has been a gradual reversion to a more traditional pattern where men work in the production industries and women in the service industries (. . .) This tendency is even more marked in the generation which had received its socialization in the Kibbutz and therefore had been exposed to no pressures which emanated from the recognition of sex differences. Women eventually showed a clear preference for the conventional female roles, in particular for childcare, and insisted on undertaking these roles despite the objections of the men. Their participation in the Assembly and administrative machinery correspondingly decreased.

Evidence of this kind provides some support for the view that there are biological bases for sex-roles — for the predilections women have for close interpersonal relationships, for communication, for the education and care of the young, as well as for the assertive, competitive, largely impersonal needs of men. Such an inductive statement is often misconstrued as prescriptive and thus taken to imply determinism (. . .) Such an interpretation, however, mistakes the nature of causes and places unnecessary restrictions on the manner of explanation. No rational scientist could be a determinist, of whatever sort, since this would imply a belief in an immutable sequence of events. The position adopted here is one that allows for the influence of biological factors in predisposing an individual to think and act in certain ways rather than others. Statements about 'causes' therefore become translated into statements about 'probabilities' and, in this particular case, hormonal exposure in early life is considered to set a certain bias in the individual's responses to his environment.

What is to be deplored, however, is the value-system which depreciates the attributes and work of women so that women underestimate their ability (. . .) Men as well as women have lower estimations of females than males (. . .) while even able women are fearful of success and what is attributed to skill in men is attributed to luck in women (. . .)

Such a value-system leads inexorably to a discriminating end.

An epigenetic* view of sex-role differentiation

Sex is the ascription to an individual of maleness or femaleness on the basis of biological features such as gonads and hormones and commonly ascertained by the external genitalia. Gender, on the other hand, is the indi-

---

* *epigenesis:* a theory of the development of the embryo which assumes that the process occurs through successive accretions and modifications brought about through the influence of the environment, and interaction of the parts. (J. Drever. *A Dictionary of Psychology*. London: Penguin Books, 1964.)

vidual's psychological identification with one sex or the other. The individual's sex is an integral part of his or her personal identity from the earliest moments of awareness. A child is named, dressed, treated and spoken of as a girl or a boy. The use of the inappropriate pronoun in reference to itself is speedily and consistently corrected by adults. In fact, the concept of self is gender-differentiated. Thus, the first aspect of its identity that the child is aware of is its gender and thereby his/her similarity to the parent of the same sex as well as to peers of the same sex. So far, the process of gender identification is seen as essentially similar to that described by Kohlberg. Once gender identity is established, many processes may contribute to further sex-role development.

As Thompson (1975) argues, there are three processes in gender development: (i) learning to recognize there are two sexes, (ii) inclusion of the self under one category or other, and (iii) the use of a label to guide sex-role preferences. Thompson found that two-year-old children used simple, physical cues, e.g. cranial hair, and clothes, to distinguish the sexes; by the age of thirty months many children were aware of their own sex and those of others and were showing a preference for same-sex pictures; by the age of thirty-six months they were using gender labels to direct their preferences.

The predisposition of young children to imitate the behaviour of same-sex peers and to show preferences for the attributes and activities of their own sex appears to be particularly strong. This tendency need not necessarily be seen in terms of a cognitive assimilation and restructuring of experience; it is more the result of an affective-conative drive to identify with the attributes and preferences of the same sex, thereby enabling the child to articulate more clearly an important part of its personal identity, vis-à-vis the opposite sex. Thus six-year-olds choose toys which they are told their own sex prefer and seven-year-olds are more attracted by and also perform better in a game when they are told it is a same-sex game (. . .) By the age of five years children already show a strong preference for same-sex clothes and objects (. . .)

Thus, the establishment of gender identity is strongly influenced by the gender assigned to the child. Where there is gender confusion it is as a result of parents' ambiguity about their own sex (as in cases of transvestism), or about the sex of the child. As Gershman (1967) points out 'The fact that the parents are clear in their belief that the infant is either male or female has permanent consequences for the child'. Where there is no equivocation on the part of parents or other adults about the child's sex, then definitive gender identification follows, as in Lev-Ran's series (1974) of sex anoma-

lies, which demonstrates the potency of the gender appellation for the establishment of personal identity, even in severe cases of hermaphroditism. Any repeal of gender is tantamount to a violation of personal identity — for John to become Jane is not simply a matter of change of gender but a change of person involving a total reconstruction of social role.

As Lewis (1977) argues, the infant manifests a concept of self during the last few months of the first year. This concept, however primitive, enables the infant to dichotomize social objects into those 'like me' and others, and subsequently to differentiate more finely amongst the category of 'like me'. Lewis regards three attributes of the self — age, familiarity and gender — as not simply being acquired very early in life but being the only ones necessary for the construction of a social matrix along which any social object can be located. Thus, gender is one of the earliest attributes of itself of which the child is aware.

Gender identity precedes the differentiation of sex-roles — the performance of sex-typical behaviours, and the adoption of sex-typical preferences (. . .) Sex-roles, moreover, are enacted with a characteristic masculine or feminine 'flavour' — a flavour which is imparted by the organizational influences of the gonadal hormones. A number of sex-role behaviours are also influenced by the natural aptitudes of boys and girls. The development of social and communicative preferences in girls has been neatly traced by McGuinness (1976): greater auditory sensitivity in infancy makes girls more responsive to many properties of sound, among them intonations and inflections of speech; hence their early focus and dependence on the linguistic mode which is further facilitated by neural programming which determines earlier and more complete cerebral lateralization of language functions (. . .) The verbal proficiency of females continues to place emphasis on communicative skills, and thence social expertise, as well as to determine subsequent preferences. A similar argument could be made for the exploratory and mechanical aptitudes of boys, their interest in the impersonal rather than the personal, their preference for the physical and mathematical sciences — all being influenced by their visuo-spatial abilities, an influence once again enhanced by cerebral asymmetry. Sensory thresholds and perceptual skills determine attentional styles (. . .) and thence influence the further processing of information. Preferences and propensities therefore are dependent on aptitude, and for many boys and men, for many girls and women, these will be of the kind already described.

Learning too may be easier for one sex than for the other, at least for certain materials. For example, performance on a memory task differed in girls and boys, depending on whether the material was presented auditorily or visually (. . .) For reasons such as these, different educational procedures for certain types of learning have been advocated (. . .)

In a study more relevant to socialization and sex-role development, Flerx et al. (1976) found that sex stereotypes were evident in children by the age of three years; in an attempt to get children to develop more egalitarian attitudes, they employed an intervention programme whereby male and female models were presented whose activities contradicted conventional stereotypes. Although this egalitarian treatment reduced some stereotyped beliefs, it was less effective with boys, who also had more stereotyped beliefs to start with. Thus environmental influences do not operate on similar entities, nor in similar ways.

The manner in which nature and nurture interact is one that concerns all developmental psychologists, yet models of development are rare. Two models which are particularly applicable to the development of sex differences have been discussed by Archer and Lloyd (1975). Taking issue with what they term an 'additive' model of genotype-environment interaction, they put forward an alternative 'interactive' model: this latter model however does little other than represent the term 'interaction' as a series of boxes and arrows — no parameters are specified, no processes are outlined, and it allows no distinctive predictions to be made.

Nevertheless, the implication of such a 'model' is that the interaction involves complex processes, unspecified though they be, which are more than facilitatory or inhibitory. But the distinction between 'additive' and 'interactive' is more a semantic than a substantive one — the epigenetic view is precisely that the basic processes of nature–nurture interaction are those of facilitation and inhibition, of accentuation or attenuation. Environmental influences in the first instance can only modulate behaviour, activity, interests and propensities that are already extant. This is conceded by Archer and Lloyd in their description of an 'interactive interaction':

> . . the initial tendency for boys to cry more than girls may interact with the mother's response to the crying in a way which amplifies and extends the original sex difference . . .

It is the essence of the argument outlined here that sex-role differentiation presupposes the establishment of gender identity; gender identity itself is the result of social factors which are most often in accord with biological ones. Thereafter upon the bases of natural aptitudes, skills and proclivities, and motivated by the affective-conative desire to acquire a stable identity,

sex-roles are developed through the processes of imitation, modelling, social learning and cognitive reorganization.

Topics for discussion

1. What evidence is there to support the view that sex-roles and sex stereotypes arise, in part, from biological differences between males and females?
2. Outline the process of gender identification.
3. What does the author mean when she asserts that 'the basic processes of nature-nurture interaction are those of facilitation and inhibition of accentuation or attenuation'?

Suggestions for further reading

1. Sutherland, M. (1983) *Sex Bias in Education*. Oxford: Blackwell.
2. Oakley, A. (1972) *Sex, Gender and Society*, London: Temple Smith.
3. Deem, R. (1980) *Schooling For Women's Work*. London: Routledge and Kegan Paul.

SECTION THREE
CHILDHOOD THINKING AND LEARNING IN THE PRIMARY YEARS

READING FIVE • Introduction to Piaget's theory: a psychological critique[1] G. Brown and C. Desforges Piaget's research into the minds of children[2] K. Sylva and I. Lunt

Many of the differences between a newborn infant and a two-year-old child are obvious. The elder child is bigger, more mobile, less dependent, has a wide repertoire of physical skills, can communicate many of his needs, has tastes, opinions, attitudes, favourite people, remembers a range of facts, names, times and promises and responds in elaborate ways to approaches made to him by others. Despite his achievements, however, he is a social, emotional and intellectual novice when compared with a four-year-old. The theorist working in developmental psychology seeks to explain these dramatic, age related changes.

In this undertaking a number of perennial issues are met. If some account is to be given of the changes as development proceeds then it is necessary to have detailed and accurate descriptions of the achievements at certain reference points. This in turn entails making choices about which part of the child's extensive behavioural repertoire to describe since it is unlikely that any exhaustive description could be possible. Given these necessarily selective descriptions of developmental attainments the theorist then has to consider how development proceeds. Will the acquisition be seen as gradual accumulations of experience or as abruptly appearing achievements, and, as a related issue, are the attainments of the four-year-old *qualitatively* different from those of the two-year-old or are they simply *quantitatively* different? Is the four-year-old's language, for example, more of the same kind of language that the two-year-old exhibits or is the elder child in possession of a radically different mode of communication? A fourth problem in accounting for development requires that the theorist explain the differential role of innate and experiential factors and of their possible

[1] The 'Introduction' from G. Brown and C. Desforges. *Piaget's Theory: A Psychological Critique*. London: Routledge and Kegan Paul. 1979 pp 1–2
and
[2] 'Piaget's research into the minds of children', in K. Sylva and I. Lunt, *Child Development: A First Course*. Oxford: Basil Blackwell. 1982 pp. 91–116

interactions. How far is the child's mode and level of intellectual functioning biologically determined at conception? How do particular life experiences interact with biological factors to enhance or limit the production of behaviours?

These problems of describing and accounting for developmental change are interrelated in complex ways. The selections made will not be random. The theorist will observe those specific behaviours which are felt to be most related to the problem he has in mind, and the conception of the problem will be informed by his stance on the nature/nurture debate, or on whether he conceives development to be a gradual and continuous accumulation of behavioural elements or a discontinuous, stepwise process of emergent functions. Of course the reverse process of influence is also true. Not only does our conception of development inform the kinds of data we select to solve problems of theory, the subsequent descriptions of behaviour in turn constrain our view of how development proceeds.

Put bluntly, the conception of a problem necessarily informs the selection of the data chosen as pertinent to the problem and selective and limited data necessarily constrain the subsequent view of the problem. In what follows, this point will be illustrated again and again. Whether, in the process of building theories of development, the above describes a vicious circle of self-confirmation or a growing spiral of understanding, we set aside for the moment.

Piaget's research into the minds of children

Ask a four-year-old to tell you the capital of France and he'll laugh and run away. Or ask a five-year-old the change he should get after paying 50 pence for sweets worth only 22. He'll look at you in surprise, as would a six-year-old asked to spell *obfuscate*. It's no wonder that young children are ignorant of geography, subtraction and spelling because these intellectual feats are mastered through lessons in school.

Now consider another case. A four-year-old falls off his bicycle and announces 'I fell off because it was Marie's birthday'. While it seems obvious to us that the birthday did not *cause* the accident, the child appears to think it did. Three years later, however, the same boy will say 'I fell off my bicycle because the front wheel skidded in a puddle and I went over the top'. Clearly children acquire sophisticated notions about cause and effect which they don't learn in class.

Teachers concentrate on numbers, letters and historical facts, paying little attention to the learning that occurs 'naturally'. But in fact the most comprehensive theory about the development of thinking focuses on 'spontaneous' rather than 'book' learning. It's the work of a Swiss psychologist, Jean Piaget. Like Freud, he did not begin his research by studying children; that was to come later.

Piaget was born in Neuchatel in 1896. He had a schoolboy passion for biology and his first nature report, published when he was 11, concerned an albino sparrow seen in the park. Between the ages of 15 and 18 he studied shellfish known as molluscs, writing several scientific papers on them while assisting the curator at a nearby museum to classify zoological specimens. As a young biologist, Piaget was concerned with the kinds of structures easily seen in the living mollusc, such as its protective shell. He was curious about various anatomical structures that helped animals cope with the environment in which they lived. Piaget was especially fascinated by evolution: how did *this* particular species come to have *this* particular structure enabling it to adapt to *this* particular environment?

After completing his zoological studies at Neuchatel, Piaget turned to other kinds of 'structures', *mental* ones, which are just as crucial for adaptation as those he studied earlier. In order to survive animals need knowledge *about* things and events (which berries are poisonous; when the sun sets) as well as knowledge about *how to do* things (how to build a nest). Mental structures consist of these two types of knowledge and Piaget was fascinated by them. Although anatomical structures are inherited through the genes, he wondered if mental ones were as well. Of course human beings have mental structures that are complex, such as the notion of 'honesty' or the ability to perform arithmetic subtraction. Are these inherited? Where do they come from?

Mental structures are more difficult to describe than anatomical ones because they do not correspond to known parts of the body. In order to investigate them, Piaget had to depart from the methods of biology.

Piaget's first attempt at the study of mental structures took place in the Paris laboratory of Binet and Simon, the birthplace of IQ testing. The assignment given the young Swiss was to standardize the French version of an English test, a tedious job but an important one since such tests must naturally present children of different nationalities with identical tasks.

While trying out his questions on children, Piaget showed immediately his unorthodox approach to intelligence. Instead of noting 'incorrect' on a wrong answer and continuing to the next question, he paused to reflect. He

in the similarities between children of roughly equivalent age. Like Freud, he wanted to unravel the immature mind, but unlike Freud, he attempted this by studying children who are prefectly normal.

In these early studies, Piaget did not manipulate variables in the manner of FORMAL EXPERIMENTATION. Instead, his early research programme attempted to *describe* the kinds of thinking characteristic of children before adolescence. He used a CROSS-SECTIONAL technique meaning that he interviewed many different children at several different ages.

Piaget questioned hundreds of children between the ages of 3 and 12 to discover how they thought about things as disparate as natural phenomena (the sun, moon, living creatures) and morality. He found that at first a child's thinking is characterized by **animism**, meaning that he considers natural phenomena to be alive just as human beings are. The sun began because 'it knew that life (i.e. people) had begun'. Lakes and pebbles act in intentional ways and all living creatures have the same feelings as we do. A little later, the child believes that some agent, either human or divine, created natural events. 'What makes the sun shine?' '. . . a big light, it is someone in Heaven who has set fire to it.'

That children have peculiar conceptions of natural events was not a new discovery. What made Piaget's research interesting was his going beyond isolated 'misconceptions' to find the systematic ways of thinking characteristic of children at various ages. One of these is *egocentrism*, the child's inability to consider events from the point of view of another. Egocentrism explains, to some extent, early animism because the child cannot conceive that natural phenomena are different from him and therefore imbues them with feelings and intentions like his own. Another is his inability to deal with *several aspects* of a situation at one time. But above all, Piaget tells us that the child before the age of six or seven is incapable of thinking logically. (Recall the little boy who fell off his bike on Marie's birthday.)

The development of logical thinking mystified Piaget. Just listening to people could account for some changes in the child's view of the world. For example, parents teach children that it doesn't hurt the log to be burnt and teachers struggle to explain the formation of rain clouds or the origin of the sun. However, logical thinking seems to develop quite spontaneously and it was to this that Piaget turned next. What are the roots of logic?

A radical and very fruitful change in method occurred in the years in which Piaget's three children were born. He turned his attention to their development, thinking that the precursors to logic might occur earlier than the years three to twelve he had studied so intensively. The clinical

found himself wishing to enquire further when a child made a mistake, probing the child's mind to see why, for him, something other than the 'standard' answer was appropriate. Of course, this is exactly what examiners at the lab were not permitted, and Piaget decided that intelligence testing was not for him.

But he did, luckily, catalogue enough wrong answers to conclude that children did not think at all like adults. Children's minds, it seemed, were organized differently from those of older people. In fact, children appeared to solve problems on an entirely different level; the difference between older and younger children was less a case of the older children having *more* knowledge than of their knowledge being of a different sort. With this discovery, Piaget began the study of the development of mental structures.

He began to think that what distinguished children's thought from that of adults was not the sheer amount of knowledge but its complexity. On the basis of children's 'mistakes' on intelligence tests, he guessed that there were dramatic shifts, during infancy and childhood, from one type of thinking to another.

Piaget returned to Switzerland to begin research of his own design. Its goals have remained constant from that time: the discovery and description of the mental structures (he calls them **schemas**) of children as they grow from infancy to adulthood. Piaget considered his lifetime's work a natural outgrowth of his early biological studies. Intelligence enables complex animals, including man, to adapt to their environments. Fundamental to intelligence are schemas consisting of knowledge *about* things/events and knowledge of *how to do* things.

Piaget began by studying children before entry into school; he asked them all manner of questions. 'Can a plant feel the prick of a pin?', 'Why does it rain?', 'Who were the first people to play marbles?' His method of interview was a far cry from ones used in intelligence testing because he gently explored the child's view of the world, tailoring his questions to the particular child he was talking to. If a child gave an interesting answer Piaget pursued it. If the child did not understand the question, Piaget clarified it. The aim of this method, called the 'clinical INTERVIEW' by Piagetians, was to follow the child's thoughts without distorting them. Although Piaget called this method 'clinical', it is quite different from the method used by Freud, and has nothing to do with psychiatry. But both of them studied one person at a time, rejecting a rigidly programmed list of questions so that they could follow the individual's thoughts. However, Piaget's interest was not in the uniqueness of individual children but rather

interview was not a useful technique with babies, so instead he had to rely on NATURALISTIC OBSERVATION — watching, but intervening as little as possible. Piaget watched his own three children, two girls and a boy, as they turned towards a finger stroking the cheek, looked at toys dangled before them, and attempted to solve 'puzzles' such as procuring a watch chain placed inside a matchbox. Such activities are commonplace in households with young children but Piaget saw them as indications of the development of intelligence. (Remember that for Piaget intelligence is not a score on a standardized test; it is that kind of mental activity that enables adaptation to the environment.)

Piaget worked out a theory that logical thinking develops in steps, broken at roughly two, and roughly seven years of age. Children, he showed, are not like vessels waiting to be filled up with knowledge. They actively construct their understanding of the world by interacting with it. At different periods of their development, they are capable of different kinds of interaction, and arrive at different kinds of understanding. The period before two (or so) he called the *sensory-motor period*, that from two to seven the *pre-operational period*, and that from seven on the *operational period* (which he subdivided into two — the *period of concrete operations* (seven to eleven years), and the *period of formal operations* (eleven to adulthood). We will now take a closer look at these periods, to see what happens in which, and how each leads on to the next.

The sensory-motor period

Think about the baby's early experiences of the breast, certainly an important object in his life. First he nestles in the crook of the mother's arm, looking towards the nipple several inches from his eyes. He makes incipient suckling actions, then his mother moves him closer so that he may take the nipple. Of course, the breast appears quite different now, and also much larger. Does the baby know that this is the same object he examined several seconds ago? Piaget says not. But the baby responds to many different images (including a finger) with sucking actions. Piaget would say he has a 'simple functional category'; that means he has a rough category of things to which he reacts in the same way — in this case by sucking. Of course, he doesn't recognize the breast in the sense of having a name for it, but he does in the sense of having a response to it, an **action pattern** for it.

Action patterns are the key to the **sensory-motor period**, since it is

through the combination of sensation and movement that the baby builds a permanent picture of the world. There follow several excerpts from Piaget's diary account of the development in Laurent of the action pattern, *striking objects*. Note that they begin when the boy was 0 years; 4 months (7) days old, and extended over one month.

> With regard to Laurent . . . striking arose in the following way. At 0;4(7) Laurent looks at a paper knife attached to the strings of a hanging doll. He tries to grasp the doll or the paper knife, but, at each attempt, the clumsiness of his movements results in causing him to knock these objects. He then looks at them with interest and recommences.
>
> The next day, at 0;4(8) same reaction. Laurent still does not strike intentionally but, trying to grasp the paper knife, and noting that he fails each time, he only outlines the gesture of grasping and thus limits himself to knocking one of the extremities of the object.
>
> At 0;4(9), the next day, Laurent tries to grasp the doll hanging in front of him; but he only succeeds in swinging it without holding it. He then shakes it altogether, while waving his arms. But he thus happens to strike the doll: he then begins again intentionally a series of times. A quarter of an hour later, as soon as he is confronted by the same doll in the same circumstances he begins to hit it again.
>
> At 0;4(15), faced by another hanging doll, Laurent tries to grasp it, then he shakes himself in order to make it swing, happens to knock it, and then tries to strike it.
>
> At 0;4(18) Laurant strikes my hands without trying to grasp them, but he has begun by simply waving his arms in the air and only 'hit' subsequently.
>
> At 0;4(19), at last, Laurent directly strikes a hanging doll. At 0;4(21) he strikes the hanging toys in the same way and thus swings them as much as possible. Same reaction on the following days.
>
> From 0;5(2) Laurent strikes the objects with one hand while holding them with the other. Thus he holds a rubber doll in the left hand and strikes it with his right. At 0;5(6) he grasps a rattle with a handle and strikes it immediately. At 0;5(7) I hand him different objects which are new to him (a wooden penguin, etc.): he hardly looks at them but strikes them systematically.

In the first three days Laurent develops a striking routine when the paper knife and doll hang above him. Piaget reminds us that the baby has acquired something more than a series of actions (locating the toy in space, raising hand to be ready to strike, executing the swiping movement, then stopping his hand's forward motion while continuing to observe the movement of the toy). He has constructed a mental structure, called an *action schema*, that guides the various steps in hitting a toy, and toy of the same sort of size. A week later at 0;4(15) he is confronted by a different doll and does not strike at it, until, by chance he happens to knock it. The sight of it swinging triggers his 'striking schema' and he deliberately strikes the new doll.

In Piaget's terminology, the schema developed with the paper knife *takes in*, *or* **assimilates** a new object. The schema itself changes little but it now includes the possibility of a new object.

In his fifth month, Laurent encounters a new situation — the toy in the hand rather than dangling above him. Whereas he could easily assimilate a new object into the schema of it dangled before him, he must now change the schema if he wishes to strike the hand-held toy. This he does, and Piaget would say that the striking schema adapts itself, or *accommodates* to the new situation. In this instance, accommodation involves coordination of two hands because now the baby must use *both* left and right whereas before he used but one.

Piaget says that a baby is born with simple schemas for sucking, grasping and the like. The process of assimilation enables him to 'take in' information about all sorts of objects he acts upon. For example, he learns about the breast, his own fingers, and a variety of toys by sucking on them. Very early in life, these things have no meaning to him except as part of his action schemas. Later, as seen in the case of Laurent in the excerpt above, some actions in the world require schemas to be adapted to suit new circumstances. As a result of this kind of accommodation, his schemas become differentiated and more complex, and so the process goes on.

In summary, Piaget began his study of children in search of mental structures that enable intelligent adaptation to the complicated world of events and people. He called these structures 'schemas' and he found that the simplest kind were present at birth. As the baby acts on the world, he assimilates objects and events to the schemas, thereby building a store of knowledge. Further, his schemas accommodate to new experiences — they become more differentiated and complex, and assimilate a wider range of objects in a wider range of ways. In a sense, the baby constructs more complex schemas by using his simple ones.

The development of the object concept *during the sensory-motor period*

By the time a child is two, the end of the sensory-motor period of intellectual development, he has an effective repertoire of coordinated schemas for dealing at the practical level with the world. These early schemas are the precursors to later ones that include **logical operations**. During the first

two years he learns much about objects, time, space and causality. We turn to the first as it has been studied extensively by Piaget as well as others. There follow observations of the three Piaget children learning about objects. At first, if you recall Laurent and the striking schema, objects exist in the child's world only as part of his actions. Later, as you will see, they take on an interest in their own right.

> At 0;8(30) Laurent, for the first time, examines a wooden hen from which hangs a ball which activates the animal's head by its movements. First he sees the hen, touches it, etc., then examines the ball, feels it and, seeing it move, strikes it immediately; he then attentively watches it swing and then studies it for its own sake; he simply sets it in motion, more and more gently. Then his attention is brought to bear on the accompanying movement of the hen and he swings the ball while watching the hen.

> Lucienne, at 0;8(10), likewise, examines a new doll which I hang from the hood of her bassinet. She looks at it for a long time, touches it, then feels it by touching its feet, clothes, head, etc. She then ventures to grasp it, which makes the hood sway. She then pulls the doll while watching the effects of this movement. Then she returns to the doll, holds it in one hand while striking it with the other, sucks it and shakes it while holding it above her and finally shakes it by moving its legs.

> Afterwards she strikes it without holding it, then grasps the string by which it hangs and gently swings it with the other hand. She then becomes very much interested in this slight swinging movement which is new to her and repeats it indefinitely.

> At 0;8(9) Jacqueline looks at a hanging necktie which she has never seen. Her hands move around it and touch it very warily. She grasps it and feels its surface. At a certain moment part of the necktie escapes her grasp: visible anxiety, then, when the phenomenon is repeated, satisfaction and, almost immediately after, something which resembles an experience of letting go and recapturing.

There is a considerable difference between the way children of four or five months act when they come across a new object, and the way the same children do four months later. The eight-month-old examines it as though it presented a problem to his mind — as though he were trying to understand it. Not only does he look at it for far longer before starting to act on it (strike it, suck it, or whatever), he also feels it, explores its surface and edges, turning it over and around. All this shows a completely new attitude: the unfamiliar represents for him an external reality — he has to adapt himself to it. It is not simply part of his action schema. He does, after taking a good look, try his schemas on it. But in doing so he gives the impression that he's trying an experiment rather than just assimilating yet another object to his schema. Piaget says '. . . it is as though the child said to himself when confronted by the new object: "What is this thing? I see it, hear it, grasp it, feel it, turn it over, . . . what more can I do with it?" '

But although children at about eight months show an active interest in *objects for their own sake*, they show no knowledge of the fact that objects continue to exist regardless of whether they are exploring and acting on them or not. Consider the following observation on Jacqueline, just coming up to her eight month 'birthday',

> At 0;7(28) Jacqueline tries to grasp a celluloid duck on top of her quilt. She almost catches it, shakes herself, and the duck slides down beside her. It falls very close to her hand but behind a fold in the sheet. Jacqueline's eyes have followed the movement, she has even followed it with her outstretched hand. But as soon as the duck has disappeared — nothing more! It does not occur to her to search behind the fold of the sheet, which would be very easy to do (she twists it mechanically without searching at all) . . . I try showing it to her a few times. Each time she tries to grasp it, but when she is about to touch it I replace it very obviously under the sheet. Jacqueline immediately withdraws her hand and gives up. The second and third times I make her grasp the duck through the sheet and she shakes it for a brief moment but it does not occur to her to raise the cloth.
>
> Everything occurs as though the child believed that the object is alternately made and unmade . . .

The observations of Laurent, Lucienne and Jacqueline demonstrate clearly the method of NATURALISTIC OBSERVATION in which the researcher does not intervene with the children he studies. But remember that Piaget was a father as well as a scientist and the informal 'experiments' he performed on his children, such as hiding a doll, were no more than familiar games played by all parents. They constituted a deliberate manipulation of the child's experiences little different from that performed by most parents. What distinguished Piaget from other parents was the theory he slowly constructed as a consequence of watching and playing with his children.

The observations also demonstrate that children during their first year change in their actions towards objects. At first they seem to use them simply as material (Piaget called it **aliment** or food) for their action patterns, and only towards eight months and beyond do they seem to be truly curious about them. In other words, at first they appear to ask 'Can I *strike* (or *rub* or *suck*, etc.) this thing?' with little concern for what the thing really is. By eight months, however, they appear to ask themselves 'what is this unique object? how can I act upon it to tell me more about its characteristics?' Finally, at nine months or thereabouts, babies do search for hidden objects, demonstrating that they know that objects exist in definite locations despite the fact that they are out of sight.

The pre-operational period, *sometimes called the intuitive period*

Sometime during the second year of life children begin to talk. At first they use single words, like 'milk' when they want a drink. Later, they string several words into sentences such as 'Daddy go bye-bye'. Before language appears, children's intelligence is practical in nature — they know *how* to act in the immediate environment. With language, their mental schemas are transformed into symbolic ones. They are no longer trapped in the here and now but can discuss events that occurred in the past and those that will occur in the future 'snow on tree' and 'Granny come'.

Because the two-year-old has words for objects and events in his daily routine, he can think about the world without acting on it. However, despite a rapidly expanding vocabulary, the child between two and seven does not think like an adult or use language in the same way. Piaget reports on one of his daughters:

> At about 2;6, she [Jacqueline) used the term 'the slug' for the slugs we went to see every morning along a certain road. At 2;7(2) she cried: 'There it is,' on seeing one and when we saw another ten yards further on she said 'There is the slug again.' I answered, 'But isn't it another one?' I went back to see the first one. 'Is it the same one?' 'Yes,' she answered. 'Another slug?' 'Yes,' she answered again. The question obviously had no meaning.

During the years between two and seven the child learns much about the physical world. He learns that inanimate objects need an outside force to set them in motion. He learns about the social world too, such as when to share and when to defend property. Some of this learning is spontaneous, while other is deliberately taught by parents and teachers. Despite the many intellectual feats of the period, children do not reason in a logical or a fully mathematical way. The girl of four will tell you that 'my sister doesn't have a sister' with no clue that the statement is logically impossible.

According to Piaget, this little girl reveals her incomplete understanding of the concept 'sister' because she fails to see the necessary reversibility between female siblings. Although she uses the same word as the adult, she has an incomplete concept rather than a mature concept.

In interviews with scores of children, Piaget found more instances of immature reasoning in young children. One child told him that the moon was alive.

> 'Why?'
> 'Because we are alive.'

This answer reveals both the **animism** (attributing life to inanimate objects) and the **egocentrism** (the inability to take into account the point of view of someone else) discussed earlier in the chapter.

Further examples of egocentrism appear in the answers of two little boys to questions about the game of marbles. These boys, who often played together, told Piaget about the rules which they followed. Much to his surprise, Piaget discovered that they followed very different rules — despite their frequent playing 'together'. Each boy played an individual game, showing that his understanding was egocentric. Children do not lose egocentricity in games before seven or eight, at which ages they can, at last, de-centre.

Children's thinking in the **pre-operational period** is characterized by what Piaget called **moral realism** as well as by animism and egocentrism. To learn about children's conceptions of morality, Piaget modified the clinical INTERVIEW somewhat. He told stories of good and naughty deeds, and followed them with questions. The stories were usually of two types: in one, the central character performed an unintentional act which resulted in a great deal of damage. In the other, the character caused a small amount of damage while acting in an intentionally naughty way. Here are two examples:

> A little boy who was called Augustus once noticed that his father's inkpot was empty. One day while his father was away he thought of filling the inkpot so as to help his father, and so that he should find it full when he came home. But while he was opening the ink bottle he made a big blot on the table cloth.

The corresponding story involving minor damage is as follows:

> There was a little boy called Julian. His father had gone out and Julian thought it would be fun to play with his father's inkpot. First he played with the pen, and then he made a little blot on the tablecloth.

After telling the stories, Piaget asked whether the children were equally guilty, or was one child the naughtier. Here are the replies from a girl of seven.

> 'Which is the most naughty?'
> 'The one who made the big blot.'
> 'Why?'
> 'Because it was big.'
> 'Why did he make a big blot.'
> 'To be helpful.'
> 'And why did the other one make a little blot?'
> 'Because he was always touching things. He made a little blot.'

'Then which one of them is the naughtiest?'
'The one who made a big blot.'

The child's morality speaks for itself; to cause a great deal of damage is to be naughty. Piaget claims that answers of this kind demonstrate moral realism because intentions are ignored while assigning guilt, and attention is focused on the realities of physical damage.

How can we summarize children's thinking in the pre-operational stage? The clinical interview allowed Piaget to conclude that it is characterized by animism, egocentrism, and moral realism. At first, these may seem disparate characteristics but they are alike in one way; they demonstrate a failure to deal simultaneously with several aspects of a situation. Animism is the failure to adopt one stance towards inanimate objects and another towards oneself. Similarly, moral realism is the consequence of viewing morality in one sense only, that concerned with damage. The young moral realist ignores intention as a contributor to guilt because he cannot consider damage and intention at the same time. And lastly, egocentrism is the consequence of the child's taking only one perspective, in games as well as in assigning kinship. The child achieves the next stage of intellectual development when at last he can consider a situation from several different aspects — in other words, he can de-centre.

> The newborn acts as if the world is centred about himself and must learn to behave in a more adaptive way. Similarly, the young child thinks from a limited perspective and must widen it. Both infant and young child must de-centre — the former, his action and the latter, his thought.

The operational period (*sub-period of* concrete operations)

At six or seven years, the child passes an important milestone when his thinking becomes logical. This does not happen overnight, of course, but in the space of a year or two the child can think on an entirely new plane. Recall that Piaget devoted his life to finding the roots of logical thinking. He discovered the early mental structures, or **schemas,** that underlie babies' sensory and motor abilities. Later, he saw how language enabled a child to represent his knowledge symbolically and to conceive of yesterday and tomorrow. But for all his apparent sophistication, the **pre-operational** child was seen to be limited in his thinking. Now consider the following scenario showing the kind of logic that *older children and adults* use every day.

The adult arranges six sweets in a row, then asks a child of seven to make a row which will be 'the same' as the original. The child carefully takes sweets from a saucer and makes a new row, parallel to the adult's and also containing six. When asked if they are the 'same amount' the child answers 'yes'. Then the adult rearranges his row by decreasing the distance between each sweet and making his row shorter in length. He asks the child to consider the number of sweets in each row. 'Are they the same now?' The child looks at the adult in amazement, and answers 'yes' without glancing at the sweets. Any reasonable person, *if he is logical,* knows that the rows must be the same because no sweets have been added or taken away. But that is precisely the point! A younger child is tricked by his perception; he would 'fail' the task.

Here is Piaget's report on a pre-operational child of five years, seven months named Per. He

> . . . had no difficulty in making a row of six sweets corresponding to the model. (Piaget uses 'model' to refer to row A, the row to be copied, and 'copy' to refer to row B.) The model was then closed up:
> 'I've got more.'
> 'Why?'
> 'Because it's a longer line.'
> (The process was then reversed.)
> 'Now there are more there, because it's a big line.'
> But a moment later, Per said the opposite:
> 'Are there more here?' (referring to the longer row).
> 'No'
> 'Why not?'
> 'Because it's long.'
> 'And there?' (the shorter row).
> 'There are more there, because there's a little bundle.' (The child meant that the shorter row was denser.)
> 'Then there are more in a little bundle than in a big line?'
> 'Yes.'
> After this, Per went back to using length as the criterion, made the two rows the same length again, and said:
> 'Now they're both the same.'

In Figure 1, Part 2, Per is 'tricked' by the appearance of things and so fails the task. Piaget calls this an experiment in **conservation** because it requires the child to conserve the number of items despite transformation in its appearance.

Note that the word 'experiment' has crept back into the text. To investigate the development of logical and mathematical abilities, Piaget had to abandon both NATURALISTIC OBSERVATION and the clinical INTER-

VIEW. He thought the latter depended too much on what the children actually said. Perhaps children knew more than they could express — perhaps his questions 'led them' to conclusions that were not theirs. He turned instead to formal experiments in which all children were presented with identical objects and events. In some instances the children were asked to manipulate the objects, such as in the following experiment (Figure 2).

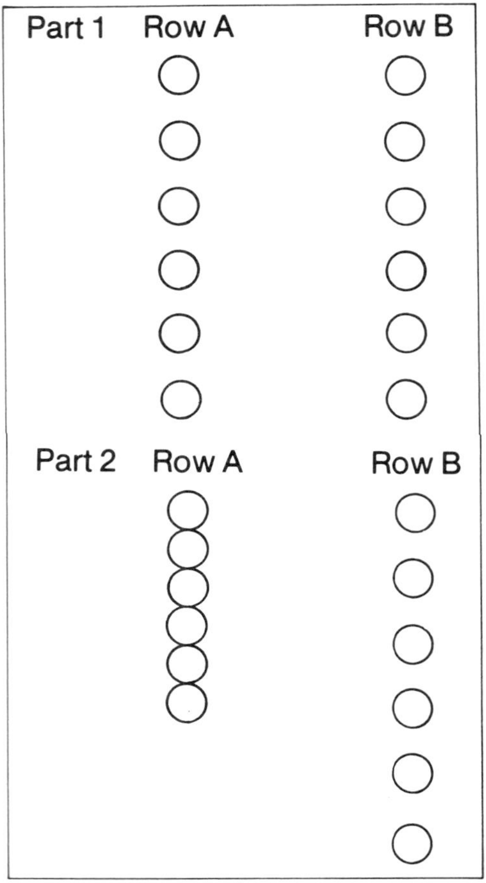

Figure 1 Piaget's experiment on the conservation of number. Part 1 shows the sweets at the start of the experiment, and Part 2 the same sweets after transformation.

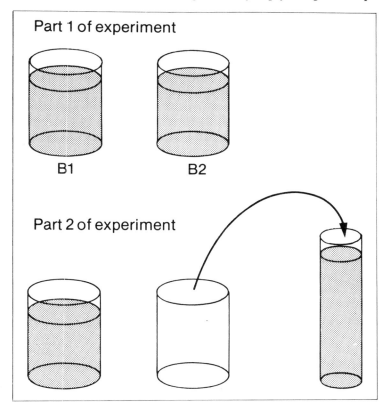

Figure 2 Conservation experiment with beakers of liquid

The child and adult sit at a table and before them are three beakers, B1, B2 and B3. Beaker B1 is filled with milk, and the adult asks the child to fill the identical beaker B2 with milk from the jug so that it has 'the same amount' as the model. The child complies, carefully lining up the two beakers so that he can see when the height of the milk is the same in them.

Next the adult produces a third beaker, B3, which is taller and thinner than B1 and B2. He asks the child to pour the contents of B2 into B3. 'Is there the same amount in this beaker (B3) as in this one (B1)?' Older children are not fooled by the task, just as they were not in the experiment with sweets. 'They are the same.'

Can younger children solve the problem? Piaget has shown that children younger than six or seven *are* fooled by the pouring and claim that B3 has 'more'. Why? Because they are fooled by the greater height in the third beaker. To them, 'lower' indicates less and 'higher' more. Of course, this rule will work with identical beakers but not with those whose shapes vary. Occasionally Piaget varied the task, pouring the milk from Beaker B2 into a B3 that was short and fat instead of tall and thin. Now, the pre-operational child would say that the third beaker had 'less' in it.

Conservation of quantity can be studied with substances other than fluids, as for instance, with plasticine. The adult rolls two identical balls in his fingers. Next, he transforms the appearance of one ball by rolling it into a sausage shape. If he compares it with the first lump of plasticine (the model), the older child will say it's the 'same amount'. A younger child will be fooled, as with the beakers, and say that the new sausage shape is 'more' (if he focuses on length) or 'less' (if he focuses on width). In either event, the younger child says that the amount of plasticine has changed because it appears different (Figure 3).

Piaget performed many other experiments on **conservation** involving weight and volume, but the results of these were not much different from experiments on conservation of number, liquid quantity, and substance. All these conservation experiments are similar because they involve first a phase in which the child judges that two similar things are equal. Most children above four can get this far. Then a visible transformation is performed. While the child watches, one of the entities is transformed in appearance by being changed in shape or transferred to another receptacle. It is quite clear that no new quantity is added to the one that has been transformed, but it now looks very different from the entity first encountered. Each experiment requires that the child must judge whether the two things are still the same or are different.

After many experiments, Piaget and his colleagues concluded that there is a sequence of development for each of the conservations. First, children do not conserve at all. They blithely tell the experimenter that 'it's more now' or 'less'. When finally capable of conservation, children are able to make the following arguments as to why the number (or liquid, volume, etc.) is still the same. 'If it were returned to the original beaker, it would still be equal.' (This is called the *negation* argument.) Another is that 'of course it is equal; it is still the same water'. (This is the *identity* argument.) Or lastly 'although it's higher now, it's also thinner and so must be the same amount'. (This is the *compensation* argument.)

Oddly enough, children do not achieve conservation all at once. Some of

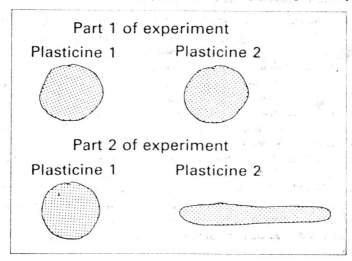

Figure 3 Conservation experiment with plasticine

the problems are 'easier' than others. In fact, children usually master conservation of continuous quantity (as with the water) and substance (plasticine) at 6 or 7, weight at 9 or 10, volume at 11 or 12. In each case, the arguments are roughly the same but the child's reasoning seems tied to particular situations and objects.

Why do school aged children succeed at conservation tasks? For one, their thought is *reversible*. Take the task with pouring of liquid amounts. The operational child can mentally reverse the pouring procedure, and so doing, realizes that the liquid is the same amount as before. The same with the plasticine; the child can mentally reverse the moulding of the sausage. Moreover, the child succeeds at conservation tasks because he is attentive to several kinds of information at the same time. He considers the height of the beaker (or the length of the row) as well as the additional information concerning width.

Children new to concrete operations may study the objects in the experiments. 'The beaker is taller now, but it's more narrow.' This is the essence of compensation. But older children, those firmly established in logical reasoning, do not bother with examination of the objects after the transformation has been performed. For them, the question 'Are they the same?' seems silly. '*Of course*, they are the same.' These children do not

believe that the question requires perceptual judgment; instead, they know that questions of logical necessity do not need verification in this way. Number or quantity remains the same despite changed visual appearance, just as the essential identity of an object remains despite its visual disappearance.

So far it has been shown that children in the period of **concrete operations** can perform the mental operation of *reversibility* and can attend to *several aspects* of a situation at once. This second skill should enable them to look at an object from the point of view of someone else — and so overcome their earlier egocentrism. This is precisely what happens.

Another experiment of Piaget's will illustrate the ability to de-centre of children over eight. A child sits at a table on which is placed a papier maché model of three mountains (Figure 4). Each mountain looks different; on top of one is a large cross, another is snow-covered, and the third is green pasture-land. The child is asked to describe what he sees and can do a good job at this task. Next, a doll is placed on the other side of the table and the child is asked 'What does the doll see?' He is shown several drawings of the mountains, and the child of eight can readily choose the view the doll sees (how the mountains look from the other side of the table). He realizes that the three mountains look different from different perspectives.

As might be expected, children in the pre-operational period think the doll sees exactly what they see themselves.

In sum, children's thinking in the period of concrete operations is logical and mathematical. It is characterized by mental actions of reversibility, ability to take into account several aspects of a situation, and de-centring. Piaget studied the further development of logical thinking in adolescence (the period of **formal operations**), and 'reflective abstraction', that very human capacity to be aware of one's own thoughts and strategies. But those are beyond the scope of this book.

Summing up the theory

Recall that Piaget was interested in the kinds of structures that enable an organism, be it man or mollusc, to adapt to its particular environment. Some are physical structures, such as the elephant's trunk or the tortoise's shell, while others are mental ones. Piaget called the mental ones **schemas**, and they are as important to adaptation as the ones clearly visible. Piaget devoted a lifetime to describing the various stages of mental organization,

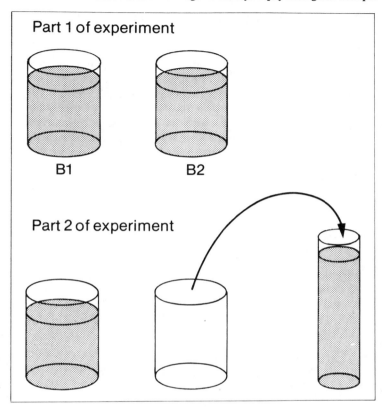

Figure 2 Conservation experiment with beakers of liquid

The child and adult sit at a table and before them are three beakers, B1, B2 and B3. Beaker B1 is filled with milk, and the adult asks the child to fill the identical beaker B2 with milk from the jug so that it has 'the same amount' as the model. The child complies, carefully lining up the two beakers so that he can see when the height of the milk is the same in them.

Next the adult produces a third beaker, B3, which is taller and thinner than B1 and B2. He asks the child to pour the contents of B2 into B3. 'Is there the same amount in this beaker (B3) as in this one (B1)?' Older children are not fooled by the task, just as they were not in the experiment with sweets. 'They are the same.'

Can younger children solve the problem? Piaget has shown that children

younger than six or seven *are* fooled by the pouring and claim that B3 has 'more'. Why? Because they are fooled by the greater height in the third beaker. To them, 'lower' indicates less and 'higher' more. Of course, this rule will work with identical beakers but not with those whose shapes vary. Occasionally Piaget varied the task, pouring the milk from Beaker B2 into a B3 that was short and fat instead of tall and thin. Now, the pre-operational child would say that the third beaker had 'less' in it.

Conservation of quantity can be studied with substances other than fluids, as for instance, with plasticine. The adult rolls two identical balls in his fingers. Next, he transforms the appearance of one ball by rolling it into a sausage shape. If he compares it with the first lump of plasticine (the model), the older child will say it's the 'same amount'. A younger child will be fooled, as with the beakers, and say that the new sausage shape is 'more' (if he focuses on length) or 'less' (if he focuses on width). In either event, the younger child says that the amount of plasticine has changed because it appears different (Figure 3).

Piaget performed many other experiments on **conservation** involving weight and volume, but the results of these were not much different from experiments on conservation of number, liquid quantity, and substance. All these conservation experiments are similar because they involve first a phase in which the child judges that two similar things are equal. Most children above four can get this far. Then a visible transformation is performed. While the child watches, one of the entities is transformed in appearance by being changed in shape or transferred to another receptacle. It is quite clear that no new quantity is added to the one that has been transformed, but it now looks very different from the entity first encountered. Each experiment requires that the child must judge whether the two things are still the same or are different.

After many experiments, Piaget and his colleagues concluded that there is a sequence of development for each of the conservations. First, children do not conserve at all. They blithely tell the experimenter that 'it's more now' or 'less'. When finally capable of conservation, children are able to make the following arguments as to why the number (or liquid, volume, etc.) is still the same. 'If it were returned to the original beaker, it would still be equal.' (This is called the *negation* argument.) Another is that 'of course it is equal; it is still the same water'. (This is the *identity* argument.) Or lastly 'although it's higher now, it's also thinner and so must be the same amount'. (This is the *compensation* argument.)

Oddly enough, children do not achieve conservation all at once. Some of

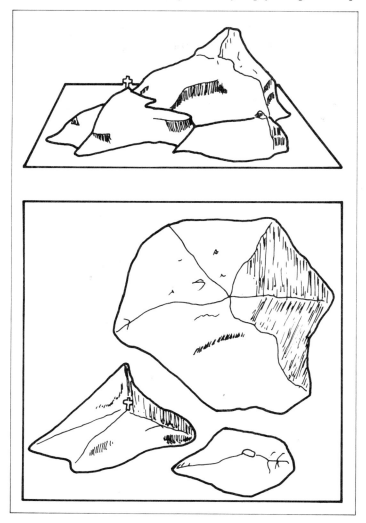

Figure 4 Piaget's model mountains, which he used to demonstrate the 'egocentrism' of young children, viewed from the front and from the top.

each more complex than the preceding one. The basic unit of mental organization is always the schema; in infancy, schemas are simple and practical, whereas later they become differentiated and complex. Examples of complicated schemas include symbolic ones such as notions of 'infinity' and mental operations such as algebra.

Where do schemas come from and how do they change? Piaget is quite explicit about this: the infant is born with rudimentary schemas, such as sucking and grasping, and these he calls *action schemas*. Through the process of **assimilation** the child uses early schemas to take in information about the world, including people, objects and events. Through the complementary process of **accommodation**, the earliest schemas become modified to fit the child's experiences. Thus, as a consequence of both processes, the infant's schemas become more complex to keep pace with his action in the world.

The twin processes of assimilation and accommodation continue throughout life. Assimilation is always the process that enables an individual to deal with new situations and new problems by using the current stock of schemas. Accommodation, on the other hand, is always the process where the individual undergoes a mental change in order to manage problems that were at first too difficult to solve.

Piaget believes that thinking is an active process. Children and adults are not creatures who passively ingest information; they actively organize experience and this activity modifies the schemas they already have. Just as an organism ingests food so that the body may be restored and grow, so does the child ingest information so that his mental structures may develop further.

Although Piaget is explicit in describing the complementary processes of assimilation and accommodation, he is less clear as to *why* a child bothers to acquire new knowledge. Piaget stresses that the child is naturally curious about the world and explores it with no prompting or reward from others. But why does he progress beyond sensory-motor intelligence? Couldn't he go on with sensory-motor exploration forever? Piaget describes a push towards cognitive development called **equilibriation**. This is a self-righting system whereby conflicts in the child's thinking are resolved by mental reorganization towards coherent system. For instance a child might know that 'daytime' comes about when the sun rises while at the same time believe that day comes because he wishes it. Seeing the contradiction will prompt the child towards a new, more mature understanding.

Central to Piagetian theory are the concepts of **stage** (each period is a stage), **sequence**, and **invariance**. Piaget divides the child's intellectual development into three main periods (one subdivided) and for this reason he is said to have devised a stage theory. A developmental period is characterized by the complexity of its schemas as well as by how coordinated they are with one another. The first stage (sensory-motor period) is characterized by practical schemas, whereas the following stage (pre-operational period) is characterized by symbolic ones. The next stage (concrete operational period) is also characterized by symbolic schemas but these are organized into a coherent network to form a logical system.

The exact ages at which children typically enter or leave a stage are only approximate, and Piaget tells us, for instance, that children may enter into the concrete operational period as early as five or as late as eight.

Although the precise ages are not important, what matters is that the sequence of stages is *invariant* — the same for each child. The invariant sequence of stages shows a progression from simplicity to mature, logical intelligence. The progression begins with the infant's sensory-motor schemas without which he could not develop symbolic ones. And without symbolic schemas, the child could not develop a coordinated network of logical, mathematical ones. In a very real sense each period depends on the one before it and this dependence is the essence of a stage theory of development.

Development can proceed in two ways. One of them, characterized by the life cycle of the butterfly, is in stages. First a caterpillar, then a chrysalis, then a sudden metamorphosis, and the butterfly appears. In a sense, it is the same creature, although in a radically different form. Mussen, Conger and Kagan (1979) have likened a *stage theory* such as Piaget's to this kind of development. Its opposite, characterized by the gradual development of a kitten into a cat, is called a *continuity theory*. Does the mind really develop like a butterfly, distinctly different at each age? Or does it slowly grow and differentiate without sudden reorganizations? This kind of problem wakes a psychologist in the middle of the night because of its vitality and our ignorance of the answer.

There is an age-old argument between those who claim intelligence to be innate, or inherited, and those who argue that intelligence is acquired through experience. Piagetian theory straddles the two camps by claiming that early schemas are present at birth, yet stressing that mature, logical schemas are the consequence of the child's self-initiated activity on the world. Is their innate intelligence? Piaget answers *yes* because simple schemas are present at birth. Does mature intelligence require experience in the world? That answer is *yes* as well because complex schemas cannot be constructed without acting on the world.

But was Piaget right?

No other theory of intellectual growth is as broad in scope or as detailed as Piaget's. Ask any psychologist who has made the greatest contribution to our understanding of cognitive development and the answer will invariably be 'Piaget'.

But was he right about everything? Did he tell us all there is to be known about intellectual development? Of course not. Much is left to be discovered; indeed, some of Piaget's 'discoveries' are clearly wrong. We will evaluate Piaget's work here in some detail for two reasons: first, he has had great influence in education, linguistics, anthropology and medicine, as well as other fields. If he is wrong, there are practical consequences. Secondly, Piaget's work provides an interesting example of how arguments go on in science.

Some important areas are not touched by Piaget's work   Piaget is often accused of being too relentless in his pursuit of logic and with being totally unconcerned with children's emotions. The first may be true, but Piaget certainly did appreciate the complicated interaction between thought and feelings. That is implied for instance in these observations.

> At 2;6(3), and on the following days, the child pretended to suck at his mother's breast after seeing a baby being suckled. This game was repeated at about 2;9.
> At 5;8(5), being for the moment on bad terms with her father, the child charged one of her imaginary characters with the task of avenging her: 'Zoubab cut off her daddy's head. But she has some very strong glue and partly stuck it on again. But it's not very firm now.'

Piaget was familiar with the work of Freud on the development of emotions and thought it provided valuable clues to the content of children's thinking. Piaget tells us at which *intellectual level* a child can think whereas Freud suggests what *kinds of things* (attraction for the parent, fear of castration) he thinks about.

Methodological problems   There are other problems with Piaget's work which have to do with methodology. For instance, his reliance on the clinical INTERVIEW is somewhat doubtful. Piaget himself tells us that it takes a year of daily practice to conduct clinical interviews skilfully with children. Because there are no set questions or set order of presentation, the interviewer might 'lead' the young child to views he does not possess. Piaget saw problems with this technique, however, and most of his later work was more rigorous in design.

Even the experiments with fixed materials and questioning have methodological problems. Some critics, such as Peter Bryant (1974), claim that Piaget designed his tasks in such a way as to make it maximally difficult for a child to give correct answers. In a series of ingenious experiments, Bryant has shown that children are capable of logical thinking well before their fifth birthdays. Where Piaget insists that even the cleverest children at this age are lost in the illogicality of the pre-operational period, Bryant believes that he is too pessimistic about their abilities and that supposed 'failures' could be due to many things — memory deficiencies, for example, or the child's not realizing that logic is called for in a particular task.

Still another critic of Piaget's methods is Margaret Donaldson (1979) who, like Peter Bryant, believes that children can solve logical problems well before Piaget thinks they can. Whereas Bryant modified Piaget's experimental tasks to make them somewhat easier, Donaldson and her colleagues retained the form of the Piagetian tasks while changing the context in which they appeared. McGarrigle and Donaldson followed Piaget's procedure with rows of sweets — but with one important difference. Instead of having an experimenter alter the two rows, a 'naughty teddy' entered the scene (contrived by the experimenters, of course) and rearranged the objects while making comic mayhem. Needless to say, the children looked with great interest at the antics of the teddy bear. When later questioned about the number of objects in the rows thrown about by the teddy bear, they easily gave the correct answer (i.e. that the number was 'still the same'). Something in the antics of the disgraceful teddy bear helped children to conserve number, despite the altered appearance of the rows.

McGarrigle and Donaldson argued that their task, identical to Piaget's except for the alteration being performed by an accomplice, was easier for children because it made sense for them to count carefully the items after wicked mayhem, whereas when the experimenter did the rearranging they didn't realize that their perceptual judgments might be wrong. Thus, argues Donaldson, children may appear to fail Piagetian tasks because of deficiencies in logic when actually they are *quite capable* of correct solutions under different circumstances.

The 'naughty teddy' experiment shows a great flaw in Piaget's work; he fails to take sufficient notice of the effect of the *context of the task* he sets before children. By concentrating on a limited number of tasks, he under-estimates children's abilities. Bryant (1974) makes this point forcefully.

> How does Piaget's theory stand today? Though every psychologist will agree that he raised some marvellous questions, many doubt that his answers are the right ones. His conclusion that children simply lack the ability to be logical for a large chunk of their childhood was surprisingly pessimistic for someone who, as a brilliantly precocious boy, published his first scientific paper at the age of 11.

Are the periods psychologically 'real'? The criticisms from Bryant and Donaldson point in the same direction: Piaget's stages of development are based on children's ability to perform certain tasks at certain ages. When they fail his tasks, he claims it is because they have not reached the appropriate stage and lack the requisite mental structures. But Bryant and Donaldson have shown that, at least in certain instances, children fail Piaget's tasks because they do not realize that it is appropriate to apply skills (such as conservation) that they already possess. No one would argue that children are born with the capacity to conserve or to de-centre — it is rather that the steps between the periods, which Piaget says are extremely clear-cut, are really blurred. A step-wise sequence of development may be a consequence of particular tasks chosen for study, rather than biological patterns of child development.

Still, no one would argue that the minds of babies are organized in the same way as those of schoolchildren. And many would agree with Piaget's description of characteristic thought patterns of children (egocentrism, moral realism, and the like). Perhaps it's best to conclude that intellectual development consists of sequential stages of structural organization, but that the 'stages' blend into one another rather than comprising a stair-like pattern.

Piaget's concepts are rather vague The abstractness of concepts such as 'schema', 'assimilation' or 'accommodation' is at once a strength and a weakness. On the positive side, Piaget looked at apparently quite different actions and sequences of behaviour to find what they had in common beneath the surface. This is easy to see in infancy, as for example the baby's underlying striking schema which is the basis of different actions in keeping with the object being struck, its location, whether it is motionless or swinging, and so on.

It is more difficult to discover underlying structures as the child grows older. Piaget found a similarity between the child's moral reasoning at four and his failure to take into account the perceptual view of another person. Beneath both moral and perceptual judgments is the child's prevailing egocentrism — his inability to see things from the viewpoint of someone else. Instead of concluding that children 'say funny things' or that they 'make mistakes', Piaget described the kind of thinking common to both events.

By focusing on the structure of thought rather than momentary actions or words, Piaget was able to describe the characteristic thought patterns of children at different ages. This stage theory allows us to see the essential changes in intellectual development, the sequence from simple action schemas to symbolic and then logical ones. Only a notion as abstract as the *schema* could be applied to the thinking of both infants and adults. If one term is used to describe very different things, it is bound to be abstract — even vague. Piaget was in fact courageous to insist on looking for deep, underlying similarities between all sorts of logical (or less logical) behaviour, at a time when other psychologists thought it unscientific and quite unpardonable to stray from behaviour that could be seen and measured on the spot.

On the negative side, abstractness and vagueness are undeniably a problem. Piaget, and others since, have verified that children all over the world do indeed learn about the permanence of objects, and about conservation (to name a few) according to the sequence he described. And his way of explaining developing intelligence seems a good one. But whether there *really* is a process like for instance 'equilibriation' one can never really prove. We must infer its existence from children's performance on simple tasks such as searching for hidden keys or answering questions about amounts of liquid. The sequence in which children acquire notions of object permanence and conservation has been verified again and again on countless children all over the world.

(. . .) To conclude, one can think of Piaget's work as providing 'intellectual milestones', a developmental timetable that gives approximate dates to cognitive achievements. Why does object permanence appear when it does? Why does conservation of discrete quantity (sweets) precede continuous quantity (water)? Why do children learn about logic on their own? Piaget's theory explains the observable facts of intellectual development. Although its weaknesses have been summarized here, *in general* it is substantiated by scientific research. The task for younger psychologists now is to build on Piaget's work, eliminating the methodological flaws and working to remedy the vagueness of concepts. This is the way that science progresses.

Topics for discussion

1. Explain what Piaget means by *egocentrism*, illustrating your answer with examples.
2. What role do *assimilation* and *accommodation* play in the child's construction of increasingly complex schemas?
3. Discuss the criticisms that have been made of Piaget's work and assess the extent to which they seriously question his explanation of intellectual development.

Suggestions for further reading

1. Furth, L.H.G. (1970) *Piaget For Teachers*. Englewood Cliffs N.J.: Prentice Hall.
2. Modgil, S. and Modgil, C. (1982) *Jean Piaget: Consensus and Controversy*. Eastbourne: Holt, Rinehart and Winston.
3. Bryant, P.B. (1974) *Perception and Understanding in Young Children*. London: Methuen.

READING SIX ● Why children find school learning difficult   *M. Donaldson*

1. First, he actively tries to make sense of the world from a very early point in his life: he asks questions, he wants to know. (This is evidently so as soon as verbal questions can be formulated. It is probably true even before language appears.) Also from a very early stage, the child has purposes and intentions: he wants to do. These questionings and these strivings imply some primitive sense of possibility which reaches beyond a realization of how things are to a realization of how they might be.

'Why Children Find School Learning Difficult', from M. Donaldson, *Children's Minds*. London: Fontana. 1979 pp 86–95

2. The sense of the possible which arises in conjunction with *wanting to know* involves, first, a simple realization of ignorance ('There might be a tiger round the corner, I haven't looked') and then an attempt to use considerations of compatibility and incompatibility to extend the field of the known and reduce uncertainty. That which is possible then becomes that which does not lead to conflict with anything accepted as real or actual. Whatever does lead to such conflict is *impossible*. This is deductive inference. But note that it does not become what is normally called *formal* deductive inference until attention centres not on conflict with the real in the known world, but on conflict with what we are accustomed to call 'the given', that is, with something merely postulated, something which you *decide* to accept as the premise on which you will base your reasoning.

3. The sense of the possible which arises in conjunction with *wanting to do* involves, on the one hand, some apprehension of the goal, of the state of affairs which might be brought into being, and on the other hand some apprehension of the means, of the actions which one might take in order to reach the goal. However, it seems most probable that, in the early stages of life, awareness of the goal is dominant and that consideration of possible action — especially systematic consideration — comes later. There is a distinction to be drawn between trying different actions to achieve a goal and reflecting on these as a possible set of actions before performing them. This latter activity — the planning kind — involves the temporary suspension of overt action and a turning of attention inwards upon mental acts instead. Developmentally, the course of events is from an awareness of what is without to an awareness of what is within.

4. This is true also when we turn to the growth of linguistic skills. The child acquires these skills before he becomes aware of them. The child's awareness of what he talks *about* — the things out there to which the language refers — normally takes precedence over his awareness of what he talks *with* — the words that he uses. And he becomes aware of what he talks with — the actual words — before he is at all aware of the rules which determine their sequencing — the rules which control his own production of them. Indeed, a thoughtful adult has a very limited awareness of such processes in his own mind.

In the early stages, before the child has developed a full awareness of language, language is embedded for him in the flow of the events which accompany it. So long as this is the case, the child does not interpret words in isolation — he interprets situations. He is more concerned to make sense of what people do when they talk and act than to decide what words mean.

After all he may not be aware of language, but he is keenly aware of other people. But at the same time he is given to structuring, or making sense of, situations even when no words are uttered; and sometimes it seems that, when words *are* uttered, the child's interpretation of the utterance is strongly influenced by his own independent structuring of the context. If there is one feature of a situation which is salient for him — if it is the feature on which he himself would be most likely to comment — then this feature can exert a 'pull' on the interpretation of the words he hears. Just how powerful this pull may be is not yet entirely clear.

5. A child who is trying to figure out what other people mean must be capable of recognizing intentions in others, as well as having them himself. And such a child is by no means wholly unable to decentre. While he may certainly, like the rest of us, fail sometimes to appreciate the relativity of his own point of view, he is capable of escaping from it. Thus he is not debarred by egocentrism from communicating with us and relating to us in a personal way. Indeed personal relations appear to form the matrix within which his learning takes place.

If the picture which has just been sketched is accurate as to its main lines, the normal child comes to school with well-established skills as a thinker. But his thinking is *directed outwards* on to the real, meaningful, shifting, distracting world. What is going to be required for success in our educational system is that he should learn to turn language and thought in upon themselves. He must become able to direct his own thought processes in a thoughtful manner. He must become able not just to talk but to choose what he will say, not just to interpret but to weigh possible interpretations. His conceptual system must expand in the direction of increasing ability to represent itself. He must become capable of manipulating symbols.

Now the principal symbolic system to which the pre-school child has access is oral language. So the first step is the step of conceptualizing language — becoming aware of it as a separate structure, freeing it from its embeddedness in events.

Some children come to school with this step already taken — or at least with the movement already begun. They come with an enormous initial advantage.

Bärbel Inhelder and her colleagues have (. . .) tried to teach children to deal with Piagetian tasks such as class-inclusion. At one point in the book in which they report their findings (Inhelder et al. 1974) they turn to the question of differences between children from different kinds of homes and whether linguistic skill is relevant. They go on to deny that 'language as such' has anything to do with success, but they say they have noticed certain differences in 'attitude' towards the words of the experimenter. Children from more privileged backgrounds are more likely to pay scrupulous attention to the words of the question, reflecting on them, analysing them before answering. By contrast, the less privileged children have a strong tendency to substitute a 'more natural' question for the one the experimenter has asked.

That there exist more or less 'natural' ways of describing certain situations or events is clear. Alison Macrae points out that an adult would be much more likely to say: 'The flowers are on top of the televion set' than 'The television set is under the flowers' (Macrae 1976). And she reports that four-year-old children already appear to be sensitive to the oddity of the second version, for they tend to avoid using it even in a situation so constructed as to encourage its use. There was incidentally no doubt about the ability of the children to produce the word 'under': they gave clear evidence of this in other contexts.

Now to an unnatural statement there corresponds an unnatural question. If it is odd to say: 'The television set is under the flowers' then it is odd to ask 'Is the television set under the flowers?' Similarly, if it is odd to assert that there are more flowers than red flowers, it is odd to ask whether this is so.

The authors of the book on teaching children how to deal with Piagetian tasks — Bärbel Inhelder, Hermine Sinclair and Magali Bovet — make the remark about unnatural questions in passing; but it goes to the heart of the matter. The difference that they note amounts to a difference in readiness to treat language in some degree of abstraction from context. And it is easy to see how this would be encouraged in the more literate and intellectually sophisticated home.

As literate adults, we have become so accustomed to the written word that we seldom stop to think how dramatically it differs from the spoken one. The spoken word (unless recorded, which is another thing again) exists for a brief moment as one element in a tangle of shifting events — from which it must be disentangled if it is to be separately considered — and then fades. The written word endures. It is there on the page, distinct, lasting. We may return to it tomorrow. By its very nature it can be quite free of non-linguistic context. We can pick it up and slip it into a pocket or briefcase. Once a child has begun to learn to read he can bring his book home from school and read to his mother *the same words* which he read to his teacher in the classroom earlier in the day.

So a child's first encounters with books provide him with much more favourable opportunities for *becoming aware* of language in its own right than his earlier encounters with the spoken word are likely to have done.

Of course in some homes awareness of the spoken word is greatly encouraged. Some parents talk *about* words to their children, play word games with them and so on. But most talk only *with* words. Indeed, a great many children come to school not even aware that separate words exist — that the flow of speech can be broken up into these units. It is true, as Fox and Routh have shown (Fox and Routh 1975, pp. 331–42), that by the age of four children are not incapable of breaking speech up into progressively smaller 'little bits' if encouraged to do so. However, it is certain that many of them will never have thought of doing so. Also many five-year-olds have very confused notions of what is meant by the word 'word', as Jess Reid showed in a highly original study of the conceptions of the reading process which children bring with them to school and which they develop as the first year at school goes on (Reid 1966, pp. 56–62). These findings have since been confirmed and extended by John Downing (Downing 1970, pp. 106–112).

For many children the earliest encounter with the written word is indirect, arising in the situation where a story is read aloud by an adult. This is already in a sense language freed from context; but the experience of hearing a story is not so likely to enhance awareness as the direct grappling with words on a page. (. . .) It is a striking fact that when young children listen to stories they very seldom ask questions about the language in which the stories are told. They ask many searching questions about the intentions and motives of the characters, the structure of the plot — if you like, the meaning of the story. They rarely ask about the meanings of the words, even when these must clearly be unfamiliar.

In a set of story-time recordings of children's speech which were collected daily over a period of roughly four months only three examples of questions about word meanings and only one about any other aspect of language were found.

The three questions about word meanings were:

'What's a "howdah"?'
'What is "cud"?' and
'What's "mousey quiet"? Excuse me, what's "mousey quiet"?'

The first two of these questions were from a child of almost five, who was already learning to read although not yet at school and who showed great interest in print whenever she could lay hands on it. The third question was again from a child who was nearly five years old, and who, though she had not begun to read, came from a highly literate home.

The one remaining question about language was asked by a child not quite three. The story-teller read the sentence: 'And at last they *did* pull up the turnip.' The child asked in a very high and excited voice: 'Why is it *did*?' This appears to be a question about grammatical structure (one which, incidentally, the story-teller found very hard to answer), but it is quite isolated. Nothing else of the kind occurred at all.

Now it is not that young children are incapable of asking *any* question about the relation between words and things. One of the very earliest questions commonly recorded in a child's speech is: 'What dat?' This is frequent at the first stage of language production, commonly reached before the age of two, and it appears to be a request to know an object's name. So it seems strange that the request to know what a word means — a question dealing with the same relation but starting from the opposite end — should be so much slower to come.

It is not, however, clear that the child's early request for a name is quite what it appears to be. There are reasons for suspecting that to a young child the name of an object may be on a par, say, with the object's weight or with its colour — just an attribute among other attributes, hence more like a part of the object than a part of some separate formal system called 'language'. Vygotsky (1962) has argued powerfully in support of this interpretation, pointing out that for intellectually unsophisticated adults the same may also to some extent be true. He tells the story of the peasant who was not so much surprised that it had been possible to figure out how big the stars are as that it had been possible to discover their names.

So a request for a name does not by itself prove that language is apprehended as a distinct system. It seems that, in general, this apprehension is slow to come and that one effect of learning to read may be to encourage the conscious reflection which produces it. Vygotsky's peasant must surely have been illiterate.

It is clear that being aware of language as a distinct system is relevant to the business of separating what is *said* from what is done or from what is somehow salient in a situation — and hence to dealing successfully with Piagetian tests like conservation or class-inclusion and with many other reasoning tasks. As Inhelder and her colleagues have pointed out, some children take stock of what precisely the experimenter has asked them, while others substitute a 'more natural question' of their own.

However, while it is evident that this last strategy can hardly work, we must be cautious about drawing the conclusion that some degree of reflective awareness of language is all that success requires. For there would also seem to be, at the very least, the issue of *control* — the question of how much ability the child has to sustain attention, resisting irrelevance while he considers implications. And young children seem not to be very good at this. For instance, Lesley Hall carried out experiments in which she asked her subjects to decide whether statements were true or false in relation to pictures and then recorded eye movements as the subjects searched the pictures and reached a decision. She found that children as young as four could organize their search patterns to some extent if no irrelevant pictures were shown but that the presence of irrelevant pictures was 'more efficacious in "attracting" the gaze than was any cognitive plan in "projecting" it' (Hall 1975). In other words, the amount of deliberate control which the children exercised in this context appeared to be quite limited. This question of control is at the heart of the capacity for disembedded thinking which (. . .) involves sticking to the problem and refusing to be diverted by knowledge, by beliefs or by perceptions which have nothing to do with it.

Yet it turns out that recognition of the importance of being able to control one's own thinking may not take us so very far from the issue of awareness after all. What is now at stake, however, is the child's more general awareness of his own thought processes — his *self-awareness*. For as Vygotsky rightly says: '. . . control of a function is the counterpart of one's consciousness of it.' If a child is going to control and direct his own thinking, in the kind of way we have been considering, he must become conscious of it.

We are still not well-informed about how self-awareness grows. But Piaget has reported the results of a very interesting series of studies (Piaget 1977).

The method used was to give children a number of tasks to perform and get them to talk about their own actions. The tasks might be very simple ones, presenting no difficulty at all for the children, such as crawling on hands and knees. Or they might be problems of some complexity like the Tower of Hanoi puzzle. In this puzzle there are three sticks, one of which has on it a number of discs varying in size, with the biggest at the bottom. The problem then is to move these discs to one of the other sticks, moving only one at a time and never putting a larger disc on top of a smaller one.

Piaget's findings and arguments are complex, but one point that emerges very clearly is that awareness typically develops when something gives us pause and when consequently, instead of just acting, we stop to consider the possibilities of acting which are before us. The claim is that we heighten our awareness of what is actual by considering what is possible. We are conscious of what we do to the extent that we are conscious also of what we do *not* do — of what we might have done. The notion of *choice* is thus central.

So what makes us stop and think about our thinking — and thus makes us able to *choose* to direct our thinking in one way rather than another? We cannot expect to find any simple answer to such a momentous question — but observe how, here again, learning to read may have a highly significant contribution to make. The child who is learning to read is in a situation that is likely to encourage him to begin to consider possibilities in relation to at least one important act of thought: the apprehension of meaning. As one child put it: 'You have to stop and think. It's difficult!' Here the same arguments apply as were relevant to the growth of awareness of language itself: the critical things are that the written word is enduring, and that it can be free of non-linguistic context. Thus non-linguistic context does not here act — as it so often does with the spoken word — to determine one interpretation, shaping the meaning and excluding the need for choice; and further, the lasting character of the print means that there is time to stop and think, so that the child has a chance to consider possibilities — a chance of a kind which he may never have had before.

Thus it turns out that those very features of the written word which encourage awareness of language may also encourage awareness of one's own thinking and be relevant to the development of intellectual self-control, with incalculable consequences for the development of the kinds of thinking which are characteristic of logic, mathematics and the sciences.

Topics for discussion

1. 'Developmentally, the course of events is from an awareness of what is *without* to an awareness of what is *within*.'
   Discuss this axiom with reference to the acquisition of language.
2. How does Donaldson explain young children's preoccupation with the meaning of stories rather than the meaning of words that compose them?
3. 'Control of a function is the counterpart of one's consciousness of it.' Discuss Vygotsky's observation in relation to the child's development of *self-awareness*.

Suggestions for further reading

Clark, M.M. (1976) *Young Fluent Readers*. London: Heinemann Educational.
Reid, J.F. and Low, J. (1972) *Link-up*. Edinburgh: Holmes McDougall.
Roberts, T. (1984) 'Piagetian theory and the teaching of reading', *Educational Research*, **26**, 2, 77–81.

SECTION FOUR
ORGANIZATION IN PRIMARY SCHOOLS

READING SEVEN • Open plan primary schools: rhetoric and reality
M. Brogden

Robert Dearden (1976) wrote that the literature on the 'integrated day' could be read in one evening; having read it he found 57 Varieties of integrated day. Dewhurst (1977) described varieties of team teaching in the primary school and found a similar range of organizations which he distilled into five groups. Someone ought to investigate the other primary label, 'family grouping', but my expectation is that the Heinz principle will apply here too. Bennett (1976) analysed the open plan primary school building and produced a schedule of designs and staffing arrangements which involved some thirty-five basic organizations. I am about to claim in this paper that open plan primary schools in England are concerned with the integrated day, team teaching *and* family grouping. Mathematicians may care to calculate the permutations of varieties produced by such a statement!

The obvious literature on the open plan primary school may be read very swiftly. There are few books with 'open plan' in the title so it is necessary to read around the 'ingredients' of open plan schools to trace the rationale. This entails delving into the notoriously vague writings of the progressives and into the history of the primary school building. Seaborne (1971), Seaborne and Lowe (1977) and McNicholas (1973, 1974) have produced very useful histories.

The roots of the open plan primary school may be seen in the rural rather than the urban building. Seaborne, Seaborne and Lowe, and McNicholas show how the enclosed classroom was a phenomenon of the new urban schools of the inter-war period, encouraged by the increasing autonomy gained by teachers who had been trained. The classroomed school developed the isolation of the classes to the point that, in some designs, rooms ran like fingers extending from the hall and administration areas, with long corridors alongside (Seaborne 1971). The designs reflected a view of the homogeneity of year groups and of teaching as a largely didactic activity in

M. Brogden, 'Open Plan Primary Schools: Rhetoric and Reality', in, *School Organization*, 3, 1, 1983, pp 27–41

which pupils are passive. In contrast, many rural schools contained insufficient pupils to enable classes to be established in 'years' and, because new school building priorities concentrated upon urban housing development areas, rural school buildings remained largely untouched. As a result, many rural schools did not expand beyond the two-roomed model (McNicholas 1974). Seaborne and Lowe (1977) comment:

> It was common practice for children of varied ages and abilities to work together in close proximity to each other, frequently sharing the equipment and other facilities. Inevitably, more individual methods of learning were necessary and the village school teacher naturally adapted herself to a supervisory rather than expository role. The concept of a separate classroom for each year group was alien to these schools . . . village school organization showed that the artificiality of the distinction then current between 'class' and shared space went far beyond the concept of 'dual purpose' rooms commonly accepted for dining and practical work.

Significantly, the first school to be designated 'open plan' was rural, built in 1959 in the Oxfordshire village of Finmere (Ministry of Education 1961). This building, designed by the Ministry of Education's Building Development Group of HMI and Architects, which had been set up in 1948, influenced the design of schools for the next twenty years, along with the Group's Eveline Lowe School in London (DES 1967) which was built in collaboration with the Plowden Committee. The designers of the Eveline Lowe School had been particularly impressed with the way one of the several rural schools they visited was used. Brize Norton School (Oxfordshire again) had set up *areas* for the various activities which took place within its basically two-roomed format. The Eveline Lowe School looks very much like a series of clusters of work areas (DES 1967). The village school had been translated into the urban setting.

The theoretical basis of open plan planning may be seen in embryo form in the Hadow Reports of 1931 and 1933 which drew together the heritage of Froebel, Montessori, the McMillan sisters and Susan Isaacs (see Whitbread 1972) with such recommendations as:

> We are of the opinion that the curriculum of the primary school is to be thought of in terms of activity and experience, rather than of knowledge to be acquired and facts to be stored.

> Today (the primary school) includes care, through the school medical service, for the physical welfare of children, offers larger, if still inadequate, opportu-

nities for practical activity and handles the curriculum, not only as consisting of lessons to be mastered, but as providing fields of new and interesting experience to be explored; it appeals less to passive obedience and more to the sympathy, social spirit and imaginations of the children, relies less on mass instruction and more on the encouragement of individual and group work, and treats the school, in short, not as the antithesis of life, but as its complement and commentary.

The classroom life approximates to the nursery life of a large family where children of different ages live and play together. . .

It is not a classroom but a playground, that is to say, not a limited space enclosed by four walls and a ceiling, but an open area . . . where the interests natural to this historical stage of growth can be stimulated and pursued.

These ideals were taken up by the Ministry of Education's Building Development Group. Its brief was to design schools with more useful floor area than those built before World War 2; with more individual spaces, spaces not of uniform size but of many different sizes and shapes, some quiet and clean, others noisy and dirty; with provision for very different physical conditions in different spaces; spaces which are adaptable; 'spaces designed for children' (Morrell and Pott 1960).

Within another decade the Group was confidently concluding that these features were 'the right way of working in primary schools generally' (DES 1967), a view which had been endorsed by the 1959 Handbook *Primary Education* and by the Plowden Report. The Building Development Group had become much more than a design group reflecting the practices identified in the schools they visited; their publications were treatises expounding educational philosophies and their buildings *necessitated* teaching styles and organizational strategies to match those philosophies. Their designs, particularly at Finmere and Eveline Lowe influenced local authority architects (Bennett et al. 1980) and of course this was the object of the exercises. By 1976, 10 per cent of primary school buildings were of open plan design (Bennett et al. 1980).

My reading of the Development Group's Bulletins leads me to conclude that the open plan primary school evolved to accommodate three organizational strategies from within the child-centre paradigm. The evolution was systematic and designed; we can dismiss those cynics who declare that open plan schools are the result of cost-cutting exercises. The evidence is not in their favour; until the 1970s open plan schools offered considerably more useful teaching space than their classroomed predecessors (Seaborne 1971).

Bennett et al. (1980) came to this conclusion too and suggest that if economies were the driving forces, there were other ways of saving money than missing out a few walls.

The first organizational strategy I wish to mention is 'family' or 'vertical grouping' and by this I mean the grouping of pupils irrespective of age. Family grouping was established in some infants schools by the early 1930s (Hadow 1933) and spread into junior schools in the 1960s (Linfield 1968). The Plowden Report noted that family grouping was a minority practice found in 'two or three areas which are among those which have the most lively infant school work in the country.' HMI recently found that about a quarter of their surveyed junior classes were family grouped (DES 1978a). Little investigation has been undertaken into this quiet revolution but it is a central feature of the rationale of the open plan school. Family grouping is concerned with children making progress at individual, rather than at age-grouped or class rates (Ridgway and Lawton 1965) and necessitates flexible grouping arrangements and a relevant teaching style; open plan schools are designed to accommodate family grouping.

The second strategy is the 'integrated day'. Concern for individuals led teachers to 'family group'. The same motive led them to abandon the rigid timetable and to institute an integrated day. I have been unable to discover who coined the term, and as with all the jargon of child-centredness, it has many different meanings. The common element in definitions and descriptions of the integrated day is that children engage in a variety of activities at the same time. Brown and Precious (1968) define it as 'a school day which is combined into a whole and has the minimum of timetabling'. It is a time-management, not a curriculum-management term; in this sense it has little or nothing to do with integration of subject matter.

The integrated day is a major element of the child-centred paradigm for if the pupils are engaged in a variety of different activities, they cannot be taught didactically as a class. The teacher has to provide for individual and group levels of work and the timetable-free day allows the child to pursue the task for as long as it takes. Where there is family grouping, by its very nature, there must be an integrated day (but not vice versa). A working party of Bristol teachers reported in 1963 that 'fluid timetabling' was being experimented with in 1948 and that this had led to the design of new infants schools based on a 'family unit' of shared areas (Bristol Head Teachers 1963). Brown and Precious (1968) describe the development of the integrated day which they instituted in infant and junior schools in Leicester in 1956. In 1970 the University of Exeter organized a conference entitled 'The

Integrated Day in the Primary School' which led to the only published work (Walton 1971) to examine the concept in any depth and to Moran's (1971) survey which categorizes five models of integrated day. Inexplicably, the Plowden Report does not mention the integrated day and Bennett 'studiously ignored' it in his national survey (Bennett 1976).

The open plan school developed to provide space and flexibility for the integrated day. Its starting point may be seen in the classroomed schools where areas were set up for different learning purposes so that pupils were able to move from one to next as necessary — for example in the Brize Norton School. The pairs of rooms with shared work areas were the first modern steps to accommodate the integrated day, followed by the establishment of more workspaces, until the classroom itself disappeared and the schools became a series of clusters of workspaces.

The third of the child-centred strategies which form the rationale of the open plan primary school is 'team teaching'. Again we have a term which has as many meanings as practitioners but here I will use Olson's definition: 'an instructional situation where two or more teachers possessing complementary skills, cooperatively plan and implement the instruction for a single group of students, using flexible grouping methods to meet the needs of the children' (Olson 1968, quoted in Dewhurst 1977). Teachers had begun to spread their work into the corridors and cloakrooms. Activities had extended to the degree that 'even the best designed traditional building' was not able to accommodate them (Bower 1968). The early designs of the Building Development Group produced shared practical areas between two classes (for example: Min. Ed. 1958). These prompted teachers to work more closely together. Thus, team teaching in the primary school arose out of the integrated day, out of child-centred not class instruction principles. Several writers confirm this 'evolution' theory — Plimmer (1974) (one of the few to study 'British' primary school team teaching in any depth), Ridgway (1976), Saville (1970), Dearden (1976) — and a University of Leicester working party (Allen et al. 1975) concluded that 'team teaching is a development of working an integrated day'. Dewhurst (1977) comes to the same conclusion. Thus, teachers working an integrated day found benefits in cooperation, for example in the use of shared work areas; cooperation became formalized into team teaching arrangements; the team teaching arrangements were then provided for in the design of open plan schools. Plimmer (1974) declares that 'Each (open plan school) represents in effect a decision by a local authority that there shall be team teaching within its walls.'

If I may recap, the case I am presenting is that open plan schools have a distinct rationale which may be identified in the literature. The rationale is located within the child-centred paradigm and supports Bennett's (1976) definition of an open plan primary school:

> An open plan school is one that facilitates joint use of space and resources, leading to co-operation between teachers and flexible grouping of children.

I have extracted the three organizational strategies from the Building and Development Group's publications which would appear to form the basis of the rationale — family grouping, the integrated day and team teaching. Whilst each term carries many meanings, definitions have been given which describe the minimum concepts.

So what might a visitor to an open plan primary school, who has read the available literature, be entitled to expect to find? A reasonable expectation would be a curriculum based upon 'child-centred' philosophies, involving exploration and enquiry, concrete materials and apparatus, which recognizes individual interests and capacities; an integration of subject disciplines; an informal relationship between teachers and pupils; an understanding of cognitive-development learning theories on the part of the teacher to aid the planning of stages of work — in fact, the elements of schooling which make up the 'teaching revolution' which is said to have taken place in British primary schools, particularly since the second world war (Westbury 1973). Our visitor would also be entitled to expect to find flexible grouping and teaching arrangements based upon notions of children's needs; little didactic instruction, minimal timetabling, much cooperation between teachers and an absence of teacher territories.

In sum, our visitor might reasonably assume that he would find a form of organization as defined by many of the criteria listed by Myers and Duke (1977):

1	Vertical Grouping.	Mixed age grouping of students.
2	Horizontal Grouping.	A high degree of heterogeneous grouping within classes.
3	Use of Corridors, Grounds and Community.	Maximum mobility within school plus utilization of surrounding community.
4	Room Arrangements.	Creative arrangement of individual rooms, often in the form of learning centres.
5	Noise Level.	High but productive noise level.

6	Sense of Community.	Feeling of cooperativeness between teachers, students and parents.
7	Affective Environment.	An atmosphere marked by trust, the exercise of student responsibility, and warmth in inter-personal relations.
8	Play.	Encouragement of student play as a productive learning activity.
9	Learning Materials.	Abundant and creative learning materials.
10	Required Learnings.	Minimum number of learning outcomes required of students.
11	Student Choice.	Maximum number of situations in which students make choices.
12	Organization of School Day.	Highly flexible organization of time.
13	Instruction.	Considerable individualized instruction and small group work.
14	Evaluation of Student.	Absence of normative evaluation of students.
15	Discipline and Rules.	Involvement of students in rule making.
16	Staffing.	Multiple staffing, providing more individualized contact between adults and students.

I have set out what I believe to be the rationale of the open plan primary school, described the organizational strategies that underpin it and quoted some of the rhetoric which is attached. Now, what do we know of the reality?

Several writers demonstrate that the link between 'open plan' and child-centred practices is rather tenuous at the 'classroom' level. The Schools Council Study (Bennet et al. 1980) quotes Seefeldt (1973):

> Yet when one settles down carefully to observe and scrutinize the teaching-learning process that is taking place in open plan schools, the observer leaves with a somewhat different and disquieting feeling. Open spaces . . . do not necessarily guarantee freedom in the classrooms. Perhaps educators need to examine and re-examine what does in fact occur within open space.

This view is supported by the observations of Adelman and Walker (1974) when investigating the quality of interaction in open plan schools:

> In some of the schools we have studied we have seen the surface features of openness, but often a failure to use these to create educationally open settings.

Often systems of workcards or a proliferation of resources, are used by teachers as a way of shifting authority from themselves on to the materials. They are able to ease themselves out of what they perceive as an undesirable and difficult role, that of the 'traditional teacher' without fundamentally changing the nature of the classroom.

. . . This is perhaps the situation best described by the phrase 'innovation without change'.

. . . A new open plan school containing adaptable furniture and flexible services, small groups, individualized curricula, resource areas and community services, does not equal open education in action.

Evans (1979) studied the transfer of an infant school from its old three-decker building into a new open plan one and found that:

although practice had been diverse and idiosyncratic within the closed classrooms of the old school, the move to an open plan building produced the introduction of a time-table, subject specialization at the top of the school and a considerable amount of streaming. Thus the very barriers which the educational architects claimed were dissolving . . . were in fact reinforced and in some cases instigated in response to the new forms.

She found, in addition, that the amount of time the children spent in play and creative activity was reduced (Evans 1979).

The Strathclyde Region of Scotland (1976) surveyed eighty-seven schools (both open plan and classroomed) and found that 88 per cent preferred a one teacher one class organization on a 'split day' pattern; 'skills' in the morning, 'frills' in the afternoon. Bennett et al. (1975) studied eleven open plan schools in Cumbria and found that the *majority* of the seventy-four teachers worked independently. Derbyshire advisers (Arkwright et al. 1975) found that in their open plan schools most teachers were still teaching 'inflexibly' to class groups, particularly in junior schools and that the work areas in the schools were usually used in rotation according to a timetable. Hurlin (1975) studied four open plan schools and found *no* children engaged in enquiry/discovery work; two of the schools operated on timetables with bells to indicate lesson changes. Jarman (1977), writing of his view of some Oxfordshire schools describes mathematics as:

individual assignments and workcards with each child virtually doing a correspondence course. . . . Any sense of integration in the subject matter is lost. Art is done in the Art Room, Maths in the Maths Room and so on. Next, the timetabling necessary makes spending continuous time on a worthwhile project impossible. Added to this, the children may have neither a permanent base nor a teacher who is their own. Clearly such an organization has lost, at a stroke, all the advantages of modern primary education gained over the last half century.

The Oracle Study (Galton et al. 1980) finds less pupil-pupil interaction and considerably less pupil-teacher interaction in open plan schools than in 'box classrooms', that the quality of teacher questioning is less and that teacher-pupil feedback is less in open plan schools. The predominant teaching style is that of the 'individual monitor', a style characterized by 'the low level of questioning and the high level of non-verbal interaction consisting largely of. . . marking.' The study reveals a great deal of individual work being done by pupils but little individual attention from the teachers; investigative work is exceptional, as is higher-order questioning from teachers:

> Grouping appears to be an organizational or managerial device rather than a technique for promoting enquiry based learning using collaborative methods. . . . The move to individualization has not been accompanied by a change in direction from didactic teaching to 'discovery' learning. . . . 'Progressivism' as *per* Plowden is hardly found in practice. . . . Many classes have little or no art. (Galton et al. 1980)

The DES Building Development Group visited thirty-four schools, some of which were open plan, when gathering information for their most recent design, the Guillemont Primary School. They found 'Considerable attention to the three R's, often table and chair-based, with reorganization of the grouping for art, craft and practical investigation' (DES 1976).

The Schools Council Study (Bennett et al. 1980) found a considerable amount of timetabling and ability grouping in open plan schools, a preponderance of the 'skills and frills' approach ('basics' in the morning, other activities in the afternoon) and up to about one-fifth of a day lost in transition and administration (but mostly in transition). This latter finding seems to mean that one whole day per week is lost in moving about! The Study concludes: 'An open plan school is no guarantee of open or informal teaching whether it be located in the United States, Canada, Australia, New Zealand, Sweden or Great Britain.'

The several studies reported above suggest that the teaching and learning undertaken in many open plan schools is not child-centred in the sense that the progressive movement and the designers of open plan schools intended. There appear to be no objective studies of open plan schools which report favourably; even the 'evangelicals' have put very little into writing. A quarter of a century of development and innovation, as Adelman and

Walker (1974) note, seems to have resulted in little change. In some cases, in fact, the conclusion is bleaker — a move to an open plan building resulted in regression.

Can the difference between the rhetoric and the reality be explained? Several theories may be relevant here:

1   Sharp and Green (1975) identified the elements of the 'progressive' and 'child-centred' paradigm and then studied the workings of several class-rooms in this context. They found that the teachers' perspectives of their work and of the children were constrained by the hidden curriculum of social class and by the teachers' ambivalence of beliefs. (For example, 'The child is our first concern' versus 'I realize I'm paid to teach children to read and write.') Sharp and Green believe that the broadening of the curriculum which is associated with progressivism is being used merely to broaden the number of areas in which children may be categorized and controlled. They call attention to the paradox which

> lies in the structural underpinning and determination of the teacher's practice whereby, although they appear generally to be satisfying their own ideological commitments, they are unconsciously accommodating to a situation which renders it impossible to realize their commitments (Sharp and Green 1975).

Thus, Sharp and Green identify an issue which may be of particular importance to the organizational structures of the open plan school; how far are children merely being kept 'busy'? The Oracle Study too (Galton et al. 1980) refers to its similar findings that there is a frequent mismatch between the teachers' perceptions of their teaching and what actually goes on.

2   King (1978) found in his study of 'Mapledene School' that the labelling of children by teachers enabled prophesies for them to be fulfilled and that belief in child-centred ideologies enabled the teachers to be undemanding of themselves and of their pupils:

> By defining as real their ideas about the nature of children as being innocent, as possessing individuality and passing through sequential stages of develop-ment and also by defining real learning as being child-centred, the teachers pursued actions which tended to confirm these as realities, that is, they were real in their consequences.

King suggests that the teachers were insufficiently capable of questioning the ideas which they hold; thus the ideas became ideologies or recipes.

> Infant teachers' actions were related to the ideas they held about the nature of young children and the nature of the learning process. These ideas were

seldom explicitly expressed by teachers because to them they had the status not of *ideas* but of the *truth* (King 1978).

3   Further support for a view that teachers' views of their work (as child-centred or not) are inadequately conceptualized comes from the Schools Council's study of teachers' opinions of the aims of primary education (Ashton et al. 1975) in which a conclusion is reached that the 'individualistic' (or progressive) view has been formed not so much as a development of the traditional (or societal) view but as a *reaction* to it. Too often, educational issues are debated in terms of dichotomies. Even so, Ashton et al. show that their large sample of teachers is almost equally divided between belief in 'societal' aims and belief in 'child-centred' aims — in fact, a small marginal majority favour societal aims. Interestingly, Ashton et al. also show that graduate primary teachers and those with higher degrees are more likely to be 'less formal and narrow in their conception of educational aims and methods' and 'more often to give a lower rating to the basic skills group of aims' than certificated teachers. Similarly, Taylor et al. (1974) showed in his research that the aims to which teachers subscribe have their roots in their fundamental beliefs about the whole purpose of education. These findings emphasize the need to appoint to open plan schools teachers whose underlying philosophies are in agreement with the rationale of such schools.

4   Neville Bennett (1980) suggests that few teachers and headteachers have had any in-service training or preparation with particular reference to working in open plan schools and that local authority advisers and architects have normally not even discussed the principles or intentions of their building design with the staff appointed to run a new open plan school.

5   Constraint upon the development of the work of open plan schools is believed by Evans (1979) to be to do with 'territory':

> Many infant teachers have struggled to adapt to the forms imposed on them by resorting to the existing educational paradigm of subject specialization. The dissolution of the classroom walls may indicate the weakening of hierarchical and the strengthening of collegial control, but the effects of this have not always been fully understood. Deprived of their separate classrooms, which historically were a hard-won privilege associated with training and certification, it is hardly surprising that many have turned to an alternative power-conferring practice, whatever its educational merit in relation to the infant child (Evans 1979).

Bennett supports this view:

It would appear that for whatever reasons many teachers have been unable or unwilling to forego their territory. Walls have been replaced by other physical, or even psychological barriers. In this way the traditional 'one teacher one class' system has largely been maintained. (This) . . . throws substantial doubt on the assumption which a number of researchers have accepted without assessing its validity. It is not unusual to find researchers who have sampled open plan schools and written their report in terms of open education as if design and pedagogy were synonymous (Bennett and Hyland 1979).

Bennett's national study also suggests that a majority of teachers in open plan schools are working in *isolation* rather than in the teams which form a central part of the rationale of open planning; he shows too that a majority of teachers in open plan schools would prefer to work in box-classrooms (Bennett et al. 1980).

6   A final theory to explain the apparent failure of the open plan school to realize the 'progressive' expectations of its ancestry is that it, the open plan school itself, is a prime example of a national curriculum development project which has been widely 'sold' as a package. It has had no dissemination procedure and yet it has been handed to teachers by LEAs with little or no attention to training — with no 'negotiation' (McDonald and Walker 1976). In addition to its lack of planning for dissemination, the project has also had no evaluation procedure. In fact, the open plan school may not only be viewed as a national curriculum project, it may also be seen as the first. The Schools Council was modelled on, and developed from, the very procedures which produced the open plan school. With hindsight, we know that centrally initiated projects have little effect on the work of the teacher in the classroom, that the teacher must change before development may take place. If this is true of later Schools Council curriculum projects, it is certainly true of the development of the open plan school.

If the published research evidence represents reality it is difficult to escape discomforting conclusions. At its simplest, the work within many open plan schools may be little different, perhaps even less stimulating than that found in 'formal' box classrooms. It has been argued that it may take teachers twenty years to catch up with the buildings (Architects' Journal 1980) so the 1980s ought to see improvements taking place in the 1960s buildings. This seems unlikely, however, in the light of the dearth of in-service education related *specifically* to the open plan school; I believe I am right in saying that in my area little or nothing has been offered in the past *ten* years. This is typical of the national picture, as Bennett shows (Bennett et al. 1980).

Improvement seems unlikely too in the current staffing climate, but even before the present round of redeployments and restrictions, the correct choice of heads and teachers may not have been made. I have mentioned the need for open plan schools to be staffed by teachers whose personal philosophy is within the child-centred paradigm. Transferring even 'good' teachers is unsatisfactory; appointing as head the next ambitious person on the list may be disastrous. Both Bennett's national survey and my local one (Brogden 1980) revealed heads of open plan schools who are not committed to the rationale and teachers who are dissatisfied.

Open plan schools should be exempt from teacher transfer arrangements! Equally irrelevant to open plan schools is the sliding scale for staffing purposes. In many cases the building dictates staffing requirements that are not supported by pupil numbers. In my ex-school, for example, no space (other than the hall) can accommodate thirty children unless they are sitting on the floor. Local Authority advisers and administrators must acknowledge that open plan schools are special cases, built for specific teaching and organizational strategies which necessitate particular staffing arrangements. Those who do not agree with this need to explain why they built open plan schools in their areas.

Despite the pessimism which this paper's review of the research may generate, my personal experience enables me to be committed to the rationale and potential of the open plan school. I believe that it offers many advantages. There is a need for descriptive, if not empirical, studies of 'successful' open plan primary schools. There may be much to be gained by teachers in box classrooms from the learning atmosphere generated by some open plan schools. I have seen excellent examples in Oxfordshire, Shropshire, Berkshire and Hampshire; I am sure this list is restricted only by my failure to travel to other counties. I conclude, therefore, with a list of the *strengths* of the open plan school which are substantiated, not by research but by personal experience. The list may appear to add to the rhetoric but for a number of schools of which I have knowledge, it *is reality*.

Some strengths of the open plan primary school

Many of the following constructs were identified by teachers in my study of a small sample of Berkshire open plan primary schools (Brogden 1980). Others are my own! When organized within the rationale outlined in this paper, the open plan school promotes and facilitates:

For teachers

1 The sharing of skills, ideas and experiences, successes and problems.
2 Discussion, self-evaluation and development, joint planning.
3 Support and assimilation of new members of staff and student teachers.
4 An 'adult' working atmosphere and social benefits.
5 The sharing of problem pupils.
6 Avoidance of child-teacher personality clashes.
7 Motivation and stimulation.
8 Consistent 'discipline', reduced discipline problems.
9 Giving of one's best.
10 Access to a wide range of equipment and resources.
11 Access to a wide range of ages and abilities of children.
12 Careful planning, organization.
13 Flexibility.

For pupils

1 Flexibility.
2 Individual and small group attention.
3 Access to various teacher strengths and personalities.
4 Seeing adults relating well to one another.
5 The avoidance of child-teacher personality clashes.
6 'Comfortable', domestic surroundings.
7 Continuity of relationships with pupils and teachers.
8 A wide range of potential friendships.
9 A non-competitive, non-threatening, atmosphere.
10 Provision for individual abilities.
11 A broad curriculum.
12 Involvement.
13 The development of self-reliance.
14 The development of responsibility and self-discipline.

For parents

1 Involvement and access.
2 Seeing exactly what is happening without disturbing 'classes'.
3 Discussion with several teachers who know and have a balanced view of the child.
4 A welcoming, non-threatening atmosphere.

For headteachers
1   Close contact with the work that is being done by both pupils and teachers.
2   Seeing exactly what is happening without disturbing 'classes'.
3   A cooperative atmosphere — 'team spirit'.
4   An absence of hierarchies.
5   Curriculum discussion and development.
6   The maintenance of agreed policies.
7   The economic use of resources — sharing of equipment.
8   Involvement.

This list is not exhaustive but it represents strengths identified in some open plan schools. I should be very pleased to hear from more of the 2,123 open plan primary schools in England and Wales (Bennett et al. 1976) that the picture is not as bleak as Neville Bennett and other researchers have painted it.

Topics for discussion

1.   Discuss the proposition that the open plan primary school evolved to accommodate three organizational strategies ('family' or 'vertical grouping', the integrated day, and team teaching) from within the child-centred paradigm.
2.   What evidence is there to suggest that the link between 'open plan' and 'child-centred' practices is rather tenuous at the classroom level and that many open plan schools demonstrate the phenomenon of 'innovation without change'?
3.   Discuss some of the fundamental assumptions about child development, learning and teaching which a teacher who advocates a 'skills and frills' approach would advance to support this organizational and teaching strategy.

Suggestions for further reading

1.   Bennett, N., Andreae, J., Hegarty, P., and Wade, B. (1980) *Open Plan Primary Schools*. Windsor: NFER (for the Schools Council).
2.   Galton, M., Simon, R., and Croll, P. (1980) *Inside the Primary Classroom*. Routledge and Kegan Paul.
3.   Bell, S. (ed.) (1978) *The Organization of Open Plan Primary Schools*. Publication No. 3. Glasgow: Jordanhill College of Education.

READING EIGHT • Primary school organization: some rhetoric and some reason K. Ridley and D. Trembath

Most of us, if we're honest, have had the sobering experience of visiting other teachers whose teaching ability surpasses our own and whose capacity for creating exciting and purposeful learning environments reduces our own meagre efforts to insignificance. Sometimes this is on the scale of a single classroom, occasionally a whole school radiates this aura. Often, our natural deference to such rare excellence is accompanied by an insidious defence mechanism which, springing into action, deflects our proper regard for quality into a destructive filleting of peripheral detail enabling us to retreat into a self-protective shell, shielding our own inadequacies from the 'corrupting' influences of superior practice. Why do we do it? Are we so insecure in our professional poise that we cannot accept our imperfections and learn comfortably from each other? Are we so insular that learning by 'osmosis' within a corporate group of professionals becomes difficult and unusual? It is sadly rare to find a group of teachers able to be relaxed with one another on the basis of their own sense of personal worth, and further developing it through the professional sharing and cooperation generated by corporate group activity. If a school is to develop, then it must do so from this basis of common, collegiate responsibility for the curriculum in terms of its planning, development, organization and evaluation. Schools are incredibly complex, multi-faceted, shifting places which can only operate sensitively and responsively if the whole staff is engaged in the process of organization, at all levels, as participants rather than hierarchical 'agents'.

Having stated this, we find it remarkable that so much in schools and classrooms goes so well, given the complexity and unpredictability of classroom activity — but it is dangerously complacent to accept that 'schools are doing a reasonable job in the circumstances'. It can dull our professional sensitivity to the constant need to evaluate our practice and provide improving quality of school experience for children. Our very involvement in the taxing process of teaching and learning can stifle our

K. Ridley and D. Trembath, 'Primary School Organization: some rhetoric and some reason'. *School Organization*, 3, 1, 1983, pp 43–50

critical faculties and reduce our ability to make objective judgements.

Take, for instance, the physical environment of many of our schools, a subject we shall explore later in the article; consider the lack of quality and the limited stimulus it presents to children. Worse still, consider our relationship with parents when they are treated to ordeal by 'Parents Evening' during which masterly strategies of non-communication are operated which anaesthetize many of the unfortunate people into a state of docility and acceptance. Parents who attempt to resist the drug of 'cliché', generalizations and evasion are quietly branded as some sort of deviant and tagged for future reference. Now this derives not from the premeditated malice on the part of the staff nor from the intimidated deference on the part of parents. It has simply developed from a well-meaning if uncritical perpetuation of a practice intended to increase communication but manifestly failing to do so.

But already we are falling into the trap we mentioned at the beginning of the article, focusing on the defects and ignoring the good and worthwhile; but are we? Perhaps it is necessary to probe, to penetrate the welter of accumulated habits and conventional wisdoms that appear as the organizational basis of many of our schools.

All schools have strengths and weaknesses, good staff and bad, and ignoring the weaknesses will not alter this reality. At the same time, a school should be able to identify its real strengths, its key people, and use these as the base line for development and growth. It is the staff's corporate responsibility to do this. In a previous article (Ridley 1979), one of the authors stated that the primary school curriculum was in a mess. An extreme statement like this is always too easy to say and is of little value unless it can first be justified and then used as a starting point for improvement. Recent research, even allowing for our scepticism of much educational research, does suggest that while some good work is being maintained in the primary sector, there are areas of concern (HMI Primary Survey, DES 1978a; Galton 1980). Sometimes this area of concern is content, sometimes methodology, sometimes management, all of which suggests that the school as an institution needs to shape its curriculum consciously and rationally. If it does not, the disarray will continue until responsibility for the curriculum is taken from the school and professional practitioners and placed in the hands of external bodies who will dictate what, how and when things will occur.

It is our view that such a shift in curriculum planning would represent a devastating blow to primary education. It would be both foolish and pretentious to claim that a school should be totally autonomous in curriculum matters but the balance between autonomy and direction is one that must be jealously guarded. Paradoxically, a determination to protect this balance is best expressed by the readiness of teachers to engage in the curriculum debate both inside and *outside* the school, and this involves a willingness to shelve the 'pseudo professional' image and recognize that curriculum development is a rough game demanding intellectual rigour and professional competence. It is not the arena of myth, prejudice, jargon or conventional wisdom. While the curriculum is not the sole prerogative of teachers they are the single most potent element in the process. They possess the skill if it is tapped; they have the commitment if it is challenged, but perhaps most important of all, they have a continuing presence in schools. The granny knot of the primary curriculum and the organization required to support it can only be unravelled from within the school though it may well be helped from outside. However, it is ultimately the teacher who mediates the curriculum, who must make sense of it and who both creates and adheres to an organizational framework within which it can be expressed. Where to begin?

Above all is the paramount question 'What are primary schools for?' or perhaps it should be what can primary schools do, in the light of knowing that children are compelled to attend them?

In primary schools children should meet people, perhaps for the first time, with specific skills, beyond that of the layman, which can be used towards helping them to 'make meanings'; people who should be able to provide a range of experiences through which children are able to make both more sense of the world that they are in, and more sense of themselves. As the twentieth century clatters to a close in a period of staggeringly accelerated change, when knowledge is rendered obsolete even before it is communicated in any widespread sense, when the outside world is fixed and explained by transitory media with such slick consistency, teachers like any other member of our advanced industrial society are caught by change. They are caught uneasily in a time when change is not simply something one prepares for, and subsequently responds to, but in a time when change has been elevated to a state of being. Therefore, to view the primary school simply as a place where knowledge is transmitted from teacher to child is to be subject to a perspective which is mindlessly out of tune with the contemporary conduct of our world. It is a world increasingly better explained by a machine than it is understood by people, and in being so, the thinking mind, the creative spirit may well be more easily subjugated to the technological sedative.

The primary school then, should be the kind of institution peopled by individuals who are particularly skilled as a result of training and reflective experience, which enables children to act on their own experience of the world and literally create out of the symbolic constructs that school makes available to them, a pattern of order that both tells them something about themselves that they did not previously know, and something of the world that they are growing up in. This meeting of child and institution is manifested through 'The Learning Experience'; the environment in which this takes place; and perhaps most importantly of all, the organization that supports that environment.

Even today, fifteen years after the Plowden Report and in three years following the Primary Survey, most children in primary schools run the tedious gamut of reading and writing exercises 'alleviated' only by comprehension tests; they thrash around in the boredom of badly written mathematics work books unenlightened by practical application; they splash paint with the carelessness that is the trademark of the unskilled; they stick eggboxes and toilet roll cardboard tubes together; sequence becomes the roll call of boredom in published schemes and art becomes more subject to accident than design. Science is lost somewhere in the detritus of a nature table and fishtank, while Social Studies is reduced to a project or a topic which means endless copying out of the characteristic knowledge of 'Flight' or 'Space'. Religious knowledge, where it is not done with critical sincerity, is echoed through the story, hymn and a prayer in the tradition of Christianity.

Through all this the teacher can be heard talking; talking to, talking at, talking over, talking under, but seldom talking with and rarely listening, as any first year college student's analysis of classroom discourse will reveal. Yet, is this talk full of the wonders of the world, is it permeated by insight and wisdom, is it revealing of life's mysteries? Sadly, no! It is generally about telling children what to do, where to go, how to lay out and present work, how to respond to teacher, and generally how to behave. The learning experiences of most children are not simply debilitatingly short of firsthand experience; there are times when an incessant bombardment of secondhand representation lands on their budding sensitivities and like the patter of rain on a rock face, eventually smoothes out individual marks to a common anonymity. Why should this be?

We have already mentioned the professional defensiveness and lack of sharing on the part of teachers. How can this potential for sharing be generated to the extent that children's learning experience moves from the

A CLASSROOM LEARNING MODEL

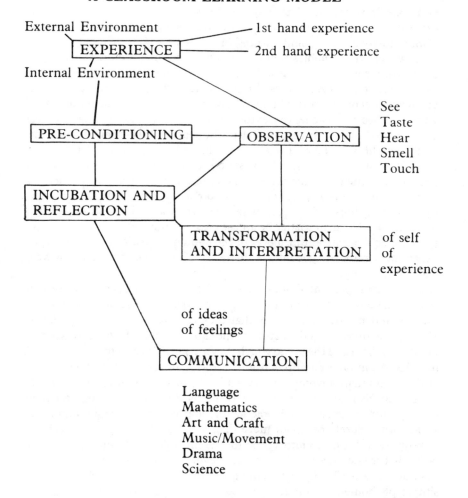

External Environment — 1st hand experience

EXPERIENCE — 2nd hand experience

Internal Environment

PRE-CONDITIONING — OBSERVATION

See
Taste
Hear
Smell
Touch

INCUBATION AND REFLECTION

TRANSFORMATION AND INTERPRETATION

of self
of
experience

of ideas
of feelings

COMMUNICATION

Language
Mathematics
Art and Craft
Music/Movement
Drama
Science

destructive certainty of boredom and repetition, to that excitement of vivid doubt in a world where the possible is anticipated and the probable examined? In terms of learning we must understand that the child is not so unlike the adult and by learning we do not suggest a sophisticated knowledge of erudite theories but a working analysis of what happens when any of us learns. The child like all of us basically (1) Experiences, (2) Reflects,

(3) Transforms, and (4) Communicates, and by experience we are reminded of Huxley's statement that 'Experience is not what happens to a man; experience is what a man does with what happens to him'. A simple elaboration of a Classroom Learning Model is shown on page 111.

However, the school system experienced by many children does not permit this view of learning to become a working reality in their lives, at least in any full sense. Almost from reception class onwards children are given a model of the world; 'This is how things are. . . . This is how things work. . .' because teachers or textbooks say so. From then on most children are expected to return that model to the teacher 'dry-cleaned' as Eisner (1980) would say. The return is assessed formally or informally on the basis of whether it meets the standards set by the teacher. These standards are largely concerned with the neatness and presentation of written or pictorial work which has often simply reproduced existing knowledge in a manner that children hope will match what teachers want. This 'work', be it a drawing of a Norman castle, or a neat page of sums, seldom becomes the personal and significant property of the child as a result of their acting on experience, rather it becomes a matter of reciprocal agreement between teacher and taught.

Before the argument about basics is raised, we must unequivocally state that no sane educator would deny that children require specific skills of literacy and numeracy in order that they can work on their experience. What we do question is the nature of the skills learned, the priority which is granted to them and the use to which they are put. To learn to read and write in order to complete comprehension exercises, or ultimately to fill in a form at the local unemployment office, while not unimportant at the necessary level of survival in a complex society, are hardly reasons enough for their often painful mastery. The practice of, and coping with our numerical system must surely be about more than work books and click wheels.

Why should it be so impossible to present individuals and groups with tasks that invite creative thought, that evoke responses to the real rather than the vicarious? Why is it seemingly so difficult to present children with simple phenomena to observe, to sense, to conjecture, hypothesize and speculate about, and to lay the surest foundations for imaginative science? Why can we not help more children to make the best possible use of materials to articulate their observation of the work? Why does tissue paper and glue continually take precedence over the careful use of the pencil and pen, or the studied concentration demanded by paint? Why is it that we insist on occupying children with mindless banality when the opportunity for real engagement with the artifacts and understandings of the world are ignored with such profligacy?

Sadly a great deal of what passes for schooling is concerned with the mediocrity of transmitted knowledge, yet it is generally recognized that young children learn most effectively through direct experience, experiences that can be clarified by contact with adults, by research, by discussion and by the transformation of that experience into new forms.

The kinds of learning we are suggesting have been the benchmark of good primary practice for many years and it is a practice requiring hard work and a powerfully supportive organization. It also means a change of attitude, a change which means confronting the significant rather than the trivial, demanding faith, a knowledgeable sensitivity and an imaginative leap that in the first instance creates the environment in which learning can take place. The average classroom, or indeed school environment, is often a matter of four walls indicating a passing concession to display. Most school staffrooms, a room that ironically should reflect the greatest taste, often suggest a paper curling chaos where melamine mugs vie for space with lost property, Union notices and plimsolls. Many of the spaces that children inhabit for a large proportion of their waking lives possess all the grace and charm of a refuse tip.

It is our view that the quality of the school environment is crucial to the process of significant learning. Its richness, diversity, challenge and structure affect the implementation of dynamic learning in a profound way, and across all parts of the curriculum. We feel that it is not impossible to create an environment that facilitates for children learning by direct experience, and while time and effort are required it is not an insuperable task to create a classroom where 'bays' exist by the simple juxtaposition of furniture; where areas exist to reflect certain distinctions of the curriculum; where display reflects taste and discretion; where there is a relationship between what is immediately apparent and visually pleasing and what children are actually doing. It requires the most efficient use of space; for example, look at the ridiculous amount of room taken up by many teachers' desks. We are not suggesting a permanent window dressing so much as a continuing theatre of communication where the marks that we all need to make in the world affirm our individual identity and our collective aspirations.

Teachers then, must develop a workable classroom arrangement which takes account of the nature of the learning process by responding in organizational terms. This means creating a highly charged, structured yet flexible and adaptable classroom that can support the diverse learning strategies employed by children. It must provide balance, sequence and appropriate 'match' as well as providing resources, content and the opportunity for developing skills.

The environment should be a subtle, interrelated mix of physical, social and intellectual elements encompassing both adults and children and it is the responsibility of the adults in the school to create the environment to which children can respond. We would ask the following questions of the environment that children learn in:

How attractive is it?
What does it declare about the nature of the curriculum, its diversity and range?
What does it say about the quality of the children's work and the teacher's response in terms of careful and sensitive display?
Is the school clean?
Is the most made of the space available?
Are the resources carefully organized and accessible to children and staff?
Is it possible to identify school priorities from the clues presented by the physical setting?
How does the environment help the social relationships?
How do children and teachers relate?
How do they talk to each other?
How do children move around the school?
Is playtime an explosive ventilator in the day or a natural phase in the rhythm of activities?

We could, of course, go on asking questions about the school environment but behind all this questioning is the assertion that the context within which children learn fundamentally affects the quality of the learning and that a necessary professional skill of any teacher concerns the creation and manipulation of an environment which stimulates learning, enhances its quality and reflects its diversity.

In analysing the significant features which together contribute to the ethos and purpose of the school, there are two overriding factors upon which success depends:

1   the positive role of the headteacher as perceived by himself and recognized by others; and
2   the absolute necessity of the staff and head working together.

These factors underpin the whole infrastructure of the school; they condition relationships, affect development and transform theory or exhortation into action. Without this participant planning and organization, progress becomes piecemeal at best and non-existent at worst.

We suggest that the good head creates a supportive framework and organization in which both head and staff alike find it possible to address themselves critically to serious educational issues. Staff meetings then become matters of professional concern rather than whether Mrs. X or Mr. Y should take their children to the Tower of London on the annual school visit.

When people create professional circumstances, they begin to behave as professional persons and out of these circumstances staff and head alike may do much worse than consider the following:

What are the aims of the school? How were they identified, when and by whom? To what extent does the practice of the school genuinely reflect them in terms of:

1 The quality of the school environment.
2 The content of the curriculum.
3 The teaching and learning strategies.
4 The effective use of resources including people and time.
5 Methods of planning, evaluation and assessment.
6 Involvement of the staff in the decision-making processes of the school.
7 On-going professional development.
8 Involvement of the wider community.

We could go on, and on, and on, asking questions is easy; answers that involve people are seldom found in any permanent sense. It is our view that the bridge between the questions and answers in terms of how we can make schools better places than they are is to create sound organizational principles that take account of past tradition, that accept the limits of the present and that anticipate the future.

Topics for discussion

1. Discuss the implications of the authors' statement that 'The granny knot of the primary curriculum and the organization required to support it can only be unravelled from *within* the school though it may well be helped from outside'.

2. Critically evaluate the ways in which different forms of headteacher leadership contribute to the ethos and purpose of the school.
3. What specific forms of primary school organizational practices would best facilitate the adoption of the 'classroom learning model' suggested on page 111?

Suggestions for further reading

1. Blenkin, G.M. and Kelly, A.V. (1981) *The Primary Curriculum*. London: Harper & Row.
2. Winkley, D. (1983) 'An Analytical View of Primary School Leadership'. *School Organization*, **3**, 1, pp. 15–26.
3. Whitaker, P. (1983) *The Primary Head*. London: Heinemann.

SECTION FIVE
CLASSROOM PRACTICE IN PRIMARY SCHOOLS

READING NINE • Junior school teachers: their methods and practices
J. Barker-Lunn

Introduction

A programme of research, sponsored by the DES and designed to investigate teaching methods, styles and practices used by teachers in junior schools, was undertaken in 1980.

The first phase of the investigation involved visits to schools and interviews with heads and teachers in order to gain a general impression of the current situation.

This exploratory study was based on visits to 14 schools in Berkshire, Leicestershire, Yorkshire, Hampshire and Durham. Thirty teachers were inverviewed in order to ascertain their aims, priorities and attitudes and to obtain information about their teaching methods and classroom practices.

The second phase comprised the development and administration of two questionnaires. The first of these was addressed to the heads of a representative sample of 732 junior schools or departments in England and was designed to yield evidence concerning their organizational policies. The findings of this survey have been published (*Educational Research*, Volume 24, Number 4, November 1982). The second questionnaire, with which this article is concerned, was intended for class teachers. In its compilation use was made of the results of the exploratory study and also of the findings of previous surveys (Barker-Lunn 1970; Bealing 1972; Bennett 1976; Bassey 1978; HMI Survey 1978). It was administered to two samples of those teachers in the 732 schools involved in the survey who taught second-, third- and fourth-year junior pupils. Sample A included teachers in large schools — those with at least eight junior classes. Sample B consisted of medium size and small schools. All teachers in Sample A and one in four of the teachers in Sample B schools received the questionnaire.

One thousand nine hundred and eighty five teachers in large schools and

J. Barker Lunn 'Junior school teachers: their methods and practices'. *Educational Research*, 1984, 26, 3, 178–188

543 teachers in the smaller schools completed the questionnaires, representing response rates of 80 per cent and 82 per cent respectively.

Nearly two-thirds of the teachers who responded to the questionnaire were female. The majority were experienced teachers: 90 per cent had been teaching for at least three years; and more than 50 per cent for over ten years.

Over 90 per cent had been trained to teach junior school pupils; seven per cent to teach pupils of secondary school age; two per cent to teach infants. Less than one per cent had no teaching training at all. Over 90 per cent had been responsible for their classes since the beginning of the school year in September 1979 (the survey was carried out in the spring of 1980).

The average size of the classes in the large schools was 30.4 pupils and 28.8 pupils in the smaller schools.

Analysis of the results

The information obtained from Sample A (large schools) and Sample B (smaller schools) was analysed separately. The data from Sample A teachers were analysed in terms of the year group taught, thus yielding three sub-groups: second-year, third-year and fourth-year juniors. The data provided by Sample B teachers were analysed with reference to the age composition of the classes (pupils from one administrative year-group) and mixed age classes (pupils of two or more administrative year groups).

In the account that follows the detailed statistical analyses on which the findings are based have been omitted. These are held at the Foundation and can be made available to anyone who wishes to examine them. Where comparisons are made and differences emphasized it is to be understood that these findings are based upon an appropriate level of statistical significance. Similarly where no specific reference is made to differences — for example between larger and smaller schools or between different types of classes — it may be assumed that no statistically significant difference was found.

The findings are presented under three main heads:

1. *Teaching method* — indicating the preferences expressed by the teachers for particular modes of instruction;
2. *The organization of learning* — discussing how teachers make provision for and superintend their pupils' classroom activities;

3. *The curriculum and its arrangement* — considering the content of what children are encouraged to learn and the priorities that are established among its constituent parts.

1. Teaching method

The teachers were asked to identify the methods they employed when teaching mathematics and English, including reading — either when they were introducing new concepts or arranging for revision. They were invited to indicate for each of the subjects separately the approximate proportions of time that they devoted to whole class teaching; teaching groups of children of similar ability; teaching groups of mixed ability; and teaching children individually. Constraints on the length of the questionnaire that could reasonably be imposed upon teachers and on the amount of information that could be accommodated by the teachers precluded questions about the methods used in teaching art and craft, music, physical education, science, history or geography or in superintending other kinds of activity. This limitation needs to be borne in mind in interpreting the results that follow.

Use of different teaching methods Table 1 below shows the extent to which the different methods of teaching were reported to be used. The figures are based on the number of teachers who used a method for a quarter or more of the total time available, either exclusively or in combination with one or more of the other methods. The proportions in each column, therefore, exceed 100 per cent.

The results show that class teaching, teaching groups of similar ability and individual teaching are all widely used, whereas more than four-fifths of the teachers in the sample reported that they made little or no use of mixed ability group teaching when dealing with the basic skills in English and mathematics. There was a tendency for more teachers in large than in smaller schools to make use of class teaching for each subject and for more teachers in smaller than in large schools to choose ability group and individual teaching.

A noteworthy finding from this section of the questionnaire was that the vast majority of teachers made use of at least two different teaching methods but not, for the most part, in equal measure.

The main method of teaching The exclusive use of a single teaching method was rarely found except that, in teaching children to read, some two-fifths of all teachers used individual teaching only, and over 90 per cent used this method for part of the time. Although reliance on one particular method was uncommon, most teachers were found to have a preferred method to which they devoted most of their time, making use of one or more of the other approaches as supplementary methods.

This preferred method was identified by examining the amount of time devoted to each method when teaching mathematics and English. (The teaching of reading was not included in this analysis because, as indicated above, there was such a marked tendency to employ individual teaching for this purpose.)

A method was designated as the main method if it was found to be used for at least half the time available.

The results show that in teaching English and mathematics there is no predominantly favoured approach. Each of the methods is chosen by a substantial proportion of teachers and a fifth of the total sample reported that they used a variety of methods in teaching mathematics. In teaching English, class-teaching is more favoured than any of the other three approaches; even so a substantial minority of teachers used each of the other three approaches as a main method.

Table 1: Teachers' use of different teaching methods (used on average at least one quarter of the time)

Use of method:	Maths		English		Reading	
	Large schools	Smaller schools	Large schools	Smaller schools	Large schools	Smaller schools
Class teaching	80%	64%	88%	80%	28%	21%
Ability group teaching	66%	69%	56%	58%	36%	38%
Individual teaching	70%	76%	63%	65%	91%	92%
Mixed ability group teaching	15%	17%	20%	22%	11%	10%
Number of teachers giving information	1903	530	1906	529	1893	526

A clear relationship was discernible, however, between a teacher's main method for teaching mathematics and that for teaching English. This was particularly marked for those who favoured class teaching for mathematics. Of these 77 per cent also used whole class teaching for English. Similarly 67 per cent of those who preferred to teach English either individually or using groups similar in ability chose to teach mathematics in the same way.

Choice of main method and type of class It is reasonable to suppose that a teacher's choice of a method of instruction would be influenced to some degree by the size and nature of the class with which she was required to deal and particularly by the range of her pupils' ages and levels of ability. A section of the questionnaire was designed to explore these relationships.

The results obtained from large schools were, first of all, analysed by year group. This showed that the proportion of teachers using each teaching method was the same whether the class consisted of second-, third- or fourth-year juniors.

The results were then analysed in terms of the range of ability or attainment within the classes concerned. In large schools, although most classes were of mixed ability, there was a sizeable minority of classes in which the range of ability had been reduced by streaming (10 per cent of

Table 2: Main method of teaching mathematics and English

	Maths		English	
	Large schools	Smaller schools	Large schools	Smaller schools
Main method:				
Class teaching	33%	19%	42%	30%
Ability group teaching	29%	32%	21%	21%
Individual teaching	20%	26%	11%	20%
Variety of methods	18%	23%	26%	29%
	100%	100%	100%	100%
Number of teachers giving information	1844	490	1816	488

Table 3: Main method of teaching mathematics in mixed ability, set and streamed classes in large schools

Type of class:	Mixed ability	Set for maths	Streamed
Class teaching	29%	39%	44%
Ability group teaching	29%	33%	14%
Individual teaching	23%	12%	20%
Variety of approaches	18%	16%	22%
	100%	100%	100%
Number of teachers giving information	1224	434	186

classes were streamed)[1] or by setting (23 per cent of classes were set for mathematics).

The results in Table 3 suggest that there is a relationship between choice of teaching method and the range of ability or attainment within a class. More teachers of streamed and set classes used class teaching as their main method of teaching mathematics than did teachers of mixed ability classes.

Nearly three-quarters of teachers of mixed ability classes used methods which made some allowance for the wide range of individual differences manifested by their pupils: 29 per cent taught mathematics to groups of similar ability; 23 per cent used individual teaching; and 18 per cent used a variety of approaches. Only 29 per cent used whole class teaching.

Very few classes used setting for English, and so an analysis similar to that used for the teaching of mathematics could not be employed. Whole class teaching was found to be the most popular main method of teaching English in both streamed and mixed ability classes. A slightly greater proportion of teachers in mixed ability classes, however, compared with those in streamed classes, chose similar ability group teaching as their main method.

The main methods of teaching mathematics and English in single age and mixed age classes in smaller schools were compared and it was found that in mixed age classes more teachers used individual teaching and fewer used

[1] The streamed classes referred to were in schools which either streamed throughout all year groups (two per cent of schools large enough to stream) or which part-streamed (16 per cent of large schools) usually taking the form of permanent remedial classes (see Barker Lunn 1982).

whole class teaching as their main method.

Although these findings demonstrate a tendency for whole class teaching to be preferred when classes are characterized by a relatively narrow range of attainment and for individual tuition or teaching children in small groups of similar ability to be chosen for classes that are of a heterogeneous kind, it should be noted that significant proportions of teachers failed to follow these trends and did not choose the teaching method that, in their circumstances, might have been expected.

For example, in a mathematics class of mixed ability one is likely to find pupils who differ significantly in their rate of progress and level of achievement and therefore in their capacity to acquire a new concept. Nevertheless, as Table 3 shows, over a quarter of teachers of mixed ability classes used whole class teaching as their main method of teaching mathematics.

Class size might be expected to be related to the choice of teaching method. In smaller schools this would seem to be the case in that those teachers who used individual tuition as their main method were found to have fewer pupils in their classes than those who opted for other approaches. In large schools, however, no relationship was found between the size of the class and the choice of teaching method.

Finally, it should be noted that no significant differences were found among teachers choosing methods in terms either of their own age or the age range of the children they had been trained to teach.

2. The organization of learning

As well as being instructed in English and mathematics children were provided with opportunities to practise the skills they had acquired and to revise and consolidate what they had learned. This section is concerned with the provision that teachers made for these activities.

Three forms of organization were distinguished: *classwork* which involves all the members of the class working on the same or similar tasks; *individual tasks* which may be adapted to suit the children's specific needs, interests or level of attainment; and *group tasks* for which provision can be made in a variety of ways.

Classwork Classwork was the most favoured form of organization for English. It featured also, but to a lesser extent, in the arrangements for activities in mathematics and even in the provision of reading tasks.

Although individually assigned tasks were predominantly favoured in the latter case, nevertheless it was found that about a quarter of the teachers in the sample set classwork in reading.

It is not surprising that an association was found between the preferred method of teaching and the arrangements made for children's learning activities. Those teachers who favoured class teaching tended to emphasize classwork: those teaching children in groups of similar ability tended to follow this up by setting work to these groups; and those who concentrated on individual teaching made provision for individual assignments.

Individual assignments Individual tasks involving children working on their own either in the classroom or elsewhere — in a library or study area, for example — were commonly assigned in all subjects.

Those teachers who organized individual assignments for at least half the time available were invited to supply further information about these activities. This was in order to establish the degree of teacher direction and control involved or, conversely, the extent of the responsibility and freedom accorded to the children in selecting and completing their tasks. The teachers were given four descriptions of individual tasks:

(a) Individual task(s) given to child by teacher to be worked on when directed by teacher;
(b) Individual task(s) chosen by child from a set of assignments to be worked on when directed by teacher;
(c) Individual task(s) given to child by teacher to be completed at a time of the child's own choosing;
(d) Individual task(s) chosen by child from a set of assignments to be completed at a time of the child's own choosing.

They were asked to indicate for each of the basic skills in mathematics, English, including the teaching of reading, the statement that best described the nature of their individual assignment.

Approximately a third of all teachers for English and mathematics, and about 70 per cent of teachers for reading, provided individual tasks for about half the time available.

The results showed that the majority of these 'individual' teachers subscribed to the first of these statements — that is, they both controlled the type of task and determined when it should be done. This control was most pronounced in the case of mathematics. Children have slightly more freedom in the choice of reading tasks but, even in this regard, only about 30 per cent of the teachers concerned permitted freedom of choice.

The practice of allowing children, after a task had been assigned or chosen, to complete it within limits, at a time of their own choosing was rare in mathematics and was adopted by about 12 per cent of 'individual' teachers (that is, five per cent of all teachers). This approach was more common in the case of reading and English: about a quarter of the (individual) teachers for reading and 20 per cent for English accepted this arrangement.

Group work Whether classes were of a heterogeneous kind or more restricted in their range of ability, it was found that teachers often subdivided them into groups for specific purposes. Some two-thirds of the teachers in the sample reported that at least for some of the time they organized their classes in this way. The groups could be given tasks in the same subject — for example all the groups might be given work in mathematics, although these might well be different kinds of task suited to the different levels of attainment of the children concerned. Alternatively groups could be set to work in different areas of the curriculum — one engaged in mathematics, for example, another in a piece of writing, a third drawing a map and so on.

Among the teachers who used grouping for classroom activities, virtually all arranged at times for work in the *same* curricular area but about half of them (amounting to approximately one-third of the teachers in the total sample) indicated that for some of the time at least they organized group work in different curricular areas. This latter approach was slightly more common in smaller than in large schools. There were no differences in this regard between teachers of different year groups.

For the most part group work involved each member working individually but some instances were found of groups working cooperatively on a common task and producing a joint output — for example, a project in environmental studies or in arts and crafts.

Cooperative group work was rare in periods designated for the teaching of English and mathematics, and was less commonly found in large compared with smaller schools, although it became slightly more frequent in large schools as the children became older.

Seating arrangements In examining the ways in which teachers subdivided their classes into groups, information was sought about the criteria used by teachers for assigning children to seats.

Approximately a quarter of the teachers reported that they allowed their pupils to choose their own seats. Nearly half seated their pupils for some of the time in accordance with their levels of attainment but roughly one-sixth of the teachers did so for all or most of the time, which is tantamount to streaming within the class.

This proportion became even greater when a separate analysis was made of those teachers in large schools who used ability grouping as their main teaching method for mathematics. Nearly one-fifth of them seated their pupils for all or most of the time in groups determined by their levels of ability.

On the other hand, 43 per cent of the teachers who used ability grouping as their main method of teaching adopted a more flexible approach in that they did not require those who formed an ability group for teaching purposes to sit together on other occasions.

There were no significant differences in regard to seating arrangements between larger and smaller schools or between classes of different ages.

3.   The curriculum and its arrangement

In considering the content of junior school education, particular attention was paid firstly to the extent to which teachers either followed their own devices and desires or were provided with a school scheme of work. Secondly, information was sought as to whether subjects were taught in a relatively compartmentalized or in an integrated fashion. Finally evidence was sought concerning the distribution of emphasis placed on various activities and parts of the curriculum in order to ascertain teachers' priorities in this regard.

Schemes of work The degree to which a teacher enjoys freedom in following a syllabus and organizing teaching procedures is determined in part by the policy of the school in such matters as schemes of work and curriculum organization.

For more than 90 per cent of the teachers there was a school scheme of work for mathematics, and a little under 90 per cent were provided with one for English. Schemes of work may be developed collectively or by a nominated teacher in consultation with others, or by the head. This aspect was not investigated. But the use that was made of the scheme of work was examined; this can vary considerably. It may be regarded as a basic syllabus consisting of a sequence of activities that pupils are required to undertake and of concepts and skills that they are meant to acquire within a specified period of time. Alternatively it may be regarded as no more than a set of broad guidelines within which teachers may cater for their pupils' individual differences.

The teachers in the sample were asked to indicate which of the following four statements best described their own circumstances:

(a) scheme of work used as a basic syllabus and followed as far as possible;
(b) scheme of work used as a guideline;
(c) scheme of work used as a very broad guide;
(d) scheme of work not used.

It was found that just over a third of teachers used their mathematics scheme of work as a basic syllabus but the majority used it either as a guideline or very broad guide. For English, on the other hand, only one-fifth used the scheme of work as a basic syllabus. Relevant here are published schemes of work in mathematics, for example Fletcher's Mathematics for School Series, and in English, for example SRA laboratories, which frequently guide work and may be a considerable influence in providing structure for work in these subjects. The origin of the scheme of work was not investigated.

The trend towards using schemes of work as guidelines rather than as a basic syllabus was found to be more pronounced in smaller than in large schools, probably because of the greater degree of heterogeneity in many of the classes in smaller schools.

Only a small minority — about 15 per cent — of the teachers reported that they regularly taught history and geography as separate subjects. Nearly 30 per cent indicated that they taught them as part of a broader subject — environmental studies, for example. The majority of teachers, however (just one half of those who responded), combined both approaches, sometimes teaching them separately and sometimes as part of a broader subject.

Teachers' priorities As a result of the exploratory interviews a list of 20 key activities and types of lesson were identified. The teachers were asked to indicate the frequency with which their pupils were required to undertake these activities, using a six-point scale which ranged from every one or two days, once a week or more, to less than once a term and never.

Although the list is not exhaustive, it is nevertheless sufficiently comprehensive to allow differences of emphasis to emerge and teachers' priorities to be revealed.

The list, shown in rank order of median score, is contained in Table 4.

Table 4: Rank order of frequency of activities

Rank	Name of activity
1	Work in mathematical computation
2	Silent reading as a class
3	Practice in learning tables/number bonds
4	Vocabulary and dictionary work
5	Comprehension exercises
6	Descriptive writing
7.5	Learning lists of spellings
7.5	Creative writing
9	Spelling tests
10	Formal grammar
11	Science
12	Practical maths
13	Individual project or topic work
14	Cooperative group work
15	Maths tests
16	Free choice periods
17	Modern maths
18	Drama
19	Dictation
20	School visits/field trips
21	Homework

Activities in mathematics It is noteworthy that a large degree of priority was given to practising *computational skills*. Such practice was provided at least once a week by 90 per cent of the teachers and nearly half of them introduced it every one or two days.

Learning multiplication tables and number bonds also featured prominently in the curriculum: about 88 per cent arranged for practice at least once a week and more than a third every one or two days.

Less emphasis was given to *practical maths* (weighing and measuring) and to modern maths (e.g. Venn diagrams, symmetry etc). Forty-five per cent of teachers made provision for practical maths at least once a week, and 27 per cent introduced modern maths at the same frequency. More than a third of all teachers gave a *maths test* at least once a week.

It was interesting to note that learning multiplication tables, and maths tests were less common in smaller than larger schools, but practical mathematics and modern mathematics were more common in the smaller schools.

As well as being questioned about the frequency with which they introduced various mathematical activities, teachers were asked whether they placed more emphasis on the basic skills such as the four rules of number, tables and number bonds than on other areas such as symmetry, shape, and probability, or whether they gave no special emphasis to any particular aspect of the maths syllabus. Eighty-two per cent responded positively to this question, declaring that they placed predominant emphasis on basic computational skills.

Activities in English Under this head, *reading* occupies the highest place in the league table. Eighty-three per cent made provision for silent reading at least once a week, and nearly half the teachers introduced it every one or two days.

An activity may be said to be receiving special attention if more than 80 per cent of teachers introduce it at least once a week. By this criterion *comprehension exercises*, (89 per cent), *vocabulary and dictionary work* (88 per cent), *learning lists of spellings* (82 per cent), *spelling tests* (80 per cent) and *formal grammar*, involving punctuation and parts of speech (79 per cent) may be said to qualify. Formal grammar tended to be less frequent in smaller than large schools.

Writing also featured prominently in the curriculum, with slightly greater emphasis on *creative* than *descriptive* writing. The opportunity for creative writing was provided at least once a week by 87 per cent of teachers and for descriptive writing by 77 per cent.

In this regard, teachers were also asked about the criterion they used in assessing written work and it is noteworthy that the majority — 75 per cent — regarded content and grammatical accuracy as of equal importance.

The aspects of English teaching that were least favoured were *dictation*, which half the teachers offered either not at all or, at most, once or twice during the school year and *spoken drama* which the majority reported as featuring two or three times a term.

Other activities Nearly half the teachers made provision for *individual project or topic work* at least once a week. This involves children in carrying out a piece of research and producing a report and often encompasses work in several curricular areas.

The proportion of classes having project work at least once a week increased from two-fifths for second-year children to three-fifths for those in the fourth year, and there was a slight tendency for this activity to be commoner in smaller than in large schools.

Free-choice periods, during which the children may decide for themselves on the activities that they undertake were slightly less common. Two-fifths of the classes were given free-choice periods at least once a week, but in a quarter of the classes these occurred less than once a term or not at all. There was no difference between year groups in this respect but, again, this provision was commoner in smaller than in large schools.

The organization of *school visits or field trips* was reported by 98 per cent of the teachers. Approximately half of them took their pupils out at least once a term, the rest less frequently. Smaller schools tended to make more school visits than large schools, and within the latter visits became more frequent as the children became older.

About 40 per cent of teachers reported that *science* did not feature in their classes as frequently as once a week, although there was a tendency for it to become somewhat more prominent when the children reached the upper age groups.

It is of interest to note that the teachers were questioned about the ways in which they introduced new concepts in science and mathematics. They were asked to choose between the statements: 'I would first let the children explore the concept with materials and apparatus' and 'I would be more likely to discuss it first with the children and then let them explore it'. The former statement was overwhelmingly rejected. Ninety per cent of the teachers indicated that they were more likely to discuss the concept first.

Summary and discussion

Each method of teaching that was included in the questionnaire claimed a substantial number of adherents, but only a very small minority of those who reported that they used a particular approach as their main method were found to employ it exclusively. A common pattern appeared to be for a teacher to use a preferred method for the greater part of the time but to supplement it on occasions with one or more other forms of instruction. The results revealed a tendency for the chosen method of teaching to be related to both the type of work or task being undertaken by the children and to the characteristics of the class concerned. Teachers were more likely to use class teaching when dealing with classes in which the range of ability or attainment was restricted, and to teach children individually or in small groups when confronted with mixed ability classes. Nevertheless a sizeable minority of teachers failed to follow this trend. (In teaching science and mathematics, discovery methods were very rarely used.)

There was an association between the preferred method of teaching and the ways in which teachers organized their pupils' learning activities. Those who favoured class teaching tended to emphasize classwork; those teaching children in groups of similar ability set work to these groups; and those who concentrated on individual teaching made provision for individual assignments.

For the most part, group work involved each member working individually. Cooperative group work was very rare in periods designated for the teaching of English and mathematics. Only about a fifth of the teachers allowed children to choose their own seats. About a half arranged for them to be seated at least for part of the time, in accordance with their levels of attainment.

The majority of teachers were provided with schemes of work for mathematics and English but, for the most part, these were used as guidelines rather than programmes to be rigidly followed.

An examination of the amount of time that teachers spent on various parts of the curriculum showed that in mathematics there was considerable emphasis on computational skills, learning multiplication tables and number bonds. In English, a considerable amount of time was devoted to the teaching of reading, and other activities that featured prominently were comprehension exercises, vocabulary and dictionary work, formal grammar, and creative and descriptive writing.

The situation that this survey has revealed is in marked contrast with the assumed stereotype that was prevalent in the 1960s and 1970s. The Plowden Committee, which was set up in 1963 to inquire into the state of primary education, lent its approval to what was described as progressive education. Its report conveyed the impression — without supplying adequate supporting evidence — that progressive methods were practised by a large number of teachers and were becoming the norm in primary schools. This became the view accepted by the general public. It was assumed — and to some extent the belief still persists — that junior schools had adopted a child-centred approach, that teachers had ceased to exercise authority and refrained from interfering in their pupils' natural development until they were virtually invited to provide such resources as the children's emergent interests appeared to require. The curriculum had become broad and largely negotiable with a diminishing emphasis on the basic subjects, and teaching methods were characterized by the disappearing dais and a heavy reliance on children's inclination to explore their environment and their capacity to acquire concepts through discovery.

This view of junior school education persisted not only in the absence of supporting evidence but even when contradictory findings were published. From 1963 to 1967 the Foundation carried out a longitudinal study (Barker Lunn 1967, 1970) which found no evidence to suggest that large numbers of teachers were practising progressive methods.

A few years later in 1973 the Bullock Committee carried out a survey of teaching practices which furnished convincing evidence that informal and progressive approaches had barely established a foothold in primary schools.

Similarly, Bennett's research (1976), which was carried out in Lancashire and Cumbria during the early 1970s, reported a scarcity of teachers using progressive methods. And a few years later, during 1975–1977, a survey carried out by HMI served to confirm the view that the earlier highly publicized account of changes from formal to progressive methods would seem to have been exaggerated and had almost certainly been confined to a small minority of primary schools.

It is equally difficult to discover evidence of changes over the years in the curriculum followed by the majority of primary schools. This would only be possible if the activities carried out in junior schools had been monitored by regular surveys using the same instruments and forms of analysis. Although this kind of accurate comparison cannot be undertaken, some evidence can be gleaned from the fact that a list of activities similar to the one included in the 1980 questionnaire was included in the Foundation survey of 1965 (Barker Lunn 1970), and the Bullock Committee made similar inquiries in 1973.

From these studies it can be inferred that the emphasis on mathematical computation was still the same in 1965 and 1980 but that increased attention was now being paid to comprehension exercises in English. The comparison with the Bullock Committee's findings yields suggestive evidence that the 1980 survey shows a heavier emphasis than was found in 1973 in comprehension, formal grammar and spelling tests.

The first part of the survey, addressed to the heads of schools, and reported in *Educational Research* in November 1982, showed that there had been major organizational changes in junior schools over the past 20 years, first in the widespread abandonment of streaming and, latterly, in the introduction of more homogeneous groups for teaching purposes, mainly by the use of setting for mathematics and to some extent for English, and by the formation of enrichment groups for the more able, and remedial groups for the lower attainers.

This latter development has made it possible to extend the use of class teaching, and the present survey indicates that class teaching has indeed become more popular in recent years and that there is an association between the use of this approach and the range of ability or attainment with which teachers have to deal.

The report of the HMI survey laid emphasis on the importance of class teaching and claimed that 'in some cases it was more efficient to teach the whole class than to attempt to teach each child' (5.65). It was further suggested that 'teachers can by working regularly with a group or the whole class, quicken the pace of mental response and encourage accuracy' (8.22).

It is suggested that the shift towards selective teaching groups (by a minority) and the attention that was given to class teaching in the HMI report may have had an influence in this regard and that the organizational changes may have been introduced in order to facilitate the increased use of class teaching.

There is an element of speculation in seeking to identify the changes in teaching practices that have taken place over the years and the factors that have brought them about. What is clear from the 1980 survey, however, is that the most recently available evidence shows that the vast majority of junior school teachers are firmly in control of their classrooms. They determine what activities their pupils will undertake; they prefer a didactic approach rather than a reliance on discovery methods; they are making increasing use of class teaching; and there is no need to exhort them to go back to the basics. Indeed the development of and practice in the basic skills both of English and of mathematics would seem to be the predominant features of junior school classrooms.

Topics for discussion

1. Discuss the implications for children's motivation and learning of the finding that 'over a quarter of teachers of mixed ability classes used whole class teaching

as their main method of teaching mathematics'.
2. What evidence does Barker-Lunn present that lends weight to the recent comment by HMI (*Education Observed, 2,* 1984) that primary school teaching concentrates too much on the basic 3Rs?
3. 'The vast majority of junior school teachers are firmly in control of their classrooms.' What are the advantages and disadvantages of close and continuous planning and surveillance on the part of the classteacher?

Suggestions for further reading

1. Department of Education and Science (1984) *Education Observed, 2.* DES Publications Centre, Canons Park, Honeypot Lane, Stanmore, Middx.
2. Barker-Lunn, J. (1982) 'Junior schools and their organizational policies', *Educational Research,* 24, 4, pp.250–61.
3. Galton, M.J., Simon, B. and Croll, P. (1980) *Inside The Primary Classroom.* London: Routledge and Kegan Paul.

READING TEN • From: The quality of pupil learning experiences
N. Bennett, C. Desforges, A. Cockburn and B. Wilkinson

Introduction

This study by Bennett and his associates is concerned with the quality of learning environments provided by sixteen able teachers of six and seven year old children. The study breaks new ground by considering the whole task process in classrooms. Attention is given to the planning and presentation of classroom tasks, their curriculum content, the intellectual demands they make on children, their appropriateness or match to the children's attainments, their continuity across change of school and the nature of teachers' explanations, diagnoses of children's work and classroom management strategies.

A short abstract of the major findings of N. Bennett, C. Desforges, A. Cockburn and B. Wilkinson, *The Quality of Pupil Learing Experiences.* London: Lawrence Erlbaum Associates 1984

The findings reveal that despite the conscientious efforts of able teachers a number of serious issues are apparent, some of which appear to be hidden from teachers. These issues are clearly identified, not for the purpose of criticism, but as a necessary basis for improvement.

The Study

In order to account for classroom learning, the processes of task allocation and task working must be closely monitored.

It is also necessary to identify the intellectual demands made by teachers on children and the manner in which children meet, avoid or adapt these demands. For each assigned task, therefore, the researchers needed to know:

(i)   the teacher's intention in assigning the task
(ii)   how that intention was manifested in the particular task set
(iii)   the teacher's task instructions, i.e. how it was presented and specified
(iv)   the pupil's perceptions of (iii)
(v)   the materials available for the task
(vi)   the pupil's task performance, including interactions with the teacher or other pupils
(vii)   an assessment of short term learning outcomes, i.e. immediately following the task
(viii) an assessment of longer term learning outcomes, i.e. at the end of each term, in order to evaluate development and retention.

The findings

The focus of the study was on task processes in classes of six and seven year old children whose teachers were rated as better than average by the advisory service in the education authorities concerned. Working closely with these teachers showed clearly that they were dedicated and conscientious people. Few with experience of working with infant teachers would doubt this description. The questions posed in the study relate to how such dedication is harnessed in attempts to provide appropriate learning experiences for their pupils.

In appraising the quality of learning experiences the demands on the children of the tasks set were first ascertained. Although there were often marked differences in the classrooms studied, tasks demanding practice of existing knowledge, concepts or skills predominated. This was particularly apparent in language work where over three-quarters of all tasks set demanded practice. A typical task was a request from the teacher for the class to write a story, usually accompanied by exhortations on neatness and appropriate grammar. Here the demand was for the practice of well-understood routines and rarely did such tasks impart or demand the acquisition of new knowledge. This staple diet of little new knowledge and large amounts of practice was rarely varied to include tasks which required either the discovery or construction of new or different ways of perceiving problems, or the application of existing knowledge and skills to new contexts.

The teachers studied held strongly to the philosophy of individualization and it was therefore expected that differential demands would be intended for children of differing levels of attainment. High and low attaining children certainly received different curriculum content but they experienced similar patterns of task demand. Thus similar ratios of incremental* to practice tasks were planned for both groups of children. This pattern was further confounded by the fact that teachers found it much more difficult to transform an intended incremental into an actual incremental task for high attainers. In reality therefore high attaining children received less new knowledge and more practice than their low attaining peers. This is the opposite pattern to what might have been expected with the probable consequences of delays in progress for high attainers and lack of opportunity for consolidation for low attainers.

The main reasons for teachers failing to implement intended demands were twofold: poor or misdiagnosis, and failures in task design. Many mismatches in demand occurred because the teacher did not ascertain that the child was already perfectly familiar with the task content. Poor or non-diagnosis thus underlay the fact that many incremental tasks actually made practice demands. Task design problems were also relatively frequent. In such cases the requirements for the performance of the task did not match the teacher's intention.

Little improvement in patterns of task demand happened as a result of transferring to a junior class or school. Here the pattern changed markedly

---

* *Incremental tasks* are concerned with the acquisition of new facts, skills, rules or procedures. *Practice tasks* demand the repetitive and rapid application of familiar knowledge.

as the term progressed. Revision tasks predictably predominated in the early weeks as the teachers ascertained the base from which to start. Thereafter incremental and practice tasks were the most prevalent.

Here too there were marked differences in the classrooms studied but in general there were more incremental and fewer practice tasks in this term than in the infant classes. This pattern was more apparent in junior than primary schools and particularly so in the language area. This would indicate a quickening pace in knowledge acquisition. However, this general pattern hid the rather surprising trend that the number of incremental tasks decreased, and practice tasks increased, as the term progressed. Thus children were rapidly introduced to new concepts and skills early in the term with little opportunity for consolidation, whereas later in the term knowledge acquisition fell away to be replaced by more and more practice.

Teachers' task intentions during this term were similar to those found in infant schools. They planned large amounts of practice and revision for high attainers and a high input of new knowledge with little opportunity to practice for low attainers, with the same predictable consequences.

High attainers also experienced, as they had in the infant classes, tasks which did not make the intended demand. Thus they received 80 per cent more practice tasks than intended, indicating little extension of concept acquisition, whereas low attainers experienced equal amounts of incremental and practice tasks which left little opportunity for consoldation. In number work the pattern was even more notable. Here low attainers received three times more incremental than practice tasks. The same problems of mis- or non-diagnosis and task design underlay the mismatching of intention and actual demand.

The quality of a pupil's learning experience is also related to the match between the intellectual demand of tasks and the pupil's attainments. In both number and language work at infant level teachers were able to provide a match on approximately 40 per cent of tasks. About a third were too difficult for the child and a little over a quarter were too easy. This general pattern masks marked differences in the classrooms studied. There was also an indication that teachers in the infant schools were somewhat better at matching than those in infant departments of primary schools. It was also very clear that the quality of matching varied in relation to the children's intellectual standing in the classroom. High attainers were underestimated on over 40 per cent of tasks assigned to them, a pattern similar to that reported by HMI (DES 1978a). But an equally clear pattern of overestimation was found for low attainers. Forty-four per cent of their assigned tasks were overestimated in both language and number work.

Matching was worse in the first term of junior schooling where the proportion of matched tasks in number work fell to 30 per cent. The incidence of mismatching was particularly severe for high attainers since three-quarters of the tasks they received were underestimates. Low attainers again suffered from overestimation, a trend which was more marked in junior schools than junior departments. It was also interesting to find that the quality of matching declined as the term progressed. In the last observation period for example most of the incremental tasks were overestimates and practice tasks underestimates.

Teachers were adept at recognizing a task that was proving too difficult but were totally blind to tasks whose demands were too easy. The reasons for this are at least twofold. Firstly the teachers' typical management style required them to be seated at the front of the class, and as a result supervision was limited to quick observational sweeps of the classroom. The usual image was of a class working cheerfully and industriously. This, indeed, is the second reason for a teacher's lack of recognition of too-easy tasks. Children always worked in this way irrespective of appropriateness of the task set. From the teacher's point of view, children were busy, and busy work equated with appropriate demands.

Thus in the short term, inappropriate work appeared to have little direct emotional or motivational consequences for children of this age. Although cognitive problems, which manifested themselves in unproductive or confusing learning experiences, were all too clearly apparent in the post-test interviews, this cognitive confusion was masked from the teachers by the children's cheerfulness and industry. The teachers avoided the immediate consequences of such confusion by rewarding individual endeavour, and by restricting their considerations of children's work to the product not the process of such work.

Topics for discussion

1. What do the authors mean by 'mismatch'?
2. Why do experienced teachers find it difficult to implement appropriate *incremental tasks* with their pupils?
3. How, according to the authors, does *teacher management style* relate to misperceptions of children's ability and, in consequence, to the mismatch of learning tasks?

Suggestions for further reading

1. Read Chapter 2, 'Knowing and Understanding Children', in, Alexander, R.J. (1984) *Primary Teaching*, Eastbourne: Holt Rinehart and Winston.
2. Brophy, J. and Evertson, C.M. (1976) *Learning from Teaching*. Boston: Allyn and Bacon.
3. Harlen, W. (1982) 'Matching', in, Richards, C. (ed.) *New Directions in Primary Education*. London: The Falmer Press.

SECTION SIX
THE PRIMARY SCHOOL CURRICULUM: PROBLEMS AND PERSPECTIVES

READING ELEVEN • The curriculum and curriculum change
D. Lawton

Two general issues emerged during the seventies which will certainly continue into discussions about the curriculum in the eighties: the content of the curriculum, and its control. Underlying both these issues are two very different approaches to the curriculum, which may be referred to as the behavioural objectives and the cultural analysis models. The former focuses on 'efficiency', the latter on justification.

The behavioural objectives model tends to take the existing curriculum pattern more or less for granted, but aims to improve it by clarifying objectives, relating these to specific changes in pupils' behaviour, and to evaluation. In that sense (and some others) it is a conservative model, likely to appeal to those worried about standards, measurement and minimal competency.

At the other extreme, the cultural analysis model is concerned with radical, fundamental questions such as 'what are schools for?', 'what is knowledge?', 'what knowledge and what kinds of experience are most worthwhile?', 'what do pupils need in order to be able to participate in our society now and in the future?'. A preference for one model rather than the other may depend on deep-rooted values, priorities and prejudices, but each has certain strengths and weaknesses which should be carefully noted.

The behavioural objectives model

The objectives model has a long history in the USA and has something in common with the 'payment by results' approach adopted after 1862 in England. From the first decade of the twentieth century, American educationists such as Bobbitt attempted to apply to school systems the industrial techniques of F.W. Taylor. This involved listing specific objectives and costing teaching processes. The results achieved by pupils were the only

D. Lawton, 'The curriculum and curriculum change', in, B. Simon and W. Taylor (Eds), *Education in the Eighties: The Central Issues.* London: Batsford Academic 1981 pp 111–123

acceptable criteria of success. This view of curriculum planning was given a new lease of life in the late 1940s by the theoretical work of Ralph Tyler. His *Basic Principles of Curriculum and Instruction* (1949) was extremely influential in curriculum theory. Tyler identified four fundamental questions which must be answered in connection with any teaching programme:

1. What educational purposes should the school seek to attain?
2. What educational experiences can be provided that are likely to attain these purposes?
3. How can these educational experiences be effectively organized?
4. How can we determine whether these purposes are being attained?

These four basic questions have been translated into the objectives model in the following way:

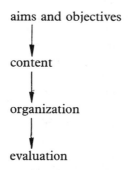

aims and objectives

content

organization

evaluation

This simple linear translation may distort Tyler's four questions; it certainly results in a very naive and simplistic view of curriculum planning. Tyler, like other curriculum theorists, was motivated by the fact that many educational programmes were extremely ill-defined and incapable of evaluation. What began as a desire for clarity has been transformed into a curriculum theory, whereby the only valid educational objectives are those which describe pupil behaviour, not teacher behaviour. So objectives must specify how pupils are to behave at the end of a teaching sequence; and these behavioural changes must be measurable.

Despite many basic criticisms both of a theoretical and a practical kind, the objectives model has flourished, especially in the USA, and has been given additional credence by such theoretical devices as the 'taxonomy of educational objectives' produced by Benjamin Bloom and his colleagues in the 1950s. Generations of American teachers (and some in England) have worked at the various levels of the taxonomy, translating what they wanted to teach into terminology acceptable to curriculum planners of the behavioural objectives persuasion. Such efforts have inevitably generated criticism. Stenhouse in Britain, and Elliot Eisner in the United States, have been particularly vocal in their opposition to the behavioural objectives model.

Stenhouse (1975) claims that it is unreasonable to pre-specify objectives in, for example, teaching a Shakespearean play because to do so ignores the nature of studying English literature. It would be possible to specify the responses a teacher wanted and then to provide feedback to inform the pupils that these were the correct responses; but this would, according to Stenhouse (and others) be failing to realize that each individual's response to a work of art is unique. This kind of teaching situation is quite unlike teaching typewriting or simple arithmetic. Stenhouse argues that to use an output model for a process where the emphasis must essentially be on the input is totally unsatisfactory and unacceptable.

Eisner (1969) argues that in the expressive arts the purpose of the teaching/learning process is to encourage the child to produce his own response, not to pre-specify what response is regarded as appropriate. This is essentially the difference between instructional objectives and expressive objectives.

Arguments against the behavioural objectives model are not confined to the aesthetic subjects. Sockett (1976) has demonstrated that a behavioural objectives model is inappropriate for the teaching of science. In science, everything is, in principle, falsifiable. If a teacher pre-specifies the outcome of an experiment, then the experiment is no longer serious — it is rendered essentially unscientific, for the purpose of any experiment is to make refutation possible. Sockett goes further and asserts that the idea of basing a curriculum on behavioural objectives is impossible. He condemns this approach to curriculum design for the same reasons that Karl Popper condemns Plato and other Utopian social planners. Sockett suggests that a Utopian in curriculum design can be identified as 'someone who believes that a thorough and comprehensive analysis of all factors relevant to a curriculum can be marshalled and embodied in a master plan. This plan will contain fully detailed objectives organized in such a way as to promote the achievement of those aims derived from the rigorous analysis' (Sockett 1976, pp. 15–16). Human behaviour is far too complex to fit such a convenient model.

There are other more practical objections to the behavioural objectives approach. Even if it were desirable, it would be quite impossible to list all the behavioural objectives connected with any particular area of knowledge. If a teacher wanted children to develop 'respect for persons', for example, it would be impossible to work out in advance all the behavioural examples likely to occur in such a way that they could be tested and measured. The debate about the objectives model is not dead, but if the model is to survive in any useful way, it will need to be altered fundamentally, in order to move away from behavioural requirements.

The cultural analysis model

This model is also American in origin, although modified in its English versions. Smith et al. (1957) and Broudy et al. (1964) put forward a view of curriculum based on the idea of common culture and common curriculum. Similar ideas have developed in Britain, but not always by curriculum theorists or even educationists. In 1961 Raymond Williams, for example, published *The Long Revolution* which together with his earlier work (*Culture and Society*, 1958) has been extremely influential. Williams represents one strand of a debate about education which stems from teachers of English and English literature in schools and in universities. Others involved in this debate have included F.R. Leavis, Denys Thompson and Richard Hoggart.

Malcolm Skilbeck came to similar conclusions from a somewhat different starting point. He refers to his own scheme as situational analysis. His curriculum model is eclectic in that it includes some aspects of the objectives approach (but not behavioural objectives). According to Skilbeck, individual schools must come to terms with the social context of the school and plan a curriculum accordingly. Skilbeck outlines a sequence of stages:

1. situational analysis
2. goal formulation
3. programme building
4. interpretation and implementation
5. monitoring, feedback, assessment and reconstruction.

In one sense, the whole of this model is an example of cultural analysis. In another, the specific cultural analysis is built into stage one of situational analysis. Skilbeck breaks down his cultural analysis into external and internal factors. The external factors of the cultural analysis include general cultural and social changes at a national and local level; the requirements of the educational system itself; changes of subject content; the potential contributions of support systems for teachers; general resources available to the school. The internal analysis consists of consideration of the pupils; the teachers; the ethos of the school and its political structure; material resources; shortcomings of the existing curriculum and other perceived problems.

Skilbeck also refers to his approach as 'cultural mapping'. He emphasizes that the map is not a still life picture from the past, but a set of features and signposts concerning the present and the future. In general, Skilbeck sees the new curriculum as something quite different from 'subjects and subject matter'. He proposes a curriculum divided into two parts, one part common to all pupils, the other providing opportunity for choice and specialization. The common curriculum would be based on a critical analysis of the main features of contemporary culture. These features will be perceived differently in particular situations, but they will include: typical work situations and modes of economic operation; social rules and patterns of social meanings including norms of conduct, value systems, and patterns of expectation; the major human symbolic systems of language, mathematics, scientific thinking, religion, the arts; leisure and recreational interests; institutional structures in both the public and private sectors; government and social policy; forms of interpersonal relationships and the management of tension and conflict; modes of individual expression and creativity.

Skilbeck has recently (1980) produced a 'core curriculum' for the Australian Curriculum Development Centre which successfully translates these principles into a document which can be understood and discussed by non-specialists.

My own approach to the curriculum is also radical rather than conservative. The curriculum is defined as 'a selection from the culture of a given society'. But who decides on the selection and by what principles? A simplified version of this approach, in a series of stages, is set out in Figure 1:

Stage 1

There are at least two kinds of question which are largely, but not exclusively, philosophical: first, epistemological questions about the structure of knowledge and how this relates to what should be taught in schools;

second, questions about why some kinds of knowledge and experience are regarded as more worthwhile than others.

There is still a good deal of philosophical disputation about the structure of knowledge, but epistemologists tend to agree that it is necessary to subdivide knowledge according to some kind of classification system. Kinds of knowledge can be distinguished by the concepts used; or the means by which concepts are built up into networks, or by different types of 'truth tests'. Most would agree, for example, that mathematics is different from science (although science makes use of mathematical concepts), and that both kinds of knowledge are in turn different from aesthetic and moral 'knowledge'.

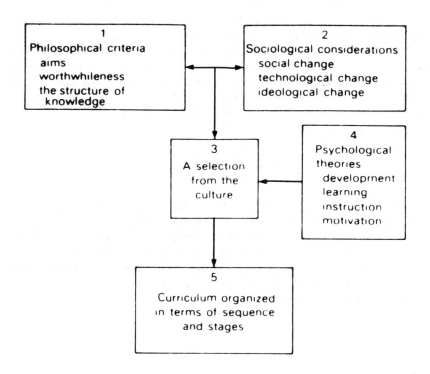

There are also good arguments to support the view that it is reasonable to regard knowledge about science as more important than knowledge about darts or cricket. This is not simply a matter of taste nor of bourgeois hegemony (see Lawton 1973, 1975).

Stage 2

Apart from questions about the structure of knowledge and worthwhileness which would apply to any society, there are also questions of particular concern in our society at present: for example, we are a highly scientific, technological, industrial society; we also claim to be a democratic society. The first has some bearing on *what* should be taught; the second has some bearing on to *whom* knowledge should be made available.

Consideration of contemporary society will enable us to draw up a list of curricular priorities, but some reference back to Stage 1 will often be necessary: without the existence of a set of criteria which are of more general applicability than our own society's, education would become a mere reflection of particular social values. Stage 2 must interact with Stage 1 before we reach Stage 3.

Stage 3

Once such questions as 'what are aims in education?', 'what do we mean by "worthwhile"?', 'what situations will pupils be faced with when they leave school?' have been clarified, we are in a better position to make a selection from the culture, based on criteria which can be made public even if total consensus is lacking. At this stage the selection is an 'ideal' selection in the sense that it does not have to take into account the limitations of individual schools (resources and teachers).

Stage 4

This stage brings into operation such psychological theories as those of Piaget on children's development, of Bruner's views on 'instruction' as well as theories of learning and motivation. Considerations of these factors would lead to the final stage of curriculum planning.

Stage 5

A curriculum based on an analysis of contemporary culture, but bearing in mind certain cultural and educational 'universals', would be very different from what is generally offered to most young people in primary and secondary schools today. For example, most schools provide some kind of curriculum in science, but offer little which would help young people to understand technology (or even the social implications of technology); similarly, most schools offer some kind of history and geography, but the majority of young people leave school almost totally ignorant of the political and economic structure of their own society.

One of the aims of the cultural analysis approach is to establish the range of knowledge and educational experience that all children should have access to. I would argue, for example, not only that there is a kind of knowledge called science which is different in important respects from other kinds of knowledge (Stage 1), but that this knowledge is of particular relevance in understanding and participating in our technological and industrial society (Stage 2). This establishes a case for giving high priority to science at Stages 3 and 5. But all knowledge is not scientific: the same process of cultural analysis would give high priority also to humanities and social science, for example, and to those kinds of experience which would help an individual to develop aesthetically and morally. An important part of this argument is that a major purpose of education is to help the young to understand and participate in their own society: cultural analysis attempts to map out the areas of knowledge and experience which are necessary for this purpose, and to identify major concepts and skills within each area as a minimum basis for understanding self and the environment. It follows that if any important 'area' is missing from a pupil's curriculum, then that individual has been inadequately educated. There is some evidence to suggest that this approach has influenced, directly or indirectly, the thinking of Her Majesty's Inspectors on the curriculum. Much of the HMI document *Curriculum 11–16* (1977) is based on the principles of cultural analysis, and there are many assumptions in the HMI *Secondary School Survey* (DES 1979) which show the same approach: for example, an assumption that all children have a right of access to important areas of experience in a common curriculum.

I shall want to return later in this chapter to the HMI approach in *Curriculum 11–16*, but before doing so, it is necessary to examine some of the concepts connected with the problems of curriculum content.

The first problem concerns coverage: a well-planned curriculum should cover all the kinds of knowledge, skills and desirable experiences defined as educational. This includes the task of bringing a curriculum up to date by including technology as well as science, politics and economics as well as history.

The second concerns the desire for a balanced curriculum, including the avoidance of premature specialization. (Premature specialization is defined as any concentration on some 'areas' which might impede adequate development across the whole curriculum.)

The third problem is that of achieving a good formula for what is made compulsory and what can be left as optional choice.

The concepts of common curriculum and core curriculum are also involved in each of these three major problems areas. It may be useful to distinguish between these two concepts at this preliminary stage. Core curriculum is a weak concept associated with the notion that there are certain basic subjects which ought to be included in all pupils' curriculum at all levels. The HMI *Secondary School Survey* (1979) showed that, while nearly all head teachers subscribed to the idea of a core curriculum, in practice, the core amounted in most schools to no more than mathematics and English. The 1980 *A Framework for the School Curriculum* attempts merely to extend this core to mathematics, English, science, modern languages for two years, together with some attempt to cater for preparation for the adult world of industry. The danger of a core is that it may become the whole curriculum or is regarded as the most important aspect of the curriculum. The idea has also been criticized inasmuch as it tends to focus on subjects rather than on more fundamental purposes or areas. In other words, it is concerned with means rather than ends, or perhaps treats means as though they were ends in themselves.

The common curriculum concept is much more ambitious and wide-ranging in scope. It is a logical extension of the idea of comprehensive education or a common secondary education for all. During the sixties it began to be argued that comprehensive schools represented very little advance on the tripartite system unless they became more than three schools under one roof. It was argued that comprehensive schools should not simply be concerned with providing an education for all pupils up to the age of 16, but should be concerned with transmitting a common culture to all pupils by means of a common curriculum. Designing a common curriculum is, therefore, concerned with establishing those kinds of knowledge and areas of experience to which it is assumed all pupils ought to have access up to the age of 16. Such a curriculum is in no sense uniform, since although 'areas' are specified as necessary for all pupils, it is not suggested that everyone should reach the same levels of attainment. Not only would that be undesirable, it would also be impossible to achieve. The common curriculum implies, however, that all pupils have access to science, for example, and that it would not be satisfactory for some to be studying physics and chemistry whilst others would be having a walk around the gasworks (unless this represented a genuine introduction to scientific concepts and understanding).

This brings us back to the first of our problems — that of *coverage*. Despite the popular concern that the basic areas of the curriculum — especially mathematics and English — are not being taught adequately, the evidence from both primary and secondary HMI surveys would seem to indicate that *too much* attention is being paid to the basic subjects and not enough to other very necessary aspects of knowledge, skills and educational experiences. In the case of the Secondary Survey, schools were again criticized for allowing pupils too narrow a range of subject matter. This was partly a criticism of the options systems (see below) but also implies that schools were not ensuring that important areas of experience were available. The examination system was also blamed for cutting out, for example, important areas of aesthetic experience.

Another difficulty is that of 'curriculum inertia'. It is often suggested that schools continue with a curriculum which might have been suited to society a generation or a century ago, but has failed to keep up to date. Thus until recently Latin and Greek tended to dominate the curriculum in many schools whilst science was comparatively neglected. More recently it has been suggested that technology should feature much more prominently in the curriculum. There is also a good deal of evidence to show that most young people leave school at 16 or 18 almost completely ignorant of the political and economic aspects of their own society. Most schools have failed to incorporate these kinds of knowledge and experience into the subject-based curriculum.

A related problem to that of coverage is the question of *balance*. Can balance be left to pupils' choice, or should it be subject to strict control by curriculum planners either at a national or a school level? One contemporary view is that, after experiencing a common, balanced curriculum up to the age of about 14, it is then appropriate for pupils to choose their own curriculum. Unfortunately, this has not worked out well in practice. The evidence of research is that pupils choose their subjects in option systems for a variety of reasons which can hardly be described as rational; most self-chosen timetables do not amount to a balanced curriculum. Evidence suggests that pupils drop subjects if they feel they are not very good at them, irrespective of whether they need them or not, or that they choose subjects because they like the teacher in charge. The option-system is the most common method of curriculum planning (or non-planning) in secondary schools in the fourth and fifth years. This tendency has been encouraged by the single subject GCE and CSE examinations which do not specify any compulsory subjects or any desirable balance. The option system has been severely criticized by HMI in 1977 (*Curriculum 11–16*) and, more recently, in the *Secondary School Survey* (1979) and *A View of the Curriculum* (1980). The discussion document *Curriculum 11–16* is the most outspoken condemnation of the 'cafeteria' curriculum, and makes a strong appeal for 75 per cent of the timetable to be devoted to a common curriculum. The Inspectors suggest that the curriculum should be thought of in terms of 'areas of experience' rather than subjects. No pupil's curriculum can be considered satisfactory unless it provides adequate coverage of the following areas of experience:

the aesthetic and creative
the ethical
the linguistic
the mathematical
the physical
the scientific
the social and political
the spiritual

The trend away from free choice and a 'cafeteria' curriculum to more restraint and guidance within a common curriculum, has come about for a variety of reasons.

The first is a reaction against the exaggerated child-centred views which were very common in the optimistic days of the fifties and sixties, and reached a climax in the Plowden Report. The prevailing view seemed to be that children given 'freedom' naturally made wise choices adequately guided by their own needs and interests. This view of the child and of the curriculum has been questioned and criticized. The paradox here is that if we want adults to be free it does not necessarily follow that we achieve this by making children totally free: the young and the immature need to be assisted towards the achievement of autonomy.

A related argument is that if the state compels children to go to school for at least ten years, thus restricting their freedom for this time, then it has a corresponding duty to set out the advantages gained by that amount of schooling. In the optimistic fifties and sixties it was sufficient to assume that schooling was an obvious benefit. This has ceased to be the case. It is now necessary to spell out the benefits of education in terms of what children should have learned by the age of 11 or 16. This need not necessarily lead us into the direction of behavioural objectives, or of a competency-based approach to curriculum planning, but it does mean that teachers should be much clearer about what they are offering, and what advantages they hope will be gained by their pupils from these educational experiences.

Recognition of this would now seem to be common ground between DES, HMI, LEAs and the teaching profession. What remains to be sorted out is the kind of 'framework' or common curriculum which can be approved nationally for implementation locally. It is not an easy task — the 1980 *A Framework for the School Curriculum* was a very poor effort — but it had to be attempted.

Conculsion

In England the debate during the next few years is likely to be about practicalities of curriculum planning rather than theories and models. But it is interesting to note that some of the rival curriculum proposals make assumptions which are identifiable either with the behavioural objectives model or with the cultural analysis approach.

The HMI document *Curriculum 11–16*, based on the idea of access to a common culture by means of a common curriculum, is firmly based, whether the Inspectors realize it or not, in the cultural analysis approach. The 1980 DES document on a curriculum framework, however, is based on the idea of a core curriculum, minimum competency, output rather than input, and testing. In this respect, the core curriculum and *A Framework for the School Curriculum* (1980) have values much in common with those of the Assessment of Performance Unit set up by the DES in 1975. Officially, the APU has nothing to do with curriculum planning or the framework for a core curriculum. The tests are there to monitor standards and not to exercise any control on the curriculum. APU officers have been careful to say that they want to minimize the backwash effect of monitoring standards by the tests which will be used. But any official test will inevitably encourage 'teaching to the test' and it is difficult to see how the APU can possibly avoid this kind of backwash. It has additionally been promised that the APU will not indulge in 'blanket testing' but work on the basis of light sampling: it will be impossible to identify individual children, classes or even schools. Perhaps a more serious danger is that the APU exercise will legitimize blanket testing by local education authorities where there will be less control over the publication of results. This would have an even greater effect on the curriculum taught in schools.

The cultural analysis ('areas of experience') approach represented by the HMI documents *Curriculum 11–16, A View of the Curriculum*, and the primary and secondary school surveys is fundamentally different from the assumptions underlying the APU methodology. Areas of experience are associated with an *input* model — that is, deciding what is sufficiently worthwhile for inclusion in every child's curriculum, whereas 'kinds of development' are associated with pre-specified norms of development which can be tested — that is, an *output* model closer to the behavioural objectives approach. Many objections have been raised about the APU, such as the use of item banking and the Rasch model, but the real danger is that testing will dominate the curriculum and eventually result in curriculum planning by behavioural objectives. Many criticisms could also be raised about the document *Curriculum 11–16*, such as its unexamined assumptions about the structure of knowledge or the omission of technology, but much more important is the fact that this document is in the humane tradition of cultural analysis. The alternative approach would take us in the direction of the worst practices of evaluation in the USA in recent years.

This chapter started with the suggestion that there are three aspects of the curriculum debate: control, content and the choice of theoretical models. It will now be apparent that these have converged to become a single debate about the curriculum. On the question of control, there is still much discussion about a partnership between DES, LEAs and teachers; but in reality, the metaphor has changed from partnership to accountability, and the DES is closer to real control of the curriculum than it has been for many years. But will the control be exercised through a flexible framework for a common curriculum or through a more rigid testing machine? Will the content of the curriculum be specified in detail, not overtly but covertly, by means of test items? The answers to these questions will depend on which theoretical model emerges as the more acceptable. Curriculum planning by behavioural objectives will take us in the direction of a core of subjects (narrowly based) backed by powerful testing; a common curriculum based on cultural analysis and an input model would take us in the direction of an improved version of the Inspectors' document *Curriculum 11–16*. There can be little argument as to which of these models teachers and educationists generally would favour.

Topics for discussion

1. Examine objections against the use of a behavioural objectives model as a basis for planning the curriculum.
2. What are the guiding principles that underlie the cultural analysis model of curriculum development?
3. Identify and discuss problems of curriculum content as they impinge upon the freedom of choice of older pupils.

Suggestions for further reading

1. Lawn, M. and Barton, L. (eds) (1981) *Rethinking Curriculum Studies*. London: Croom Helm.
2. Galton, M. (ed.) (1980) *Curriculum Change: The Lessons of a Decade*. Leicester: Leicester University Press.
3. Sockett, H. (1976) *Designing the Curriculum*. London: Open Books.

READING TWELVE • Learning how to learn and learning by discovery   *R.F. Dearden*

A universal skill?

How is *learning how to learn* different from learning how to ride a bicycle, make a dovetail joint, or use a telephone? In both cases, there is a 'learning how to' which suggests some skill as the object of the learning. But 'learning how to learn' is not specific in the way that learning such skills as how to ride

'Learning how to learn and learning by discovery', in R.F. Dearden, *Problems in Primary Education*, London: Routledge and Kegan Paul, 1976, pp 69–83

a bicycle are specific. Learning how to learn is at one stage further removed from any direct specific content of learning. It might therefore reasonably be called 'second-order' learning. There could be many such comparably second-order activities, such as deliberating how to deliberate, investigating how to investigate, thinking out how to think things out, and so on.

Then is 'learning how to learn' a super-powerful unitary skill employable in all first-order learning whatsoever? Indeed if it were a piece of learning which would really enable us to 'think effectively about any subsequent experience in life', then here would surely be the modern answer to Spencer's question about what knowledge is of most worth. But that it could be such a super-powerful unitary skill or strategy seems very unlikely as soon as one reflects on the enormously divergent variety of first-order learning. What it would be much more plausible to contend would be that learning how to learn marks out, not a unitary skill, but a family of structures of second-order learning having *wide* first-order application. Thus there would be different kinds of learning how to learn related to different general classes of more specific learning tasks.

Certainly this interpretation permits a readily comprehensible application to the notion. In fact, even babies could be said to learn how to learn more specific things, as when they learn to carry everything to their mouths, or to manipulate things, or to incline their heads so that they can look at particular new sources of noise. Later still, young children learn to ask adults for information and help as a way of learning more specific things that they wish to know. In fact, even the very traditional classroom, with its predominantly formal methods of class teaching, required that children should learn a corresponding skill of how to learn. Learning how to learn in that situation was a matter of learning to listen, to attend to what the teacher said, to control one's phantasies and wandering thoughts and to ignore external distractions. Learning how to learn was indeed present there, but it took the form of learning how to concentrate intelligently and attentively on what the teacher said by way of didactic instruction. In this way, students have to learn how to learn from lectures, tutorials and seminar discussions. Recent research into methods of teaching in higher education has made lecturers rather more conscious of this fact.

The point of drawing attention to these applications of the notion of learning how to learn is certainly not to show that there is no new thing under the sun. It is rather to show that the recent emphasis can only be an emphasis on one new *sort* of learning how to learn, not a new emphasis on it absolutely. And the sort of learning how to learn in question is learning how to learn for oneself, independently of the teacher. The switch here is quite comparable to the historical switch of emphasis to experience and activity in educational methods. For all educational arrangements involve some sort of experience and activity, even if it is only that of sitting still and listening. But in this case too there was a shift in what was stressed, and not an absolute innovation. The shift was towards practical and concrete experience, and towards physical and manipulative activity.

The recent emphasis on learning how to learn, then, is neither absolutely new, nor does it imply the discovery of a single super-powerful skill of absolutely universal application. On the contrary, the term picks out a class of skills or strategies having in common only that they are of more or less wide application in facilitating relatively more specific sequences of learning. The relevant class is of such skills or strategies as a child might independently employ in learning, as opposed to the more traditional general skills and strategies for learning directly from teachers. And it is this connection with independent activity which makes the connection with autonomy that is of interest to child-centred theorists.

However, closer inspection of some of the recent advocacy of learning how to learn reveals that it is not just one type of skill or strategy that its advocates have in mind. Different writers have at least five rather different things in mind, which have not commonly been distinguished. First of all, there is learning how to get information on a given topic. The skills involved here mainly include knowing how to use libraries, for example how to exploit classifications, contents lists and indexes, reference books and atlases. Of course, such learning is limited by the reader's capacity to understand what he reads and by the ideas that it will occur to him to pursue. Plainly there is a danger of mere verbalistic copying of material from the books consulted. Often a topic will be suggested by browsing amongst given books, rather than being pre-chosen and used as a criterion of relevance in going to books. But, within limits, and especially at an earlier and less systematic stage of primary schooling, this sort of learning how to learn does seem to be valuable.

A second possible meaning of learning how to learn would emphasize the learning of general rules and principles which can be applied to the solution of a wide range of more particular problems. An elementary example of this would be using a phonic approach to the teaching of reading, where each phonic rule serves for decoding a corresponding whole class of unfamiliar new words. Scientific and moral principles of a general character could be seen as serving a similar function. For instance, the principle of the electrical circuit can be applied in solving a variety of problems concerning switches, wiring patterns, testing to find conductive materials, and so on. Moral principles can similarly be applied in coming to a more adequate and considered judgment on particular actions or rules. This sort of learning how to learn is, however, not new, and so cannot be distinctively illustrated from contemporary thinking.

A third and currently much emphasized species of learning how to learn concerns the 'logic' of different forms of inquiry. Here what is required is that, instead of applying his mind to learning a mass of particular findings in a given subject, the learner should master the methods of inquiry which have produced those findings. He should learn the sorts of questions which can be asked, and the criteria by which different claims can be validated or their particular content verified. In mathematics, for example, the learner has to learn the axioms of arithmetical or geometrical reasoning, and the transformations which count as valid. Concrete analogues may facilitate coming to such an understanding, especially in the early stages. The logic of scientific inquiry has similarly to be learned, including the decisive role of observation and the importance of experimental control over known variables in a situation. Again, with historical or social studies, the sorts of questions which can profitably or sensibly be asked, the moves which count as valid and the checks which need to be made are what have to be learned. Of course, a full understanding of such principles of inquiry could not be gained quite apart from going through any particular inquiries, but the emphasis and results of such an approach would be very different from a more traditional fact-memorizing approach. The pupil would not simply have learned this and that, but would have learned how to learn in that particular field. This type of learning how to learn is an important bridge between child-centred attitudinal aims and the aim of giving a general education.

Yet a fourth meaning concerns what might be called the self-management of one's learning activities. The object here would be to learn how to exploit one's capacities to greatest advantage in learning. It would include, for example, retention strategies such as spacing practice, seeking structural meaning and summarizing in one's own words. Heuristic strategies could be included, such as taking care that one had clearly perceived the problem, checking that one's assumptions were safe, breaking the problem into parts, using diagrams, sleeping on problems. Also included would be learning how to organize one's time and to use one's effort most economically and advantageously. This species of learning how to learn has fullest application at the advanced student level, but it does have some application at every stage of formal schooling.

A fifth and final meaning which can be culled from recent thinking would more perspicuously be called, and often is in fact called, simply 'learning to learn'. For what is learned here is not so much how to do something as an habitual disposition to do it. 'Learning to learn' in this sense is analogous to learning to behave, learning to avoid the rush hour, or learning to enjoy music. Learning is itself something which one learns to do, as being perhaps intrinsically rewarding. Where this is stressed, as in the Plowden Report (CACE 1967), then such motivations as the satisfaction of curiosity, the enjoyment of discovery and of problem-solving, the excitement of new ideas, and the gaining of a sense of mastery will be highly regarded. But though a connection can easily be made between this and learning *how* to learn, strictly speaking it is something different, and in that case we have really distinguished four senses, and not five, of 'learning how to learn'. To summarize, these might be called: (i) information-finding skills; (ii) general substantive principles; (iii) formal principles of inquiry; (iv) self-management skills. We are now in a position to make some general observations about learning how to learn, and to consider its links with autonomy.

Learning how to learn and autonomy

A person is autonomous to the degree that he shows initiative in making independent judgments related both to thought and to action. His actions stem from and execute his own plans and deliberations. Now if this is so, then clearly learning how to learn in its various senses will be of great value in aiming to develop autonomy in children. For to the extent that they become capable of learning for themselves, and exercise that capacity, to that extent what they learn is determined by themselves. There are, however, some general observations which need to be made on this preliminary remark.

Making learning how to learn an objective does not dispense with the need for teaching. At the very most, it shifts the content of what is taught from particularities to the skills, principles and methods of general application which constitute having learned how to learn. Furthermore, this shifting of the object of teaching from first-order content to the second-order equipment of autonomous finding out involves rather more than just teaching what these second-order skills and strategies are. It involves training and practice in their use, with accompanying habits of persistence, patience, tolerance of frustration, delaying gratification and concentration. Neglect of this executive aspect of the new emphasis results in disappointments and unjust inequalities. Teachers who make the transition to the new classroom regime without regard to the need for support and plain pressure are likely to be disappointed. And children coming from homes where no habits in harmony with these new arrangements have ever been developed will be at a disadvantage by comparison with children from homes where habit-training and analytic language modes have already created a readiness for what the school can more systematically offer.

Again, however successful a teacher may be in training children to learn for themselves, there will remain much of a first-order character which, for reasons of empirical necessity, still has to be directly taught. This may simply be for greater efficiency in the limited period of schooling available, or because failure, muddle and confusion have resulted from self-directed learning, or because consolidation and practice of past learning are now needed. Self-styled progressive teachers and educationists seem now to be recognizing, with the air of bold admission, that such a degree of direct first-order teaching is still necessary. And to the extent that this is so, as also to the extent that the skills of learning how to learn have themselves to be taught, then learning how to learn in the more traditional uncelebrated sense will still have a place, i.e. learning how to learn from a teacher, by attention, listening, setting aside distractions and so on.

One way in which a connection can be seen, then, between learning how to learn and autonomy is that the former is justified as an educational policy by its value for the latter. Learning how to learn is a means to the development of autonomy, and it is so not just contingently, through some causal connection which might have been otherwise, but logically, through being already a partial instantiation and progressive realization of autonomy. A secondary, though very important, justification of learning how to learn in the classroom is of a more clearly instrumental kind. For once a child has achieved, through teaching and training, a measure of self-direction of this sort, then he becomes less teacher-demanding in his activities. This is very valuable in a class of mixed ability, or in a class organized along the lines of the 'integrated day', because in those circumstances it is a difficult organizational problem for the teacher to divide his teaching time adequately and fairly between several groups or individuals. A further gain is that the impossibly polymathic demands of the teacher's knowledge are eased, especially through the training in the information-getting skills referred to earlier. What a teacher need not be expected to know he may yet be expected to know how to find out.

The current emphasis on learning how to learn has yet another important aspect, so far not touched upon. This relates to what Postman and Weingartner (1971) identify as the most striking feature of modern, developed societies: constant change, both technological and social. One aspect of this is that everyone is likely to have to change his job, or to change in his job, not just once but several times in his lifetime. Life has become a process of continuous re-learning. It has virtually ceased to be possible to learn anything in a way which will be permanently valid or valuable. This has dizzying implications for schooling in its aspect of 'preparation for life', since the 'life' which will actually be lived is in many respects unforeseeable. Specific vocational training is likely to be for a job that has changed or even disappeared by the time that the training is completed. In these circumstances of Heraclitean flux, the notion of learning how to learn has found powerful favour as offering something that can be taught of more permanent value. At this level of second-order learning, a stability may be found which is only chimerical at any first-order level.

But this situation can induce a curiously misconceived relativism. This is well illustrated in the work of Bloom (1956) when he says: 'we recognize the point of view that truth and knowledge are only relative and that there are no hard and fast truths which exist for all time and all places.' But surely, if a fully specified proposition 'p' is true, then it is part of our concept of truth that 'p' is true for all times and all places (though not of course *of* all times or *of* all places, e.g. Bonn can truly be said to be the capital city only of West Germany, and only since the Second World War). It is not that the world *was* flat and now *is* round; rather it is opinions about the world's shape which have changed, from false to true opinions no doubt we would say.

There are, however, acceptable senses in which knowledge can be regarded as relative. Certainly something can be known at one time or place, and not at another, or to one social group and not to another. But these are really sociological points about the distribution of knowledge rather than logical points about the knowledge-status of what is believed. Again, certainly something *thought* to be true at one time can be refuted or corrected at another. Thus we now think that the world is round (or very slightly pear-shaped, in fact), and we now think that we have a more adequate understanding of the atom, the nervous system and mental illness.

Often of course, it is not so much that some piece or field of supposed knowledge is refuted or corrected as that it is discarded as useless. The technology of the steam railway locomotive is not falsified by the introduction of diesel or electric traction, but simply set aside and forgotten as being no longer relevant to social and economic needs. Furthermore, no more permanent value could be found in learning how to learn if the particular things then learned were not in fact true, or at least a fair approximation to truth. Valuing learning how to learn for its many changing and more particular employments would then be incoherent.

But these misconceptions about relativism aside, it is clearly the case that much that we learn is later discredited, discarded or improved upon. There is a large element of obsolescence in what we learn of a more particular kind. Road systems, public transport timetables, locations of offices, addresses of people — all are likely to be changed in a short period of time, and often even by the next time that we want them. Jobs change in their requirements almost daily, often suddenly disappearing altogether.

A new twist is thus given to Spinoza's perception that autonomy makes us less the creature of fortune. For if learning how to learn equips us to cope with change by helping us more efficiently to re-learn our jobs, or to re-orientate ourselves in changed circumstances, or to learn new jobs, then to that degree we are less at the mercy of fortune and more the determiners of our fates. It is worth adding, however, that in curriculum terms this new emphasis has rather more validity in relation to mathematics and the sciences than it has for the arts. One's enjoyment of Jane Austen, Tennyson, Rembrandt, or Beethoven is not suddenly made redundant, or invalidated. New interpretations of works of art cannot destroy the fact of one's actual enjoyment in the light of understanding one already does have. But the notion of learning how to learn nevertheless has applications here too, in relation to how we can find our way into an appreciation of new work or form of art.

In one way, however, this aspect of the importance of learning how to learn would militate against autonomy. For Postman and others tacitly concede all the initiatives to socio-economic-technological change. As individuals, it is tacitly assumed that all we can do is respond more or less adaptively and self-directedly to these external changes. This obviously detracts from personal autonomy in that much in our lives is then conceded to be properly externally determined at least in its occasion and pressure on us. This, however, perhaps underestimates schooling as also being to an extent an end in itself, and not just a preparation for some future of kaleidoscopic change. It underestimates educational institutions as being to an extent themselves autonomous institutions in a society. At this point, however, developing autonomy as an aim passes beyond simply equipping people with a capacity to learn how to learn. It points to the necessity of having some sociological and perhaps also political awareness of the social process, and having a value-perspective on that. It may well point to a rather special significance of social studies for the development of autonomy.

Learning by discovery

Closely related both to the development of autonomy and to learning how to learn is the notion of learning by discovery. In fact learning how to learn and learning by discovery are not always distinguished in current educational literature. But distinguished they should be, though it can be conceded at once that there is some overlap between the two notions, both in content and in background concerns. The present chapter will therefore be concluded with some discussion of learning by discovery.

So often with educational ideas, to go for the word is to miss the substance. Usually, the word gives only the vaguest indication of what all the fuss is about. Who, for example, could ever guess, simply from a good knowledge of the English language, what the 'integrated day' was? If 'discovery' is taken literally, then it would be a very simple matter to show that children have always discovered things, and that there is no subject or activity that is not full of possible discoveries for children to make. Children discover where it is warmest in the classroom, how Mr Jones reacts to noise, what happens if you mix red and blue powder paints, what sounds different objects make, when the class has a television lesson, and so on.

All of this is discovery, but not much of it is to the point: the substance has been missed by concentrating attention on the word. Nevertheless, it is not by mere chance or accident that the label 'discovery' has become attached to the new emphasis in learning which the fuss really is about. The ordinary meaning of the term is not irrelevant. And so in learning by discovery we may reasonably expect children to learn something new: to them, at least, if not to the teacher or in relation to human knowledge generally. We may also reasonably expect children learning in this way to do so through some initiative of their own. But to go much beyond that means looking at the actual preoccupations of the educational debate, and not just scrutinizing a word.

Three things in that debate strike me at once. First, it is primarily the learning of facts, concepts and principles which is at issue, not usually the learning of skills, techniques or sensitivities. In curriculum terms, the subjects and activities of most relevance to discovery learning seem to be mathematics, science and studies of the local environment. 'Creativity' is the corresponding preoccupation in most other areas of the curriculum. Second, a broad and obvious contrast is drawn in the debate between learning from direct teaching, whether from instruction, demonstration or explanation, and learning through a more self-active mode of mental operation, such as achieving an insight on one's own, or through a personal initiative in finding out. Often, this insight or finding out is to stem from some concrete and practical experience, but it may also result from going to books. Finally, this learning by discovery is not envisaged as something that typically just happens. It is designed to happen, as a result of a definite teaching method or strategy. At least five different strategies can be distinguished, which it may be useful at this stage to describe.

Type A

For the most part, the teacher is a mute presence. His task is to 'structure the environment', or to provide 'structured apparatus'. The children are then to learn the relevant facts, or are to abstract the relevant concept or principle, in the course of self-chosen activities. The 'method' consists of providing and arranging suitably enticing materials. For example, through playing with a blob of plasticine the conservation of volume is to be discovered. Through investigating a tray of assorted materials and magnets, facts about magnetism are to be discovered.

Type B

This is broadly similar to Type A, except that the teacher supplements the self-chosen activity with her own seemingly casual commentary on it. She asks questions about what is being done, supplies information, suggests further activities, and draws attention to certain features. Visits to building sites, museums, farms, waterways and churches well illustrate this form of learning by discovery.

Type C

This is principally concerned with books or, more broadly, with textual resources. Through referring to these resources, a wide range of facts may be discovered. Those anxious to give grand names to simple things may speak here of 'research', daring anyone to contradict. For example, if the topic is 'tea' then books will be consulted, the Indian Embassy may be written to, Assam will be discovered in an atlas, and so on.

Type D

With this variation, a task is set or proposed by the teacher. But the task requires independent activity for its completion. How it may be completed is left open, and the sort of result to expect is not very precisely indicated. 'See how far back a ball bounces from different heights. Try different sorts of ball and different heights.' 'Look for a quick way of adding up all the whole numbers from 1 to any given number.' The now familiar traffic census could be another example.

Type E

This final type might be called 'Socratic questioning', after the episode with the slave boy in Plato's dialogue the *Meno*. The teacher hints, provokes, asks leading questions, confronts the learner with the implications of what he thinks, or prods him into framing some hypothesis. The object is to stimulate active, searching thinking in some specific direction, but always to stop short of actually telling anything. An illustration would be an exchange with a group of children leading up to the formulation of a definite hypothesis about where plants extend themselves in growing.

These, then, are five strategies for stimulating learning by discovery that I have come across. Some of them overlap or differ only in emphasis, of course. And there may well be other types that I have missed altogther. But there are, I think, sufficient examples and types here for us now to attempt a critical assessment of learning by discovery.

A general but very important question to begin by asking is What things could, at least in principle, be genuinely discovered by children? It seems clear that there is much in any ordinary curriculum which certainly could be discovered, but not everything. For instance, it is not possible to achieve an insight into something that is true only by convention, such as the gender of French nouns, or the English system of weights and measures. Again, an upper junior should be able to work out for himself the spelling of a strange word such as 'compensation', but not the spelling of 'manoeuvre', because it follows no rule that he could have inferred. With structured apparatus, such as Cuisenaire rods, it is possible to discover such facts as that two yellows are the same length as one orange, but not the conventions as to what layouts and placings will represent the operations of addition, multiplication, and so on. Such conventions are best straightforwardly taught. This limitation set by conventional truths shows the doctrinaire absurdity of the maxim 'never tell a child anything'.

Another doubt that I have about what could be discovered is much more important but very hard to present sharply. It particularly concerns Type A discovery from a 'structured environment', and also Type B if it is carried on for too long. The validity of these approaches is no doubt best seen in a good nursery, infant or first school, where children can and do discover an immense amount from a fairly free exploration of a carefully designed physical environment, or from a well-chosen outside visit. They discover how balls rebound, how people react, their own physical powers, the properties of sand, water and dough, how to get the toy that they want, what lives round the edges of a pond and so on. All of this is very important, but it is in a sense superficial: it lies on the surface of things, open to natural curiosity. My doubt concerns whether such more-developed and differentiated forms of understanding as mathematics and science could be learned in quite the same open-eyed way.

What the teacher may see as 'structured' in a particular way can always be seen (and used) in very many other ways. How can the teacher's seeing it as structured in that way guarantee by itself that children will see it in just the same way? It is just as open to them to assimilate it to already familiar concepts and uses, which will be misuses only in relation to the teacher's intentions. For instance, there is a wealth of mathematics to be seen in the fifty-pence piece — if you are familiar with Reuleaux curves. Otherwise it is just the queer-shaped coin. Certainly 'mathematics is all around us', but you need more than eyes and natural curiosity to see it.

Forms of understanding such as mathematics and science are cultural achievements. Their insights have been historically accumulated and have often needed genius to attain. All of this cannot be rediscovered by a confrontation with objects, no matter how carefully structured or expensively produced they are, or how actively they are manipulated. If discoveries are to be made here, and many can be, then they must be made by a limited reaching forward from within a growing understanding of these ways of thinking. They require the definite guidance of articulate teachers, or teacher-substitutes and teacher-extensions such as television or workcards. And this in turn presupposes that the teacher will himself be sufficiently familiar with these forms of understanding. Without that familiarity, how is he to ask opportune and fruitful questions, or even to recognize when a genuine discovery has been made?

Discoveries do have to be discoveries, and not just exciting errors, muddles, confusions or blankness. There is an objective side to making a discovery, as well as the subjective satisfaction. Only ironically can a child be said to have 'discovered' that heavy things sink. (How about an aircraft-carrier or an oil tanker?) Respect for truth is involved here, as well as personal satisfaction. Again, external discipline may meet with impatience and frustration, as well as enjoyment and success. An opportunity to discover is also an opportunity to fail to discover, which is likely to make learning by discovery slower and less certain than learning from intelligent instruction and explanation. In this, as in everything, children will no doubt come to school very differently prepared by their home backgrounds in terms of curiosity, general knowledge, acceptance of an independent role, and familiarity with analytic modes of thought and talk.

Everything in education always has its drawbacks. Therefore having some is never by itself a knock-down argument against anything. Where discovery learning is concerned, we should now ask what possible merits might outweigh those drawbacks. Some say that retention of what is learned will be much better, and also that 'heuristic strategies' of more general value will be learnt. But there is no clear evidence to favour either of these two contentions, and neither seems obviously likely to be true.

The Plowden Report's strong backing for discovery methods is in terms of the Piagetian doctrine that 'the child is the agent of his own learning'. What that doctrine means, I take it, is that each child actively constructs his own mind through a process of interaction with his environment. Certainly the spontaneous construction of reality in babies is deeply impressive. But the truth of the Piagetian doctrine cannot be used to justify preferring learning by discovery to learning from instruction, because the doctrine is compatible with *both* ways of learning. The learner just interacts with something different in each case.

Learning language is an actively constructive process, often displaying intelligent mistakes ('I maked', 'he holded', 'mouses'). But, as a set of conventions, it is not learned by discovery from things. Parents instruct children in 'what we say' and provide speech models for imitation. The 'agent of his own learning' actively makes sense out of that direct teaching. Instruction, intelligently adapted to the learner and coupled where appropriate with suitable concrete and practical experiences, could also satisfy the Piagetian doctrine. It *must* satisfy it, since children do in fact often learn in that way.

Perhaps the distinctive merits of learning by discovery are to be found by looking for different sorts of objectives, rather than in arguing over comparative efficiency in achieving the same objectives. The characteristic objective of instruction is that a certain amount of knowledge should be passed on and learned. Remembered content is the criterion of success. Learning by discovery is more concerned with attitudes, even if that difference is never absolute but only one of emphasis. Learning by discovery characteristically aims to engender intrinsic interest, both in what is learned and in the process of learning it. It also emphasizes the satisfactions of learning independently. But the development of both intrinsic interest and independence in learning are extremely important liberal educational aims. If a method in the hands of some teacher is successful in achieving these aims, then it has much to be said for it, at least as one valid method amongst others.

Topics for discussion

1. What *sort* of 'learning how to learn' does Dearden focus upon and what, in practice, is it seen to consist of?
2. How does 'learning how to learn' relate to the growth of pupils' autonomy in the classroom and their 'preparation for life' in the wide society?
3. 'There is a wealth of mathematics to be seen in the fifty-pence piece — if you are familiar with Reuleaux curves.' Discuss Dearden's argument concerning the limitations of 'learning by discovery'.

Suggestions for further reading

1. Cohen, L. and Manion, L. (1981) *Perspectives on Classrooms and Schools.*

Eastbourne: Holt, Rinehart and Winston, pp. 282–314, 'Open Education'. See especially Box 9.2 page 289, 'Assumptions about children's learning'.

2. Anthony, W. 'Progressive learning theories: the evidence', in Bernbaum, G. (Ed.) (1979) *Schooling in Decline*. London: Macmillan.

3. Stephens, L.S. (1974) *The Teacher's Guide to Open Education*. New York: Holt, Rinehart and Winston.

SECTION SEVEN
THE PRIMARY SCHOOL CURRICULUM: POLICY STATEMENTS

READING THIRTEEN • The curriculum in primary schools
Schools Council

By the time children enter primary schools at about 5 years of age most have learnt to behave in a reasonably social way, though they may be unaccustomed to being members of such a large community as a school. They are likely to have acquired the basic structures of their mother tongue, not always English, and be aware of and interested in the shapes, sizes, colours and quantities of things about them.

Individual differences and common needs

Each individual brings a different set of experiences to bear on his schooling. These differences arise from variety in the surroundings in which children are brought up, from the degree of support and encouragement they have had from adults, and from differences in what their powers of imagination and intellect have allowed them to make of their experiences. At 5, a few have a vocabulary that is barely sufficient for their daily needs, while at the other extreme a small minority have a wide vocabulary, can detect fine shades of meaning and have begun to recognize written words; and a few have started to write.

At one level of generality, all children in primary schools need to be occupied in a programme that will enable them:

to engage with other children and with adults in a variety of working and social relationships;
to increase their range and understanding of English, and particularly to develop their ability and inclination to read and write for information and imaginative stimulation;
to acquire better physical control when they are writing, or exercising utilitarian skills and engaging in imaginative expression in art, craft, music, drama or movement generally.

Appendix B 'The curriculum in primary schools' in, *Primary Practice: a sequel to the Practical Curriculum*. Reproduced with permission of the Schools Council Publications from Working Paper 75, pp 184–189, Methuen Educational, 1983

Furthermore, if they are to extend their powers of language, children must be brought into contact with new experiences and ideas or look afresh at old experiences through discussion with teachers and through the use of books, role playing and audio-visual material. Studies of the beliefs and ways of life of historical characters and of people and communities who live today in other parts of the world, or indeed elsewhere in Britain, provide opportunities for language development through discussion, reading and writing. Moreover, these studies are valuable in their own right. This is especially so in a country that is multicultural. Learning about the nature of materials and about the needs and life cycles of plants and animals provides further opportunities for the extension and application of language and of mathematical skills and ideas. It also helps children to appreciate the world around them and provides an early introduction to the industrial and scientific age in which they live.

Some necessary differences of programme

When described in these general terms, the curricula of primary schools show close conformity. Differences that occur from class to class, and even from pupil to pupil within a class, are in the particular topics chosen for study, the methods of study employed, the weight given to each part of the curriculum and the level of difficulty to which each part is taken. There are good reasons why, to some extent, this should be so.

The first arises from differences between children, such as those de-scribed earlier. For example, a child entering school who has already begun to read soon requires books covering a wide range of topics and stories and may well be able to progress quickly with only a modest amount of supervision. Another child, before he is ready to begin to read, will need to acquire a surer grasp of spoken language, skill in noticing relatively small differences in sounds and shapes, and the habit of looking at printed material in an orderly way. Even then much patient help and encourage-ment may be needed if the second child is to gain in skill and confidence. To treat both children the same is to do an injustice to one.

As children make progress their interests diversify and what is a stimulus to one may be a barrier to another. If the necessary skill or the underlying idea can be presented as well in one way as another then it may create unnecessary difficulties to use the same way with all children.

Teachers as well as children differ in their abilities and enthusiasms.

Schools differ in the resources available to them both because of the purchasing policies of present and past incumbents and because of the accidents of locality. A school in Lincoln is better placed to develop historical studies based on Lincoln cathedral than is one in St Albans.

The development and use of local opportunities, the special skills of teachers and the enthusiasms of children should be used to enhance the quality of work beyond what might come from a simple uniformity of practice; though such uniformity may have the advantage that the work to be covered becomes very familiar to teachers, what is done may be only a loose fit to local circumstances and soon become threadbare. When teachers make good use of their particular interests and strengths they can take children much further than is now common.

Conditions required for the inclusion of a modern language

The presence of a teacher with strength in a subject does not necessarily justify the inclusion of the subject in the curriculum, even if the children are capable of studying it. In the short term, French can be taught successfully in a primary school where there are sufficient teachers who speak the language well enough, who know how to teach the subject to young children, and who have the resources necessary for the work. However, these conditions are only the first that must be satisfied if the time and effort spent is to be worthwhile in the long term. Additionally, there should be a reasonable expectation that the teaching will be continued even if the teachers now responsible for the work leave. It should also be possible to continue the teaching in the secondary school in such a way as to profit from what has already been done. This may be difficult and even impossible if children in other primary schools in the area have had no opportunity or substantially different opportunities for learning the language. Unless conditions are favourable in all these respects for including the subject, it is best excluded from the primary school curriculum. Plainly, there is need for agreement between schools in a neighbourhood and the LEA on whether and how the teaching of a foreign language is conducted in primary schools.

Levels of difficulty in the work

In other parts of the primary school curriculum the decisions to be taken more usually concern the range of what should be done, the choice of priorities within the range and the level of difficulty of the work. In each of these, local circumstances and the differences between individual children and individual teachers have to be taken into account, but some common requirements remain.

Skills

All children should learn to use English better as they grow older, and to read and write English with a growing sureness. Some children come to school with little or no English. It is essential for them to become fluent in English but, whatever is done to achieve this, the child's interest and pride in his mother tongue should be preserved.

A minority of children of 11 years of age can manage only simple reading texts made up of short sentences using common words. They as much as anyone require appropriate reading material on almost all aspects of the curriculum so that they may better appreciate the importance of reading. The great majority of children should learn to use books, fiction and non-fiction, in the sense that they improve their powers of comprehension, that they learn how to find the books they want on the library shelf, and that they learn to use a contents page and an index. The full range of reading skills required by the more able 11-year-olds is much wider than this . . .

Learning to read and learning to write go hand in hand, and the majority of children should, by the time they are 8, be able to write stories and accounts of events in their own words. As they go on through the primary school many children should become accustomed to writing which involves presenting a coherent argument, exploring alternative possibilities or drawing conclusions and making judgements. Children should learn, in the course of their work, to spell the words they use, to employ acceptable forms of grammar and sentence structure and to begin to develop styles of writing appropriate to the task in hand.

In mathematics, priority should be given to acquiring familiarity with whole numbers up to 100 by gaining skills in relating them to one another — including the speedy recall of the commonly used addition, multiplication, subtraction and division facts — and by applying them to circumstances that occur in everyday life. But nearly all of the children should go far beyond that. They should begin to appreciate the simpler spatial relationships and they should make a start on work requiring a relatively explicit application of logic as with some popular games and puzzles . . .

Over the course of the primary school years children should learn how to observe and to measure with increasing precision. They should also learn to use these skills with common sense; for example, when measuring or weighing, to use a degree of accuracy that is appropriate to the circumstances. They should learn to record — and to interpret and comment on — what they have seen, heard or otherwise learnt. They should gain from increasing control over their nervous and muscular systems so that they can use tools, instruments and a variety of small equipment in drawing, painting, modelling, music-making and games in such a way that they feel a sense of achievement.

Content and concepts

A wide range of skills, not least those concerned with the development of good personal relations, are relevant to the education of each child, though each makes progress at a different rate. The skills are learnt in the context of developing concepts and in the acquisition of information . . . Some appropriate historical, geographical and scientific concepts are discussed in the following paragraphs.

When topics are being selected for inclusion in the programme a number of factors should be taken into account. These include the characteristics of the children, the knowledge of the teachers and the availability of suitable resources and facilities. The information to be covered should be worth knowing and useful in providing further insights into some more general idea or in improving a skill. There needs also to be some agreement between teachers in a school, with teachers in the secondary schools, and with teachers in neighbouring primary schools so that if a topic is to be studied twice or more in the course of a child's school life, the second and later occasion will build on previous experience.

On the national level it can be said that all primary schools should help their pupils to appreciate that today's world grew out of yesterday's, and to acquire some sense of historical chronology, even if the topics studied are not presented in chronological order. The children should learn to distinguish between fiction and historical fact and some should begin to recognize that historical evidence may itself be partial or biased. The youngest children's introduction to the past might concentrate on the immediate circumstances of their own families and friends and the paraphernalia of daily life. But today's world cannot be understood without some knowledge of Britain's role overseas today and in former years, and reference to this should certainly be included in the later primary school curriculum in a balanced and sensitive way as a means of helping children to understand our multicultural society.

The lives of the children and their parents are also conditioned by the geographical circumstances under which they and others live. As they go through primary schools, children need to become more aware of local features, of the formation and characteristics of the earth beneath their feet and of the weather. They need to learn something of the major differences in the conditions under which children live in other parts of Britain and abroad, and of the consequences of those conditions. They should also learn of the importance of routes and other means of communication between human settlements.

Skills of observation, listening and touching need to be developed so that children possess information on which their imaginations can work and be expressed through painting, modelling, music-making, dancing and story-telling. They need to be developed more than is now common in such a way that children are introduced to scientific ideas about stability and change in living things and materials; about reproduction, growth and development in succeeding generations; about forms of energy sources and storage; and about factors which influence personal and community health, including safety. Children should grow to respect and care for living things. In the course of the work they should learn how to observe systematically and carefully, to note similarities and differences and to make reasonable generalizations; they should conduct, and some should learn to devise, simple experiments to test out hypotheses.

Religious education has a statutory place in the curriculum of all maintained schools and the agreed syllabus system makes it possible to provide a framework of advice and guidance for this aspect of the curriculum in county and voluntary controlled schools. However, it is necessary for schools and teachers through their schemes of work to decide how that framework is to be adapted to the capacities and experience of the particular children with whom they are concerned.

Through religious education children can begin to learn something of the characteristic practices and beliefs of Christianity and of other major world faiths, and the influence these faiths have on the life and conduct of the believer. On another level, also important in the growth of attitudes and of an appreciation of human behaviour and achievement, it is necessary to introduce children to suitable examples of literature, drama, music and the graphic arts. Of these, literature offers an especially rich source and the children should be introduced to books by the major authors who have written for, or whose books have been adopted by, children. Some of the books should have been written by authors alive today.

Summary

Current practice is such that discussion on the primary school curriculum does not need to concern itself so much with the total range of work as with the extent to which parts of the curriculum are developed, especially for the more able children. It is only provision of observational and experimental science that is seriously lacking in many primary schools; and the teaching of French that is sometimes attempted when conditions are not suitable. More extensive discussion is required on the levels to which work could and should be taken, at least for some children, in the various parts of the curriculum; for example, the identification of the skills and ideas associated with geography and history that are suitable for primary school children should help teachers to ensure that the day-to-day programme is organized so that children become acquainted with these skills and ideas, and should help to improve continuity from one class or school to the next — whether or not these subjects are shown separately on the timetable. Working parties of teachers, LEA advisers, inspectors and others have already shown what useful guidelines can be produced for parts of the curriculum, particularly, but not only, in mathematics.

Anxiety is sometimes expressed that maintaining a wide curriculum in primary schools may be possible only at the expense of the essential, elementary skills of reading, writing and mathematics. The evidence from the HMI survey of primary education in England does not bear out that anxiety. A broad curriculum can include many opportunities for the application and practice of the skills of reading, writing and calculating. It should be planned to include them, and every opportunity should then be taken to improve children's abilities in these essential skills.

Topics for discussion

1.   What are the implications for the practising teacher of the comment that 'More

extensive discussion is required on the levels to which work could and should be taken, at least for some children, in the various parts of the curriculum'?
2. How does the policy statement resolve the apparent problem of providing a common programme for all yet avoiding uniformity of practice in primary classrooms?
3. What, in your view, is the most critical comment that Her Majesty's Inspectors make about current practice?

Suggestions for further reading

1. Blenkin, G.A. and Kelly, A.V. (1981) *The Primary Curriculum*. London: Harper and Row, Chapter 5.
2. Schools Council (1983) Working Paper 75. *Primary Practice: a sequel to 'The Practical Curriculum'*. London: Methuen Educational.
3. Kelly, A.V. (1980) *Curriculum Context*. London: Harper & Row.

READING FOURTEEN • The curriculum
Department of Education and Science

The basic skills

8.16 High priority is given to teaching children to read, write and learn mathematics.

8.17 The teaching of reading is regarded by teachers as extremely important, and the basic work in this skill is undertaken systematically. *The levels of ability of the children inevitably vary, but those who find learning to read difficult are more likely to be given work suitably matched to their abilities than the children who are more able readers.*

8.18 The survey also makes it possible to say, on the basis of the scores in the NFER reading test, NS6, that the results of surveys conducted since 1955 are consistent with gradually improving reading standards of eleven year olds. It is only in the reading performance of eleven year olds that

DES, *Primary Education in England: A Survey by HM Inspectors of Schools*, London: HMSO 1978. 'The Curriculum', reproduced with permission of the Controller of HMSO.

earlier data exist for statistical comparisons to be made with the findings of this survey.

8.19 *It is vital that the careful work already being done to ensure that children become literate should continue and be further developed. Future marked improvement in the general level of performance in reading, however, probably depends on developing a more systematic approach to teaching average and more able readers to find the books they require and to use the contents page and index to decide whether to skim or to study a text thoroughly; to follow a line of argument critically; and to look out for the implications of what is written, as well as to note the explicit information the passage contains. For this to be achieved children need to be introduced to a wide range of reading material in connection with many aspects of their work.*

8.20   In writing, considerable effort is made to teach syntax and spelling. *It may be that because this work is often based on isolated exercises, the rules are too often forgotten when children write in their own words, as they frequently have the opportunity to do. What is written is often descriptive or narrative in form and, while these forms are important, by eleven years of age more children might be expected to develop an argument or to explore an idea when writing than is now the case. Furthermore, the time spent on writing should allow for the correction and improvement of initial attempts.*

8.21   The children spend a considerable amount of time on mathematics and the work in this subject is better matched to their abilities than is the work in most other subjects — though the more able children often work at too low a level. In the light of these efforts, the scores achieved in the NFER mathematics test, E2, are disappointing.

8.22 *It seems clear from this part of the survey that individual assignments should not be allowed to replace all group or class work in mathematics. Teachers can, by working regularly with a group or the whole class, quicken the pace of mental response and encourage accuracy. They may also, in these circumstances, more readily draw children's attention to general rules in the work they do and so help to create a better understanding of the ways in which numbers behave. Children need to practise mental and written calculations in the four rules of number, including whole numbers and, when they are ready, decimals and fractions. They also need to use numbers in connection with practical activities. The forms of questions and the forms of answers required ought to be varied so that children are not put off by an unusual word, or combination of words or symbols. More of the examples worked by children could usefully lead to multiple answers. The work in mathematics should not be confined to the four rules of number: children in those classes where the programme included all mathematical items*

taught to 80 per cent of classes for the age group did better in the mathematics test.
8.23 *The evidence of the survey bears out the view that the effective application of skills, including their use in practical activities, is important. The teaching of skills in isolation, whether in language or in mathematics, does not produce the best results.*

Other aspects of the curriculum

8.24 The curriculum as a whole provides many opportunities for pupils to apply basic skills, and it contains other elements that are important in their own right. The programme of most classes included work on plants, animals and man-made objects and materials. The children were taught about the historical and geographical context of the society in which they live, and the moral values that underlie it. Unless their parents asked for them to be withdrawn, they took part in religious education based on Christian beliefs. *More might be done to make all children aware of other beliefs and to extend their understanding of the multicultural nature of contemporary society. In the course of work on these and other matters, children acquire information and learn to respond imaginatively to what they see, hear and otherwise experience.*

8.25 *Curricular content should be selected not only to suit the interests and abilities of the children and to provide for the progressive development of the basic skills, but also because it is important in its own right.* This requires a considerable knowledge of the subject material, going far beyond that which is to be used explicitly in the classroom. The teacher's need for a thorough knowledge of the subject becomes more marked as the children get older.

8.26 *Observed practices in some parts of the curriculum show the difficulty that a considerable proportion of teachers have in selecting and utilizing subject matter. Science is the outstanding example and one in which no individual item of observational or experimental work occurred in as many as 80 per cent of the classes at any age; this is the only aspect of the curriculum of which this is true. Craft is also making a smaller contribution to the work than is desirable. The lack of progression and the amount of repetition in the work in geography and history probably result from a lack of planning, though the mere presence of a scheme of work is no guarantee that a subject is well taught; over 40 per cent of the schools had schemes of work in science but there was little evidence of these programmes being implemented.*

8.27   Physical education was given about as high a priority as mathematics. Music, of which more will be said later, was also given relatively high priority. *It is interesting to notice that both of these subjects were among those for which there were frequently teachers with posts of responsibility.*

The range of the curriculum

8.28   It might be argued that if some parts of the curriculum are difficult for class teachers to deal with it would be better to narrow the range of the curriculum. That view does not seem to be borne out by the findings of this survey. The basic skills are more successfully learnt when applied to other subjects and children in the classes which covered a full range of the widely taught items did better on the NFER tests at nine and eleven years of age; also, for all three age groups the work of children in these classes was better matched to their abilities than was the work of children in other classes. This finding has to be interpreted with care, because the remaining classes did not necessarily have narrower curricula; the teachers may merely have been more idiosyncratic in their choice of items. *Nevertheless, there is no evidence in the survey to suggest that a narrower curriculum enabled children to do better in the basic skills or led to the work being more aptly chosen to suit the capacities of the children.*

8.29   *The general educational progress of children and their competence in the basic skills appear to have benefited where they were involved in a programme of work that included art and craft, history and geography, music and physical education, and science, as well as language, mathematics and religious and moral education, although not necessarily as separate items on a timetable. There is no justification for differentiation between the curriculum for boys and for girls because of traditional differences in social roles; such differentiation as does still occur, for example in craft work which limits girls to using soft materials, is unusual and should cease.*

8.30   *It remains important to establish priorities and to keep the curriculum within realistic limits. Agreement on these matters should be sought far more than is now done with other schools in the locality, primary and secondary, and in accordance with national needs.*

8.31   *Such agreement makes it easier to ensure that the programmes of primary and secondary schools are attuned, and that there is continuity as children move from one stage to the next.*

Differences amongst children within a class

8.32 Especially in the basic skills, but also in other parts of the curriculum, children are frequently divided into groups, or provided with individual assignments of work. In the basic skills, the main objective is to give work that is of an appropriate level of difficulty. In some other parts of the curriculum the groups are based on common interests or on friendship. The almost universal occurrence of grouping and individual work indicate the concern that teachers have for individual children.

8.33 The evidence of the survey shows that children's needs are more successfully catered for in some parts of the curriculum than in others; and throughout the curriculum, the needs of some children are more often met than are the needs of others. *The relative success that teachers have in matching the work in the basic skills for the slower children has already been mentioned in this chapter. Otherwise, it is broadly the case that the more able children within a class were the least likely to be doing work that was sufficiently challenging.*

8.34 One reason may be that it is difficult for a teacher to keep track of what every child in a class is doing if each is engaged in a different activity. *Certainly children who were customarily given some — though not too much — mathematical instruction in groups working from the blackboard with their teacher were at an advantage in completing the NFER test.* This advantage may have come about because a teacher could afford to spend more time explaining a process to a group than to a series of individuals, or because the group contact enabled the teacher to inject more pace into the work, or because the children learnt from each other's questions, or all three. *Some potential loss of precision in matching the work to individuals was compensated for by other factors; in practice, the loss of precision in the grading of work for groups as compared with individuals may be negligible.*

8.35 Another reason why teachers find it more difficult to match the level of work to the abler than to the slower children in their classes may be that these children are more demanding with regard to subject content. *It is particularly interesting in this connection that the work in music, for which specialist teaching, including peripatetic teaching, is most common, is the area of the curriculum in which the work of the able, average and least able children is most evenly matched to their abilities. It is also striking that classes in schools where the holders of posts of special responsibility have marked influence were much more successful than others in matching the work to the abilities of all children, including the most able.* Furthermore, the better match that is achieved in the basic skills may well occur because all the students who intended to teach in primary schools are given some training in the teaching of these skills, because carefully graded materials are available, and because dealing with children who find it difficult to learn to read is another common area of specialization in primary education.

Some children in inner city schools

8.36 In recent years efforts have been made to provide for the special needs of some children in inner city schools. In the survey, inner city schools generally had a more favourable staffing ratio than similar schools in 'other urban' areas, and in some of these schools resources were noticeably better than average.

8.37 Some of the schools in inner city areas contained a larger proportion than most of children whose home language was not English, and also of those children from some indigenous families who find it difficult to gain as much as they should from their schooling. While both the HMI survey and the NFER tests indicate that standards of performance are lower than average in these schools, neither can show whether the efforts made in recent years have improved the levels of performance. *The survey indicates that children in inner city schools are more likely than others to be underestimated by their teachers and least likely to be given work which extends their capabilities. This strongly suggests that further improvement in the children's performance is possible.*

8.38 *Further study is required of how improvements may be brought about. Some research has already been undertaken in this field but more is necessary in primary schools, particularly to identify conditions that are likely to be effective in teaching children from these areas.*

8.39 *The need to raise teachers' assumptions about children's capabilities has special relevance here. It may also be that in these schools, with a preponderance of children who find learning difficult, special care should be taken to support and encourage those children who make average or good progress, not least in order that they should set a standard of work at which others may aim. This may require yet more teachers and resources. The slower children still need painstaking and thorough attention if they are to reach minimum standards of literacy and numeracy; and children who come to school with little or no English cannot be expected to make progress in school unless, as a result of careful teaching, they achieve a sufficient command of English, which is for them a foreign language.*

Topics for discussion

1. 'It remains important to establish priorities and to keep the curriculum within realistic limits.' *Who*, in your view, should do this and *how* might it best be accomplished?
2. What can be done to achieve a better matching of levels of work across the range of ability in primary school classrooms?
3. In what ways might 'class teaching' be contrary to the child's interests, particularly perhaps, after the early primary years?

Suggestions for further reading

1. Taylor, P.H. and Richards, C.M. (eds) (1984) *An Introduction to Curriculum Studies*, NFER-Nelson, 2nd edition.
2. Alexander, R.J. (1984) *Primary Teaching*. Holt, Rinehart and Winston, part I, pp. 9–47.
3. Schools Council (1983) Working Paper 75. *Primary Practice: A sequel to the Practical Curriculum*. Methuen Educational.

SECTION EIGHT
THE PRIMARY SCHOOL CURRICULUM IN ACTION

READING FIFTEEN • Personal and social development
Schools Council

Children spend more time at school than anywhere else except home. They follow the formal curriculum, take part in the extramural life, and are exposed to the ethos of the school. Schools cannot avoid, and no teacher would wish to avoid, a large measure of responsibility for their pupils' personal and social development.

The words 'personal and social education' encompass a vast area, hard to describe, and hard to map. (. . .)

It may be helpful to draw together phrases (. . .) used to describe what schools might aim for. The suggestions relating to personal qualities and relationships with other people come near to providing schools with usable checklists.

Personal qualities
1. qualities of mind, body, spirit, feeling and imagination
2. capacity for enjoyment
3. lively enquiring minds, the ability to question and argue rationally, and to apply themselves to tasks and physical skills
4. the will to use knowledge, skills and practical abilities
5. a reasoned set of attitudes, values and beliefs
6. habits of self-discipline and acceptable behaviour
7. a sense of self-respect, the capacity to live as independent, self-motivated adults
8. achieving as much independence as possible.

Relationships with other people
1. tolerance of other races, religions and ways of life
2. to understand the interdependence of individuals, groups and nations
3. an active participant in society and a responsible contributor to it

'Personal and Social Development', reproduced with the permission of Schools Council Publications from *'Primary Practice: A sequel to "The Practical Curriculum"* ', (Working Paper 75). London: Methuen Educational 1983, pp 91–105

4. the ability to function as contributing members of cooperative groups
5. awareness of self and sensitivity to others

Religious education
1. respect for religious and moral values.

Moral education
1. awareness of moral values
2. respect for religious and moral values
3. acquire a set of moral values and the confidence to make and hold to moral judgements.

To the extent that these summaries do describe satisfactorily a school's long-term aims, teachers need to consider next what they can and should do to help their pupils develop these abilities.

Personal qualities

In this area of education more than most teachers need a clear view of what they are trying to achieve and how to do it, because there is unlikely to be a separate slot in the timetable for developing personal qualities. Most of what schools can do will arise from the teaching of other parts of the curriculum, and from the school's organization and ethos. Many different strategies are needed. It may be helpful for example to tell children what behaviour is acceptable, and to teach them how to question and argue rationally. Teachers may need to work hard to provide opportunities for every child to succeed at some things, and to develop a sense of self-esteem. But developing lively enquiring minds is perhaps more a matter of encouraging and setting an example of lively enquiry. Young children, like other creatures, learn by imitating older members of the species and may depend heavily on their teachers as models of self-respect, self-discipline, application and enjoyment. The fact that teachers are so important to young children, as models, as surrogate parents for much of the waking day, as founts of advice and information, may make it particularly difficult for teachers to make opportunities for their pupils to practise independence.

Relationships with other people

The teacher's high authority makes it easy and natural for teachers to develop effective one-to-one relationships with pupils. It may be somewhat harder for teachers to help their pupils to develop effective working and social relationships with their peers, their juniors and their seniors. Children need practice as members of cooperating groups, contributing to group discussions, analysis and activities, taking the lead or accepting the leadership of others when appropriate, and, perhaps especially as leader, finding ways of accommodating the interests and preferences of other people. There are of course many such opportunities in the playground and the park, but children are not all equally active or successful in outdoor play. They all need similarly enlarging experiences in their normal work. Creating suitable conditions for this kind of experience is not easy. Sitting children in groups round small tables may look like group work but may turn out to be merely another way of arranging children doing individual work. Strenuous efforts are needed to ensure that groups of children do work collaboratively, and that each child has practice in making different contributions and playing different roles. Creating an environment in which specific skills like politeness, empathy, social competence and helpfulness can flourish is the key task.

Religious education

The 1944 Education Act gives religious education a unique place in English and Welsh schools. All county schools are required to provide religious education, and to do so in accordance with an Agreed Syllabus adopted by their local education authority. There are no similar requirements in any other area of the curriculum, and those for religious education now raise some difficulties because the assumptions which lay behind the 1944 Act can no longer be taken for granted. This is partly because active participation in the life and work of a Christian church is less common than it was forty years ago, and partly because many families of other faiths have now settled in Britain.

In these circumstances the rationale of religious education needs to be restated in convincing terms.

The introductory handbook produced by the Schools Council Religious Education in Primary Schools Project suggests that

> religious education can build upon the desire to make sense of life. It tries to help pupils to enter imaginatively into the experience of a believer so that they can appreciate the importance to him of what he believes and does. It can

provide a basis of understanding and appreciation upon which reasoned assessments and informed decisions can be made. In short, religious education is helping pupils to understand religion. However, such an understanding is not quickly acquired; for many it is a lifelong process. So, in the primary school, teachers are concerned with laying foundations, with the question of the extent to which we can equip children with the tools for understanding.

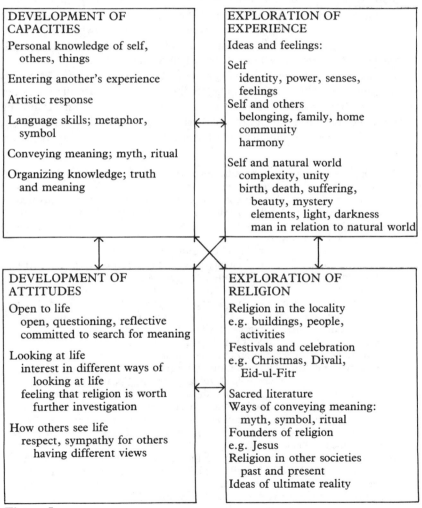

Figure 5

It goes on to suggest four ways in which teachers can help. They can interest children in different ways of responding to and interpreting life, help children to develop capacities necessary to understand religion, encourage children to reflect on their experience, and help children to explore various aspects of religion. The handbook goes on to suggest more detailed objectives corresponding to each of these four strands in religious education. These objectives are set out in Figure 5.

If primary schools can devise programmes of activities which contribute to these objectives they will have made a useful start in helping their pupils towards understanding religious ideas, feelings and activities.

That is, of course, the underlying aim of education in religion. As well as reassurance about how they can help, teachers may find it useful to consider exactly what religious education is, and what it is not. The following statement of principles from a recent Agreed Syllabus tackles this question, and may be a helpful starting point for others who wish to clear their own minds.

1. Religious education is the education of children in religion. It is not primarily social education or education in personal relationships. Nevertheless, as the aims show, there are opportunities for both within this area of the curriculum. Neither is religious education directly concerned with political and non-religious philosophies, except in so far as such philosophies relate to religion.

2. Religious education should not be confused with moral education. Morality is not necessarily dependent on particular religious beliefs, but can exist independently of them. Responsibility for moral education should run across the whole curriculum. The overlap of religious education with moral education occurs when children are exploring the ideas, feelings and actions involved in the ethical teaching of religious traditions and in the moral conflicts that may arise in the life of the believer.

3. Religious education is concerned with the spiritual growth of the individual, with those feelings and beliefs that arise out of experience and that influence the search for meaning and purpose to life. For some, such experience will be interpreted in religious terms. Spiritual growth is the concern of both the school and the faith community. The latter will encourage spiritual growth in accordance with its own tradition. The school's task in religious education is to enable pupils to become aware of a wide range of religious interpretations of personal experience and their importance to believers.

4. Religious education must include the study of Christianity. It is the example of religion most readily available in our society for study; and it is the religion that has most influenced our culture, giving rise to social institutions, moral codes and patterns of behaviour.

5. Religious education must also develop some understanding of the religious

beliefs and practices that affect the attitudes and actions of people through-out the world. Many examples are to be found in the variety of beliefs and ways of life that are accepted and practised in Britain today.

6. Religious education, to be educationally acceptable, must be characterized by open enquiry and awareness of prejudice. It should help children to appreciate that religion offers a distinctive interpretation of life. It should also encourage them to think honestly for themselves about their own beliefs and values.

7. Religious education seeks not only to impart knowledge but also to develop understanding of religious experiences, feelings and attitudes. The use of the imagination is an essential tool for exploring religious beliefs and practices.

In so far as education is involved in the development of the whole person, religious education fosters the personal search for meaning and purpose to life in the wider context of the religious traditions of mankind. In so far as education is a preparation for life in a changing society, religious education clearly has a part to play by introducing pupils to society's religious traditions and to its present plurality. In so far as education is concerned with disciplines and areas of knowledge, religious education offers a distinctive area for study. It stands, therefore, in its own right within the curriculum of the school, making a unique contribution to the education of children.

The lack of a detailed syllabus may seem strange to teachers who grew up with very prescriptive Agreed Syllabuses. The following example shows how one junior school in another local authority which had adopted a similar framework of aims and objectives used the framework to shape a detailed programme of work. The suggested objectives for children of 8 to 12 were as follows:

To enable pupils:
a to develop a sense of their own identity and worth
b to understand some features of human groups and communities
c to become aware of different forms of verbal communication
d to appreciate that symbols and artefacts can express human feelings and ideas
e to explore the natural world and various human responses to it
f to extend their awareness that people commit themselves to beliefs and causes.

The teachers listed various activities and topics which might contribute to these objectives and then arranged these in a programme which was intended to cover the six main objectives and to match the developing capacities of the children. Table 7 shows the suggested programme for the first year. It was not intended as a blueprint for every subsequent year even in that school, but other schools may find it helpful in their own discussion of an RE programme.

As in other areas of the curriculum teachers are quick to respond to circumstances in their own school and the community it serves.

The following example comes from a junior school with about 250 children. Built seventy years ago in a small county town, the school now serves an industrialized area with a canal, an airport and numerous factories. The area has attracted a good many West Indian and Asian families, and a third of the children are Asian, mainly Sikh but some Hindus and Muslims, and about 7 per cent West Indian. Most of them seem to have strong religious affiliations at home, but their parents are happy for them to join in every aspect of school life. 'The English children seem to have little or no contact with organized religion.'

Celebrating the school's seventieth anniversary created a new sense of excitement and purpose and a new sense of interest in the community. This, and the associated infant school's concern about religious education and the deputy head's attendance at a short course on world religions, led to a joint review of aims for religious education in those two schools. The teachers agreed on five objectives:

1. We wanted to introduce the children to the experience and ideas of community.
2. As the children explored what is of importance to various communities we would encourage them to respond as individuals and to reflect upon themselves as individuals.
3. Man's relationship with the natural world would be explored as a result of looking at patterns of interdependence.
4. The importance of attitudes, especially of tolerance and of interest in the idea of religion.
5. Developing skills appropriate to this and other areas of the curriculum, particularly sharing through words, art, music and movement what the children felt was important.

The teachers found it difficult to work out a detailed programme of work so they charted important areas of exploration to provide a balanced programme for each year. Their suggestions are set out in Table 8.

The chart does not bring out the extent to which this school took advantage of its multicultural make-up, though the programme is broad enough to allow the ethnic minorities to contribute their own experiences and insights. Teachers without that advantage may have to make a greater effort to introduce faiths other than Christianity to their programme of work.

Such a programme of religious education might involve close links with studies of the local environment, and work in language and art. Bringing out such connections will help children towards understanding, and may lead helpfully to some economy in time and effort. The power of these connections is revealed in the following account of how some children in a Roman Catholic school in Northern Ireland visited two local churches, one Roman Catholic and one Church of Ireland.

> The same questionnaire was used for both visits which surprised the children as they had not realized how much the two buildings had in common. They looked at the shape and furnishing of the churches, learning the names of the various parts of the buildings and of the objects and their significance in the life of churches. The minister from the Church of Ireland church visited the school to answer questions. He had a gift for talking with children and the interview was a great success.
>
> The patron saints of the churches were St John the Baptist and St John the Evangelist. The children used the Gospels and other books to find out about the lives of these two men.
>
> At the same time they carried out a survey among their friends and relations and discovered both Catholics and Protestants among them. This realization contributed to a discussion of the idea of 'neighbours' when applied to people of different faiths living in the same community. They became very interested in peace movements and visited the Corrymeela community. They made a collage to convey their feelings about the divided community in which they live and showed great interest in the situation in Northern Ireland and the part religion played in it.
>
> The teacher felt that visits to the two churches were important; they suggested a number of points for discussion. The children were interested in the idea of visiting an unfamiliar church. It was a new experience for many of them. They thoroughly enjoyed their talk with the Church of Ireland minister, and it was important to meet somebody associated with the church building they had visited.
>
> Attitudes are difficult to evaluate, but the teacher has noticed that these children have shown a more positive attitude to 'the other side'. There was some realization that beliefs and practices, although different from one's own, are important and meaningful to those who hold them. Certainly, they learnt more both about their own church and the one down the road which previously had been just another building to them.

This example illustrates how a teacher can organize experiences which contribute to the different strands of religious education mentioned on pages 190 and 191. The challenge for other teachers is to find similar examples in their own community.

Table 7

	1st Year	2nd Year	3rd Year	4th Year
	Belonging home, school, club roles, rules.	*The world around* trees – life cycle, as a resource, use and misuse (Harvest)	*Food* dependence, interdependence, plenty, want; symbolism: care, unity, celebration. (Harvest)	*Creation myths* making sense of the world, myths compared, place of origins, motifs.
A U T U M N	*Guy Fawkes* colours, sounds, dark, light, fire, customs, rituals, symbols.	*Autumn* turn of year, Fall, patterns of death and renewal.	*Hallowe'en* ghosts, witches, spells, real and unreal experiences, dark, shadows, fears, good, evil, heaven, hell.	*Festivals* motif – *light* Celtic
	What is precious favourite things, people who are important, what is precious?	*Background to life of Jesus* Synagogue school, Jewish Bible, Hebrew, types of writing, poetry, law, stories, Festivals, Passover in Jerusalem, pilgrim songs.	*Exploring myself* X-rays: inside, outside, doing, thinking, imagining, feeling; conscience.	Divali Hanukkah Advent
	Christmas (Santa Claus)	*Christmas* (exploring customs)	*Christmas* (meaning of celebration)	*Christmas* (light)

SPRING

Background to the life of Jesus growing up in a Jewish home, family life, Passover meal, Synagogue, stories from Jewish Scriptures.	*North American Indians* patterns of community life, dependence on nature, customs, myths, stories, rituals.	*Life in a mining village* coalmining – methods and history, being a miner, underground, pit disaster, life in the village.	*Cortez and the Aztecs* Aztec society, way of life, festivals, rituals, myths, the coming of Cortez, clash of cultures.
Spring plants and animals, new life and growth.	*Night and day* light and growth, nocturnal animals, time and seasons, sun and moon, stories and myths, light and dark.	*How the Bible came to us* translation, transmission, William Tyndale, James Evans.	*Jesus* as others saw him (friends and enemies) at the end of his life.
Easter →	*Easter* →	*Easter* (customs) →	*Easter* →

SUMMER

Communication (non-verbal) 'language' of music, dance, art, expressing ideas, feelings, Beethoven.	*Man and animals* pets: care, companionship, animals for food, work, clothing, animals for sport.	*Living with others* using *The Diddakoi* to explore: acceptance, rejection, homelessness, death of animal.	*Maccabeus* history. Greeks and Jews. Zealots, dying for beliefs.
The world around a local stream, water and life, dependence on water, pollution.	*Signs and symbols* road signs, flags, mathematical signs, codes, metaphors, symbols, cross, Star of David, crescent.	*Religion in the locality* the local churches – building, communities, leaders.	*Time and space* using *A Wrinkle in Time* to explore ideas of time, travel through space, overcoming evil.
			Growing up looking back and forward, changes, going to secondary school.

Table 8

The Infant Years	1st Year	2nd Year	3rd Year	4th Year
Favourite Things e.g. games, toys, stories, people, colours, sounds, smells, sensations (enjoyed through out senses). *Feelings* e.g. happiness, sadness, excitement, fear, loneliness (explored mainly through movement and other creative activites). *Happy Times* e.g. birthdays, parties of different kinds (an opportunity for children to share their experiences). *Homes and families* ideas of home and family from the experience of some of the children, children's literature or through themes such as 'People who care for me' or 'People who help me', 'Babies'. *Pattern* the turn of the seasons. *Living Things* growing things and animals cared for in the classroom.	*Things that make me feel happy, sad, etc.* e.g. time I will always remember *Celebration* looking at different kinds of celebration – weddings, christenings, festivals, for example. Drawing out ideas, e.g. the giving of gifts, special food and clothes. *The Family of the School* e.g. doing things together, people who contribute to the school community. *Change and Pattern in Nature* e.g. life cycles, frog, butterfly, the patterns of flower petals and snow flakes. *Living Things* small animals, e.g. insects, large animals, e.g. dinosaurs.	*Who am I?* beginning with a simple physiological study, e.g. the senses – looking at what marks an individual, his 'outside' or his 'inside'? *Homes* looking at children's homes and countries of origin where appropriate, what's important there? customs, festivals, the stories that are told. *Night and Day* to be explored creatively, imaginatively, scientifically. *Animals and Plants* looking at animals and plants as a result of or in preparation for visits to the zoo and local botanical gardens.	*Things that make other people feel happy, sad, etc.* explored through literature and the arts. An opportunity to look at the stories behind some religious festivals, e.g. Easter as a time of great happiness for Christians – why? – the origins of the festival. *A local study* patterns of interdependence in the neighbourhood, important places in the neighbourhood (e.g. sacred buildings) and important people (visiting speakers). *Light and Dark* exploring the importance of these ideas especially for religious festivals, e.g. Christmas, Divali, Easter, etc. *A changing world* looking at adaptation to the environment or in the environment, taking examples from the natural world and various cultures, e.g. Eskimos, Vikings, Man's responsibility, pollution, conservation.	*Important People* their motivation and how they have motivated other people – the children's own particular heroes and introducing others including Jesus as others saw him. Who is St Peter? (The name of the local church). Guru Gobind Singh (of great importance to the Sikh children). *Exploring a culture or community outside our own* e.g. Ancient Egyptian. What motivates them? How do they communicate their ideas? behaviour, celebrations, sacred writings, myths, rituals. *Change in the children's lives* looking forward, looking back, change and continuity, making decisions. *Creation* to be explored creatively, imaginatively, scientifically, and mythically.

Moral education

Like religious education, moral education is one of the most important aspects of personal and social development. They have much in common, but one important difference. As Charles Bailey put it in a contribution to *Personal and Social Education in Secondary Schools*: 'It cannot be the aim of a state school in a pluralist society that all its pupils necessarily become religious, but it should be its aim that all its pupils become moral.'

It is necessary therefore to agree what being moral is, and see whether there are stages in becoming moral as there are in becoming a scientist, a musician or a gymnast, and see what schools might do to help children through some of these stages.

The first question is what we mean by a moral person, or what we mean by acting morally. It is not enough just to do things which are themselves right. If a burglar decides not to burgle a house because there happens to be a policeman outside, no one would regard his decision as a moral one. A decision is moral only if the intention behind it is a moral one, and only if the person performing the action is a free agent. If you are thrown from a window, fall on someone else and kill that person you are clearly not responsible for your actions. Concepts like 'telling the truth' and 'keeping a promise' involve more than just a set of words. They involve also ideas of intention, understanding and responsibility. You cannot tell a lie by mistake. It seems therefore that the ideas of intention and responsibility are both bound up in what we mean by a moral action.

To behave morally in the way we have outlined a person needs sympathy, to be able to identify with other people, and insight, to be able to understand other people's feelings as well as his or her own. To be moral a person needs to be able to understand the consequences of his or her actions, and on the basis of this insight and understanding to be rational enough to formulate a set of rules or principles to govern both relations with other people and personal conduct. Above all, of course, a moral person will live up to his or her principles, having both the ability and the will to translate rules and principles into action. A morally mature person seems to be one who is altruistic, rational and morally independent.

This attempt to describe what we mean by being moral may seem rather theoretical and remote from the classroom. But we hope teachers will use these ideas to shape their own thoughts about the long-term aim of moral education.

The next step is to relate this to what we know about children's development. As far as we know children are born without any moral awareness. Their first ideas of morality come from parents, teachers and other people. They become morally independent only over many years, and some may never reach that stage. Most observers and thinkers agree in recognizing about six stages altogether. In the first children behave in the approved way to avoid punishment, and in the second they learn to conform to obtain approval and rewards. These two essentially pre-moral stages lead on to two in which children begin to act independently. They learn to conform first in order to avoid the signs and marks of disapproval, and then to avoid their own feelings of guilt if and when they are censured by other people. Only after that do they reach the stage of understanding and adopting rules and principles of their own free will. First they make contracts with other people, and avoid violating the agreed rights of other people. Then at last they develop their own principles, to which they conform to avoid having to condemn themselves.

These stages of moral development should not cause teachers any great difficulty. They correspond to the stages we recognize in intellectual development. The problem teachers face is relating the ultimate aims of moral education to what they know of children's development, to shape an appropriate programme. In this task teachers need to bear in mind the three dimensions of moral education in schools, the formal curriculum, the informal extramural activities of the school, and its ethos and values, the hidden curriculum of assumptions, rules, procedures and practices. Even within the formal curriculum, as *The Practical Curriculum* said, 'Sometimes the mode or process of learning has its own lessons, more potent than the formal subject-matter of the lesson.' If the aim is to help children to become responsible, rational, independent decision-makers, we have to ask whether it is enough to instruct them in these matters, or whether they need opportunities to practise these skills. As Ken David says in *Personal and Social Education in Secondary Schools*, young people come to know and live under many rules and principles emanating from parents, teachers and others. If, however, the young person is to be involved in these rules and principles from the point of view of moral education, rather than that of convenient social control, then he or she must be involved in them in an educative way. There may be some room for discussion about the age when children should be so involved, but some children will be able to make some responsible, rational and independent decisions when they are quite young.

Even, or perhaps especially, those who have not reached that stage need appropriate models of moral communities. A school's rules, regulations and expectations about behaviour 'must be shown to be part of a rationally justifiable structure, attached to the educational purpose of the school, rather than the arbitrary likes and dislikes of those in authority'. Teachers may find that it is much more effective to help a child to think through some disapproved action and its consequences than to punish it. Toilet training, tidiness and good manners may be necessary if children are to develop the habits and standards which are needed for moral thinking. But long hair, jeans and jewellery may not prevent children from developing moral standards. Every school should examine its rules from time to time to see whether they still meet this test. Children may find it difficult to understand, for example, why infants are free to go straight to their rooms when they arrive at school in the morning, whereas juniors have to wait outside until ten to nine. They may see the point of rules about keeping to the left and walking in the corridors, but be puzzled why only some teachers insist on ruled margins and ruled headings. They may be puzzled about the equity of whole class punishments when they know only a few are responsible.

Schools are small societies, and like all other societies they develop conventional systems of behaviour and reward. It is important for children's confidence in these systems to be consistently maintained. It is important, too, that teachers themselves, quite possibly the children's most respected adult models outside the family, should appear as the mature adults described earlier.

What we have described is a counsel of perfection. We know that teachers need to know where and how to make a start. The ten points which follow may be a useful starting point for thinking about practical methods.

1. The pupil's need for a secure framework in terms of a group identity.
2. His or her need for a personal identity in terms of feeling confident, successful, useful, and wanted, particularly in the case of underprivileged children.
3. The importance of close personal contact with adults.
4. His or her ability to develop moral concepts, and to communicate linguistically.
5. The relevance of rule-governed activities and sticking to agreements.
6. The importance of parent-figures and of a firm and clearly defined authority, which is consistent.
7. The need to channel or institutionalize aggressive feeling.
8. The merits of cooperation and competition.

9.   The need to enable the pupil to objectify his or her own feelings.
10. The importance of getting the pupil to participate, and to make the educational situation 'come alive'.

If the whole staff can accept this as the starting point they may need a brainstorming session to find practical ways of moving ahead. The following questions may help to stimulate discussion about the context in which moral education takes place.

1.   Is the concept of moral education properly understood, and the task undertaken responsibly?
2.   Are the school's ground rules based on the appropriate sort of criteria?
3.   Are the rules and the points of the rules clear to the pupils?
4.   Do the pupils have any means of self-government, or involvement in making decisions?
5.   Are there opportunities for the pupils to let off steam and channel aggression?
6.   Do all the school's criteria of success allow everyone to succeed in something, and win some prestige and self-confidence?

The following questions refer to the content of the curriculum:

1.   How can the teaching in other curriculum areas be designed to increase awareness of other people in the class, and in society?
2.   Is sufficient opportunity made of music and drama to present moral issues in an objective way, and to give the pupils opportunities for imaginative role play? Are music and the arts used in ways which allow children to express and objectify their emotions?
3.   Do the pupils have opportunities of discussing moral questions, and learning to handle them precisely and calmly?
4.   Do the pupils have opportunities to play games, to see the point of rules and procedures, to act out ideas of equality, honesty, duty and justice?
5.   Do the pupils have opportunities of helping younger children, old people, the poor, or animals, so that they feel needed and develop powers of sympathy?
6.   Do they take part in activities like swimming, and school journeys, to see the need for prompt and precise discipline in certain situations?

These questions illustrate the interdependence of moral education and the growth of personal qualities and interpersonal relationships.

Topics for discussion

1. What more can you do to ensure that what you teach and how you teach helps to promote each of the personal qualities your school is aiming at?
2. What more can you do to create opportunities for each of your pupils to have practice in different kinds of relationship, and in particular of different roles within a cooperative group?
3. Compare the statement of principle about religious education on pages 192 and 193 with the principles on which your own school's work is based. Does your practice satisfactorily reflect the principles?

Suggestions for further reading

1. Department of Education and Science (Assessment of Performance Unit) *Personal and Social Development*. London: HMSO. See especially Figure 3.1 (page 7) which purports to provide a 'map of the territory' of personal and social development for teachers' use.
2. Lowenfeld, V. and Brittain, W.I. (1982) *Creative and Mental Growth*. New York: Macmillan.
3. Pring, R. (1984) *Personal and Social Education in the Curriculum*. London: Hodder and Stoughton.

READING SIXTEEN ● The place of mathematics in primary schools: planning the mathematics programme
Department of Education and Science

The place of mathematics in primary schools

Mathematics, at least in the form of arithmetic, has had an important place in the education of young children since well before the Education Act of 1870. The obvious reason for this is that numbers are a part of everyday life and adults find it useful to calculate at work, while shopping and when

DES *HMI Series Matters for Discussion 9: Mathematics 5–11 A Handbook of Suggestions*.
'The place of mathematics in Primary Schools', 1979, pp 3–6, Appendix 1, pp 77–79
and
'Planning the mathematics programme' pp 7–11.
Reproduced by permission of the Controller of HMSO.

engaged in sports and pastimes. Nearly all primary school children are capable of learning what is necessary for most of these purposes.

For many years, speed and accuracy in working out sums on paper helped some people to obtain clerical jobs that were more secure and physically less arduous than many others. Today, with a widespread use of mechanical and electronic aids, speed is governed by the machine operator, but it is all the more important in offices and factories to know whether the answer arrived at is reasonable, or whether it has been distorted by a slip on the part of the operator or a fault in the device used. Consequently, there is a special need for understanding of the processes used, and for the ability to estimate what might reasonably be expected as an answer. Both can be improved by working at written calculations in which the method is displayed. Moreover, it would be foolish to rely completely on mechanical or electronic devices. Facility with mental arithmetic is as important as ever.

Children should also be able to weigh and measure with a degree of accuracy appropriate to the task in hand, and given suitable opportunities the majority of primary school children can learn to do so.

In recent years it has become more important to understand the various ways in which mathematical information is presented. Graphs of various kinds and statistical tables are commonplace in the newspapers and on television. They are often introduced into primary schools now and quite young children can both get pleasure and acquire insight, if the work is suitable and its implications are sufficiently probed by the teacher.

The learning of the necessary skills in mathematics is certainly part of the basic course in primary schools. Not all the children who might acquire them do so and, as later chapters of this booklet suggest, care has to be taken in pacing the work and in providing the right preparation and range of activities for it.

But there is a good deal more that mathematics can do for children if the teacher is sufficiently knowledgeable to be confident in the subject. Clearly, it is not essential that every man in the street should know that the ratio between the circumference and diameter of a circle is about three and one-seventh and is represented by the Greek letter π. Most people manage to get through life reasonably well without realizing that the shell of a nautilus, the florets in the head of a daisy and a spider's web are all arranged, nearly enough, in the form of equiangular spirals. Still more often, they get by without knowing that the number of left turning spirals is different from the number of right turning spirals in the head of a daisy, and, what is more, that the two numbers appear side by side in an interesting mathematical sequence named after the greatest of medieval mathematicians, Leonardo of Pisa (nicknamed Fibonacci). People who have been made aware of these curious but orderly aspects of nature may gain more pleasure in life as a result. There is a whole range of relationships and patterns of a mathematical kind that can catch children's imagination and, though they are not essential, it is a pity if some of them are not included. They cannot however be allowed to oust the essential, and there is no sense in introducing them if the teacher feels uncertain of the material, or under strain. Certainly there should be some way of providing such aspects of mathematics for children who have a flair for them — not always those children who are quick and accurate when doing sums.

In the course of learning mathematics children have to learn a good many other things. For example, they have to learn to be neat and tidy, for muddled working may produce a wrong answer. They need to learn to be careful and they ought to learn to be discriminating. They should learn to check what they have done; they should also learn that understanding and knowing how to do something is as important as getting the right answer.

The purpose of teaching mathematics

The need for schools, both primary and secondary, to provide their pupils with a good foundation of mathematics has been argued on three main grounds. Mathematics is useful, mathematics is part of our culture, and mathematics trains the mind. There are many other arguments but they nearly always reduce to variations of these three; and the three interrelate with one another.

The utilitarian argument can be presented in both narrow and broad versions. At one extreme each person needs to know enough arithmetic to make simple purchases, count change, check wages and understand a popular newspaper, but it can be fairly claimed that he has no basic need for very much else. The broad utilitarian case goes much beyond this. It can be argued that mathematics is of fundamental importance for the understanding of the physical sciences and technology, that it is increasingly employed in the social sciences, business management and social administration, and that the person with a knowledge of mathematics has the key to many other areas of knowledge as well.

The arguments for mathematics as a cultural subject can also be presented in a variety of forms. Different people may define *culture* in different and unnecessarily divisive ways; our problem is not so much to define utility or culture, but to establish common objectives towards which teachers with differing outlooks can work. If a sufficiently broad view is taken of utility on the one hand and culture on the other, then these two arguments for teaching mathematics reinforce each other. We teach mathematics in order to help people to understand things better — perhaps to understand the jobs on which they might later be employed, or to understand the creative achievements of the human mind or the behaviour of the natural world. It is the particular power of mathematics that its central ideas help us to do all of these things.

The third argument, that mathematics is a training of the mind (quite apart from any use of the actual material studied), has some validity, but it is open to abuse. Mathematics can provide a valuable mental training, but many other things can do this just as well; and mathematics cannot be justified on this ground alone if it deteriorates into stereotyped working to rule, with the higher functions of the mind neglected. Mathematics can be justified as a training for the mind, but the training also needs to serve other purposes which can be understood by the pupil at the time. There is something wrong with the teaching if the reply to 'Why are we learning this?' has to be 'You will understand later on!'

The mathematical aims

Aims are essentially declarations of intent that give direction and shape to a scheme of work or teaching programme. Although they may lack detail or precision, they should remain in the forefront of the teacher's mind at all times when he or she is considering the provision of experiences which lead to the mathematical development of the child. The formulating of *aims* and then of *objectives* is necessary before attempting to draw up a scheme of work.

Listed below are some of the *aims* within the primary school from which *objectives* will later be derived. It is not an exhaustive list and the order is to some extent arbitrary. It will however allow the teacher to consider their relative importance and to encourage discussion with colleagues who share in the planning of the work throughout the school.

The general *aims* should be to develop:

    i. a positive attitude to mathematics as an interesting and attractive subject;

ii. an appreciation of the creative aspects of the subject and an aware-ness of its aesthetic appeal;

iii. an ability to think clearly and logically in mathematics with confi-dence, independence of thought and flexibility of mind;

iv. an understanding of mathematics through a process of enquiry and experiment;

v. an appreciation of the nature of numbers and of space, leading to an awareness of the basic structure of mathematics;

vi. an appreciation of mathematical pattern and the ability to identify relationships;

vii. mathematical skills and knowledge accompanied by the quick recall of basic facts;

viii. an awareness of the uses of mathematics in the world beyond the classroom. Children should learn that mathematics will frequently help them to solve problems they meet in everyday life or under-stand better many of the things they see, and provide opportunities for them to satisfy their curiosity and to use their creative abilities;

ix. persistence through sustained work in mathematics which requires some perseverance over a period of time.

Finally, there is the overriding aim to maintain and increase confidence in mathematics, shown by the ability to express ideas fluently, to talk about the subject with assurance and to use the language of mathematics.

The objectives

Having decided on the general *aims*, teachers also look for ways of achieving them, and for classroom practices which accord with these aims. It is therefore essential that aims should be converted into more detailed de-scriptions of performance which teachers can accept as evidence of learning and as 'milestones' along the path of progression and development. These can be regarded as *objectives*. In forming objectives, we are categorizing evidence of learning in terms of performance and achievement, i.e. think-ing, remembering and understanding. The objectives of a programme can usually be set out precisely and clearly in terms of what the children are intended to learn.

Listed in Appendix I are the *concepts* and *skills* which children are normally expected to acquire before leaving the primary school.

It must be recognized that the objectives listed in the appendix will never be achieved within the primary school by some children, particularly those with special educational difficulties. On the other hand these 'milestones' should have been reached by the age of 11 years, by perhaps 75 per cent of children, and surpassed by some.

In view of the present diversity of practices and aims, and the current criticisms of the standards being achieved, it would have been very attractive to seek improvement by establishing a central core or agreed minimal goals. But a discussion of standards and quality implies pre-established criteria; at the present time primary teachers are not all agreed on common aims and objectives in mathematics. Some stress factual knowledge to the exclusion of other objectives; others emphasize the importance of processes and understanding, and the enjoyment of mathematics. The formulation of minimum requirements could be a helpful step but, unless the formulation is accompanied by continuing attempts by teachers to develop their professional judgement, minimum standards could too easily become an accepted norm. Any statement of minimal goals needs to be accompanied by some non-prescriptive indication of the broader range of work which might be appropriate for most children.

Appendix I

Objectives
These should be considered to be the main objectives for the majority of children at the age of 11 years:
  i. The development of appropriate language; qualitative description, the recognition of objects from description; discriminating, classifying and sorting of objects; identifying objects and describing them unambiguously;
 ii. The recognition of common, simple mathematical relationships, both numerical and spatial; reasoning and logical deduction in connection with everyday things, geometrical shapes, number arrangements in order etc;
iii. The ability to describe quantitatively: the use of number in counting, describing, estimating and approximating;
 iv. The understanding of whole numbers and their relationships with one another;
  v. The appreciation of place value, the number system and number notation, including whole numbers, decimal fractions and vulgar

fractions. The ability to recognize simple number patterns (odds and evens, multiples, divisors, squares etc);

vi. The appreciation of the measures in common use. Sensible estimation using the appropriate units. The ability to measure length, weight, volume and capacity, area, time, angle and temperature, to an everyday level of accuracy;

vii. The understanding of money, contributing to a sense of the value of money, and the ability to carry out simple purchases;

viii. The ability to carry out practical activities involving the ideas of addition, subtraction, multiplication and division;

ix. The ability to perform simple calculations involving the mathematical processes indicated by the signs $+$, $-$, $\times$, $\div$ with whole numbers (maintaining rapid recall of the sums, differences and products of pairs of numbers from 0 to 10);

x. The ability to carry out with confidence and accuracy simple examples in the four operations of number, including two places of decimals as for pounds and pence and the measures as used;

xi. The ability to approximate and to check whether the result of a calculation is reasonable;

xii. A sound understanding of place value applied to the decimal notation for numbers. The ability to carry out the addition and subtraction of numbers with up to two decimal places and the multiplication and division of such numbers by whole numbers up to and including 9;

xiii. The multiplication and division of numbers with up to two decimal places by 10 and 100;

xiv. An appreciation of the connections between fractions, decimal fractions and the most common percentages;

xv. The ability to use fractions in the sequence $1/2$, $1/4$, $1/8$, $1/16$, or $1/3$, $1/6$, $1/12$, or $1/5$, $1/10$, including the idea of equivalence in the discussion of everyday experiences;

xvi. An appreciation of the broader aspects of number, such as bases other than ten and easy tests of divisibility;

xvii. The ability to use and interpret the following: diagrams; drawings; tables; simple networks; maps, scale drawings; diagrammatic, pictorial and graphical representation, statistical charts and three-dimensional representation;

xviii. An appreciation of two- and three-dimensional shapes and their relationships with one another. The ability to recognize simple properties; to handle, create, discuss and describe them with confidence and appreciate spatial relationships, symmetry and similarity;

xix. An ability to read with understanding mathematics from books, and to use appropriate reference skills;

xx. An ability to write clearly, to record mathematics in statements, neatly and systematically.

Extension of concepts and skills

Further skills and concepts which experienced teachers with the appropriate knowledge might consider appropriate for some children include:

i. calculations involving the four operations using numbers with up to two decimal places, and the addition and subtraction of vulgar fractions;

ii. further measures, including speed, force, pressure and density;

iii. simple ideas of probability;

iv. a simple approach to topological notions (ideas of connectedness, as explained in a number of mathematical topic books for children);

v. an extended appreciation of broader aspects of number such as modular arithmetic, index notation and standard form, number sequences, number games and puzzles;

vi. symbols of algebra for stating logical patterns, following abstraction and generalization in arithmetic.

In developing any skills and concepts, it is important for teachers to appreciate that *there is no value in techniques which outstrip a working understanding and sense of purpose*, e.g. if division of fractions is to be introduced, it needs to be a gradual development through examples where the result is 'obvious'. A standard procedure may be employed later, when the child can appreciate that it is correct. It is also an advantage if the child has opportunities to make use of this newly acquired skill through realistic applications.

Planning the mathematics programme

Introduction

The primary teacher today is faced with a considerable task, brought about by the changes which have taken place in the teaching of mathematics. These have involved new content, new terms, new concepts and what many regard as a new approach to the teaching of the subject (although this approach has a very long history).

Today, the child is encouraged to make enquiries, investigate, discover and record; learning is not looked upon only as something imposed from without. It is recognized that it is through his own activity that the child is able to form the new concepts which will in turn be the basis of further mathematical ideas and thinking. These early experiences provide the foundation on which future learning is built.

The school which concentrates single-mindedly upon arithmetical skill alone is neglecting the whole range of important logical, geometrical, graphical and statistical ideas which children can meet before the age of 12. The school which stresses 'modern' topics and practical work for its own sake at the expense of consolidating number skills, systematic thought and learning, is equally guilty of neglecting its charges. The challenge is to encourage children to develop their mathematical education along a broad front of experience while ensuring systematic progression and continuity.

The primary teacher, confronted with the task of providing a wide experience for her children, can be bewildered by the wealth of apparatus, material and equipment which are now available. *She must be capable of informed choice, bearing in mind the needs of her individual class within the school.* Planning is vital; and it cannot be achieved by teachers in isolation. Infant and junior teachers need to plan together within the school and between schools.

Although most schools have a scheme of work for mathematics, in many schools this needs to be revised; what is perhaps a greater problem is that large numbers of teachers experience difficulty in translating the scheme into an effective mathematics programme.

Within some primary schools today, teachers are endeavouring to work for some of the time in such a way that subject barriers are not emphasized. Many 'integrated' studies, resulting from this way of working, lend themselves admirably to the introduction of mathematics. This mode of working requires understanding of the mathematical potential of a wide variety of situations, and this in turn demands more mathematical knowledge than many teachers possess. As a result, the opportunities for developing mathematics from an integrated topic are too often under-developed. The thematic approach is unlikely to motivate all the mathematics which most children need to cover within the age range 5–11 years; it is necessary to provide adequate time for mathematics, to cover a scheme of work systematically, and to include sufficient regular revision of those skills which have been identified as necessary for further progress.

Organization

The school or classroom organization can be critical in determining the effectiveness of mathematical learning. Any decision on organization needs to take into account the aims and objectives decided by the school or by teachers themselves.

It is essential for the teacher to intervene appropriately and give support and help, not only in the later stages of mathematical learning but also in structured 'play'; otherwise these activities are not fully utilized and can easily become meaningless and result in time wasting and a lack of progression. An activity which does not have the teacher's attention can seem to be less important to the children. In addition, if the only work which draws the teacher's attention is that written in a book, it is quite natural that children should desire to work in this way, however inappropriate it may be, in order to attract the teacher's approval. There are occasions, particularly with the younger children, when the teacher needs to recognize that participating with the children in the activities she arranges might sometimes be the best use of mathematical time.

When the activities of a class are well organized children are able to work with much less direct supervision and teacher support. This allows the teacher to work with smaller groups and individuals within groups. Class organization which allows children the opportunity to exercise an informed choice need not override the wish of the teacher to withdraw a group of children in order to teach them. Indeed, professional time can easily be wasted if on one day a teacher finds that she needs to introduce or teach the same skill eight times with eight individuals separately. In general, it is the extremes in classroom organization which militate most acutely against the effective learning of the subject.

Forms of organization which require children and their teacher to change their activity after a set period of time inhibit sustained work in mathematics. This is particularly true if the child has been working constructively with material or apparatus and needs an extension of time to complete his task before the equipment is packed away or used again for something else. A child will often work with deep concentration and effort on a task which has interested him, and to ask him to move off quickly on to some other area of experience can be unwise. If it is decided to impose timetabling restrictions these should be interpreted flexibly, bearing in mind the needs of the individual child. Over-fragmentation of the child's day should be avoided.

A further cause for concern is the quality of mathematical education which is available to those children who are able in the subject. Too often, schools present an insufficient challenge to the more able or highly gifted. In primary schools the problem is as important as at the secondary stage.

The efficacy of an organization for mathematics can be judged by the following criteria.

Does the organization provide opportunities for:

i. direct teaching of individuals, groups of various sizes and the whole class,

ii. practical work with appropriate material in a range of situations,

iii. children to use mathematics across the curriculum and to see the relevance of mathematics in the different areas of study which mathematics pervades,

iv. discussion and consolidation of mathematical ideas with individuals, groups and the class,

v. project work or studies,

vi. effective remedial work for a variety of ability levels,

vii. extended experiences for the more able pupils,

viii. children to reflect on their experience and the kind of thinking they are engaged in, so that they are aware that the activities in which they are involved are mathematical,

ix. children to learn relevant work skills;
    recording and clear presentation, including an understanding of why this is important,
    the use of reference books,
    the use of measuring instruments.

Assessment

If teaching is to be successful, it is essential that the teacher should assess what is happening. *Assessment, evaluation, diagnosis* and *prescription* are all important and should feature in the planning of work in a school, in a particular class or for groups or individuals. These forms of assessment are essential if children are to learn mathematics effectively and to make progress that is in accord with their ages and abilities.

Responsibilities at various levels Responsibility for assessment operates at different levels — national, local authority, school and teacher.

There was not, until recently, a standardized system for judging the attainment of pupils on a national level. The Department of Education and Science (DES) set up an Assessment of Performance Unit (APU) in 1976 to provide for this. Mathematical attainment began to be monitored in 1978 by the National Foundation for Educational Research on behalf of the APU.

Local education authorities (LEAs) have discretion with regard to their own procedures for monitoring attainment and many authorities are taking steps to establish systems of their own. In the future, it is possible that many will use material related to the national system of monitoring as these assessment procedures become available. LEAs have freedom to employ their own methods and this provides opportunity for various systems to be tried and for practice to develop. Nevertheless, there could be disadvantages if the schemes they adopt are too widely disparate.

Assessment in the school Schools and individual teachers have problems at other levels, and it is with these that this booklet is mainly concerned.

As a first step, the school should decide the purpose of its assessment procedures. The aim may be to grade children in order to assist transition to the next stage of education, and in this case there is little choice. A uniform scheme devised by the LEA would seem almost essential. Where the school has discretion, assessment may be part of a philosophy which embodies a belief in the stimulus of competition, or its purpose may primarily be diagnostic (seeking to reveal the learning problems of individual children), or it may be part of a more general strategy seeking to modify the future teaching planned for a group of children in the light of the collective progress made. All of these objectives imply different types of tests and appropriate record-keeping procedures.

It is necessary to evaluate what both individuals and groups are learning; the results may or may not reflect what the teacher believes she has taught. These procedures demand great courage and professionalism. A teacher should not feel a failure if, on occasion, what has been taught has not been learnt, providing that assessment is continually being carried out. Following the evaluation of the work done by pupils, it may be necessary for the teacher to diagnose the difficulties of a group of children or of a single child within a group. When a difficulty has been identified a prescription which gives specific help should follow, if success is to be achieved.

It is all too easy to restrict assessment to those aspects of mathematics teaching which are most easily tested. Efforts should be made to broaden assessment procedures to include as many as possible of the initially planned objectives of the course.

It is essential to know the ability of the child to apply skill and knowledge to problems associated with the world in which he lives. The teacher needs to know the child's attitudes towards mathematics, his perseverance, creativity (elaboration, fluency, flexibility and originality), his understanding, visualization and psychomotor skills. At the present time, skills which are described as mathematical are applied across the curriculum. It is necessary to assess this — to assess the ability to generalize, to classify and to identify and select the essentials which determine the solution of a practical problem.

Formal examinations, based on syllabus content, frequently limit the teaching of mathematics to that which is to be tested. Objective tests, although they give a wide coverage and facilitate rapid marking, seldom reflect good methods of teaching or satisfactory levels of learning. In addition, the existing tests in no way assess mathematical creativity.

Oral questioning is an important method of checking, particularly for some areas of the curriculum and for some pupils. Certain aspects of the work can be reliably tested particularly well in this way (for example, rapid recall of number facts). For other work, judgement based on this type of testing, unless very carefully prepared, can be unreliable. Oral questioning is usually very time consuming.

There are certain long established standardized tests. The use of a well validated test will not of itself be helpful unless the teacher takes the trouble to learn the purpose of the test, studies the appropriate method of administration, and appreciates the limitations. Some teachers prefer to plan their own assessment tests, believing that such tests can be more closely related to the teaching objectives. Where this is the practice, an attempt should be made to learn something of the expertise laboriously acquired by professional testers over many years, and to apply it appropriately.

It is also necessary for schools and for teachers to evaluate the teaching methods and materials they use. This involves the careful scrutiny of materials, schemes of work, textbooks, work-cards, equipment and apparatus, to see if they are providing what is required.

Assessment might be regarded as a procedure which challenges the teacher to define aims and objectives more clearly, and subsequently leads to more effective teaching and learning. It allows the teacher to check if the aims have been achieved and the objectives reached. Most learning experiences need to be planned, and it is at the planning stage that the fullest assessment (evaluation, diagnosis and prescription) is important if the experiences are going to meet the real needs of the children. For this there are no standardized tests, and the teachers involved must rely on their professional judgement. This judgement can often be sharpened by collaborative work within the school or at a teachers' centre.

Finally, no methods of assessment are sacrosanct. From time to time, the methods themselves require reappraisal in order to decide whether or not the purposes they are intended to serve are being achieved.

Teacher development

As headteachers, advisers and organizers of in-service training know, a problem almost as large as that of the initial training of teachers is that of helping teachers already in post to acquire the necessary knowledge and skills. In spite of the great efforts which have been made over recent years, it is still the case that too many teachers have to teach mathematics without knowing enough about the subject, or about current ideas of teaching it. Additional provision of in-service training is only part of the larger problem of enhancing the quality of the teacher's professional life. Teaching innovations fail unless the teachers are fully conversant with, and convinced by, the reasons underlying the innovation. In-service training must be directed above all to the development of the teacher's own capacity to make judgements.

The primary teacher today needs all possible help, support and encouragement in teaching mathematics to those for whom she has responsibility. Whereas, for some subjects, teaching groups within which there is a wide range of ability give rise to few difficulties, in some aspects of mathematics they can present major problems for all but those who have substantial mathematical background and are both experienced and skilful teachers.

Individual and group work is essential and there is a need to provide and supervise a range of different tasks each lesson and to keep adequate progress records for each child. These demands make the problem of classroom organization difficult and support is often needed by those teachers who are insecure or less experienced in the subject. Some success is being achieved in schools which have one teacher on the staff with special knowledge of and interest in mathematics, who has some responsibility to undertake the in-service education of the other members of staff. Support at this level is vital if the primary teacher is to gain the knowledge and confidence she needs to carry out her task.

In schools where the mathematics programme is of some quality, the head supports his colleagues and gives them a positive lead in what is for many a difficult area of the curriculum. *It is essential that there is a coherent and systematic policy for mathematics throughout the school.* The head also needs to ensure that the appropriate resources are as far as possible made available within the school to serve the teachers' needs. Where a teacher has been given special responsibility for mathematics, it is necessary to provide appropriate opportunities for her to work in a way which makes it possible to carry out her responsibilities — once these have been defined — in giving support and help in the classroom to her colleagues and in arranging that meetings of staff are planned and occur regularly.

Topics for discussion

1. The publication from which these readings have been selected attempts to 'distinguish between those parts of mathematics which are required by all — or virtually all — children in primary schools, and those that can usefully be tackled by children who show a flair for the work with the help of teachers confident and knowledgeable in the subject' (DES HMI Series: *Matters for Discussion: Mathematics 5–11 A Handbook of Suggestions*, p. 75). Is this distinction on the right lines or would another be more appropriate? Discuss.
2. Discuss the importance of 'assessment', 'evaluation', 'diagnosis' and 'prescription' in the planning of work in a school if children are to learn mathematics effectively.
3. What organizational and teaching strategies might be used to ensure that there is a coherent and systematic policy for mathematics throughout the school?

Suggestions for further reading

1. Dickson, L., Brown, M. and Gibson, O. (1984) *Children Learning Mathematics: A Teacher's Guide to Recent Research*. Eastbourne: Rinehart and Winston.
2. Shuard, H. and Rothney, A. (1984) *Children Reading Mathematics*. London: John Murray.
3. Choat, E. (1978) *Children's Acquisition of Mathematics*. Slough: NFER.

READING SEVENTEEN • How can children's progress in science be monitored, recorded and evaluated?   *B. Davis*

Introduction

Within primary science teaching, the area most neglected by schools and individual teachers is the monitoring, recording and evaluating of children's work. First of all let me define these terms as I see them.

Monitoring is looking at the activities offered to children and the attitudes, skills and concepts which are being formed so that a *record* can be made of progress and development. From this, *evaluation* of the children and teaching can take place.

1 Why check up?

A survey started in 1976 (Clift et al. 1981) found that very few primary schools kept records of progress in science. In visiting a considerable number of schools recently, I also found there were very few records of pupil progress in science. With the increasing demands made upon a teacher's time, perhaps this is understandable. However, it shows that many teachers are not clear about why they should give time to science. This chapter attempts to provide some ideas about what to look for, and ways of carrying out these checks.

B. Davis, 'How can children's progress in science be monitored, recorded and evaluated?', in, C. Richards and D. Holford (eds) *The Teaching of Primary Science: Policy and Practice*, London: Falmer Press. 1983. pp 71–81.

Monitoring can be carried out for the following reasons:

   (i) to assess the extent to which a balanced programme of science activities is provided;

  (ii) to assist in the planning of future work, revision and reinforcement;

 (iii) to try to determine the level of development of each child in the class;

 (iv) to match the work to the pupils' level of development.

After checking up, teachers should have a clearer picture of the scientific experiences which they are offering within the class, and this should help to formulate aims and objectives in the teaching of science (referred to later). Checks can also avoid situations such as the one I came across recently. A newly appointed teacher had carefully planned a topic on food, only to find out too late that the children had worked with this topic in the previous term. No record of this had been available to her and the time and energy spent in preparation were wasted.

2 Finding out what children are doing

The easiest way of monitoring what children are doing is by observation. The Progress in Learning Project (Harlen et al. 1977) picks out the following five aspects which can make a teacher aware of children's thinking.

   (i) *Dialogue*, when we and children freely exchange views, ideas, feel able to ask and answer questions, and listen to each other;

  (ii) *Questioning*, when we ask 'open questions' to find out what children are thinking and feeling, questions which do not need a particular response such as, 'Why do you think these leaves have gone brown'?;

 (iii) *Listening*, when we let children do most of the talking and do not break in with such comments as 'do you mean?';

 (iv) *Watching actions and working processes*, when we observe children's behaviour and work patterns, for example, cooperation with others, responsibility and perseverance;

  (v) *Looking at children's work*, when we look at all the aspects of each child's communication, for example, art, writing and number work, we can get an indication of the difficulties experienced and the child's way of working.

As this information is gathered a teacher builds up an overall picture of each child. However, we must be aware of two dangers. The first is that our observations cannot be completely objective. Secondly, inferences can only be of value when made from observations over a time. Factors such as motivation, the behaviour of other children in the group and physical fitness, could radically alter our perception of each child on a particular day.

3 Recording

Observation does not necessarily lead to recording, but there are several reasons why we should keep records:

   (i) one cannot assume that progress is being made by the children;
  (ii) we must not become complacent and assume we are offering the right experiences;
 (iii) carrying information in one's head may leave the teacher confused about children's development and progress;
 (iv) records properly kept and passed on will save the teacher of the next class or school from starting afresh.

However, there is no point in record-keeping for its own sake. Records must be used to be of value. I shall return to methods of recording later.

4 Evaluation

Having observed and recorded children's work, we then need to make judgements about the science programme, the children's progress and our own teaching. Before these judgements can be made, schools and teachers will need to consider why time should be given to science, and which experiences children should be given. The process of evaluation can only be attempted when a basis of aims and objectives has been established either by the school or the individual teacher. One book of the 'Science 5–13 Series' (Ennever and Harlen 1972) looks at objectives, and there is further help at the end of each unit of the series.

What are we looking for?

It is now recognized that science education is concerned with a way of thinking and not primarily with the transmission of facts. The scientist is concerned with seeking information and making judgements, in order to arrive at a closer approximation to the truth.

In primary school we attempt to make progress towards a scientific way of thinking by involving children at increasingly greater depth. We try to get them to investigate in the following sequence:

   (i) making observations;
  (ii) recording these;
 (iii) making generalizations on the basis of (i) and (ii);
 (iv) designing investigations (experiments) to test these generalizations;
  (v) recording new observations;
 (vi) drawing conclusions.

This is generally called the *process* approach which can also be applied to investigations in other areas of the curriculum as well as science. 'Investigations' in this chapter is another word for 'experiments'. It does not mean, for example, looking up facts in a book. Scientific investigations are distinguished from all else by the need to set up experiments.

The level at which each child will be able to perform the sequence above will depend on the stage of development. In the infant school, children will start with observing and recording, moving on to investigations as they develop these skills. So much of the work we do in primary schools is based on observing and drawing conclusions that it is important that the children have the opportunity to develop this process approach in all areas of the curriculum, for investigations are just as likely to arise in maths, history or art as in a more scientific topic.

1 Guidelines

Many teachers lacking the confidence to include science in their classroom activities need some sort of guidance to give them a much greater sense of security and purpose. Being told to 'incorporate science in the curriculum' because 'not enough is being done' does not help to get science started. Guidance in the form of guidelines should state the school's interpretation of primary science, the reasons for teaching it, the experiences considered suitable for the children and how science is organized and evaluated. It will require considerable time and discussion for a whole staff to develop these. 'Science 5–13 Series' and the ASE primary publications (1974, 1976) give particular help with this.

It is generally agreed that the aims of primary science can be divided into three sections: the development of (i) attitudes; (ii) skills; (iii) concepts and knowledge.

Let us look more closely at these three groups of aims.

2 Attitudes and skills

Which attitudes and skills are developed during *science* activities? If we wrote down our own lists I have no doubt that they would be similar to those produced by teachers in the Schools Council Progress in Learning Project. For younger children these attitudes were:

curiosity, originality, perseverance, open-mindedness, self-criticism, responsibility, willingness to cooperate, independence;

and the skills of:

observing, raising questions, exploring, problem-solving, finding patterns in observations, communicating verbally and non-verbally, applying learning and classifying.

As children grow older and become more experienced 'raising questions' and 'exploring' might become 'proposing enquiries, experimenting and investigating'. Developing 'critical reasoning' might also be added to this list.

3 General and specific skills

The skills which are developed through scientific investigations are both general and specific. The general skills are common to other areas of the curriculum; these are the skills such as observation, recording and communicating. The specific skills are more wholly science-based, such as the use of controls and identifying variables.

Children must first have the opportunity to develop general skills such as observation and exploring, for without these skills they cannot develop the more specific ones. As children build up these general skills we can start to put them into situations where they are required to develop the more specific skills. This development will come from asking children the right questions, such as, 'Is it a fair test?', and from encouraging them to set up experiments. In the later years of the primary school the specific skills must not completely replace the general skills for both will need to be developed together.

A recent list of skills based on the process approach has been developed (APU 1981). This is more clearly defined and more specifically science-orientated than the previous one. The skills are divided into six categories:

   (i) *Using symbolic representation:* children's ability to record and interpret information using graphs, tables and charts;
  (ii) *Using apparatus and measuring instruments:* children's ability to handle simple measuring and science equipment, such as a ruler, tape measure, hand lens, thermometer, etc.;
 (iii) *Using observations:* the selection and recording of observations, looking at similarities and differences using keys and interpreting observations;
 (iv) *Interpretation and application:* seeing patterns and relationships in data, identifying assumptions and applying science concepts;
  (v) *Designing investigations:* children's planning and investigations, recognizing variables and controlling them and being critical of their own proposals;
 (vi) *Performing and investigating:* performing an investigation, planning, measuring and observing.

This list contains both general and specific skills and was produced by the Assessment of Performance Unit (APU) of the Department of Education and Science to monitor nationally a sample of children aged 11, 13, and 15.

It is not possible to test our pupils' performance using the APU tests, nor would this be useful. If teachers had the test questions available so that children could be monitored there would be a danger of teaching skills just to achieve a good result in the test. However, these categories can be used to help identify the experiences which we should provide for our children.

At the upper junior age the APU categories are more appropriate than the earlier list of skills, since they help to direct attention towards specifically science-based skills. Since becoming involved in trials of APU tests, I have noticed that children are less successful at the science-based skills, not because they are beyond their capabilities but because we teachers are not so aware of them.

The first APU report for 11-year-olds (APU 1981) indicates that children are developing general skills but not those which are more specifically science-based. Harlen (1981) has noted that the better performance in general skills is probably attributable to the effectiveness of an active approach to teaching and learning in general in our primary schools.

To improve primary science we must focus more attention on the skills which are science-based. The most important are: recognition of patterns in observation; explanation of events using science-based concepts; use of controls in investigations; identifying variables; making predictions; checking results and planning experiments.

Recently two children in my class investigating how fruits lost weight as the water content evaporated, observed and accurately measured the change in weight. They came to conclusions consistent with what they had observed, but the results were not valid because they had not controlled the temperature of the fruits by putting them all in the same place. In discussion with me the children became aware of the mistakes they had made. They were able to use the general skills of measuring and observing, but needed more experience in the use of controls.

We need to monitor and evaluate our teaching to see if we are giving opportunities to develop the more complex skills. Children do not need a deep knowledge of science facts but they do require some understanding of the scientific process. The experience of good teachers of primary science indicates that quite young children are capable of following this process through, providing that the context is concrete, fairly simple, and related to topic and interest areas. Attention must still be paid to general attitudes and skills, as well as specific ones, throughout the later primary years. Both will need to be related to the level of each child's development.

4 Concepts

Science knowledge and facts cannot be ignored, although in the process approach they will be secondary to the development of attitudes and skills. Each teacher or school will need to consider which concepts the children might need to grasp. The list might include: volume; length; area; cause and effect; life-cycles/circuits; time; speed; energy; force.

The APU report shows that by 11 children are well able to apply concepts about the properties of living things and the environment to new situations, but find difficulty in explaining the reason behind a particular application. Is this because it is beyond the power of the age group to do so, or because we are not offering children the right quality of experience and prompting them to set up experiments?

5 Areas of study: topic or specific content?

The choice between a topic approach or a syllabus of specific content is one of the problem areas of primary science (. . .) My own view should already be clear. I favour the development of attitudes and skills through topic work. However, some teachers still prefer a syllabus approach for the following reasons:

(i)   they feel more secure with content lists and a supporting text;
(ii) set content allows skills and attitudes to develop in a proved and tested framework;
(iii) set content allows the teacher to develop a balanced programme of science activities;
(iv) children need to be taught content from which scientific knowledge can be gained as an early foundation which can be built upon;
(v)   children must be given a body of knowledge early in their school life as there may not be enough time or opportunity to do this at secondary schools;
(vi) adults are the best judges of the experiences and knowledge a child will require.

Those in favour of the topic approach think that a syllabus tends to:

(i)   discourage children from following their own interests and designing their own investigations;
(ii) give less opportunity for individual interest;
(iii) make it virtually impossible to provide a variety of experiences at the right level which are required by different children in a group; a child unable to understand becomes bored;
(iv) increase pressure upon a child to conform and avoid questioning what is taught. The topic approach allows the child more opportunity to find out and question;
(v)   relate less easily to other areas of the curriculum

There is, however, a need for a compromise. Teachers, particularly those who are uncertain about science, need some guidance on the choice of activities for children, and the scientific investigations which can be extracted from different topics. One way of combining content and topic areas is to list those areas of scientific investigation which children might experience in different topics during their primary school years. One such list might be the following.

The environment (weather, water, soil/rocks, air, planets/sun/stars, conservation)
Materials (wood, plastic, metal, food, building, structures)
Moving things (flight, transport, friction, machines, floating and sinking, etc.)
Magnetism and electricity

Light and colour
Heat and energy
Ourselves

Animals and plants
Sound and music

How do we go about it?

1 Recording areas of work

In schools using a thematic or topic approach it is necessary to record the lines of investigation taking place. A central record, either in the head-teacher's office or the staffroom, would help to ensure that this was so, and that children were not merely retracing their steps if the same topic were used twice. This record would allow the headteacher to rectify omissions, coordinate themes in progress and maintain a balance of science with topics in other areas. In some schools records might be kept as a termly forecast but this does not account for children focusing on other aspects of a subject, or teachers overestimating what they can cover. This may mean amendments at the end of a topic or term. It would, therefore, be better to record areas investigated at the end of a period by means of a flow diagram or a statement of general areas covered in each subject in relation to the topic as in the following example.

Topic	Canals
Maths	Volume, capacity, scale plans, measurement
Science	Floating/sinking, loading boats, properties of water, bridge/tunnel structures, porosity of materials — clay, sand, soil, rock, water plants and animals

Environmental	Development of canals, costume, horses and horse-drawn barges, canal and boat equipment, canal architecture, maps, mapwork local and national
Language	Factual and story work, discussions, play about a barge family
Visits	Stoke Bruerne Canal Museum, Edstone aqueduct, Oxford canal — lock, canal basin, cantilever bridge

At the same time each teacher should keep a record of what activities each child or group of children has experienced. One way of doing this would be to list and letter-code all the activities which the class has undertaken, and then on another sheet of paper list those activities each child has followed, by putting the code letters by the name. The two sheets could then be stapled together for easy reference, as in the following.

Activities Sheet

A Sorting different materials that float and sink; altered materials from sinking to floating (such as plasticine);

B Investigating which shapes move most easily in water; investigating the wash made by different shapes at different speeds;

C Loading marbles into different floating containers; trying this in different water solutions, for example, fresh water and salt water;

D Weighing objects in and out of water;

E Making a working model of a cantilever bridge and investigating the strength of different structures used for bridges and tunnels.

etc.

Record Sheet
CANALS

Name	Activities				
J. Brown	A	B	E	G	
M. Smith	A	B	C	E	H

Though this record is an outline it should prevent repetition of areas of study and particular activities. Floating and sinking may be repeated with the same group, but the work can then be at a greater depth or placed in a different context such as a study of a harbour or port.

Recording the type of investigation undertaken in different topic areas also allows us to evaluate the depth and width of experiences we are offering our children. This record can be matched against content guidelines by asking the questions: Have the children had the opportunity to see . . .?; or Have they had the experience of . . .?

2 Children's development: the idea of matching

If the attitudes, skills and concepts are monitored and recorded, the results can then be used to match children's level of development to their experiences. Matching means giving a child an experience which promotes some step forward in his development. Judging the amount of forward development is important; too big a step forward and mismatch is created. Given that the experiences offered to a child should be matched to his level of development, we must first ascertain that level. Before matching can take place a teacher needs to determine that level through careful observation of the attitudes and skills attained. Once this is determined, how important is the match? Without it problems arise in a number of ways. Children of limited ability will easily become frustrated and bored if the work they are given is beyond their capabilities at that time. When frustration and boredom set in, the child either gives up or becomes a nuisance. Conversely, children asked to do work well below their capabilities are likewise reduced to a state of boredom, frustration and underfunctioning. Attempts to match work to children's level of development will reduce these problems, although it is not an easy matter and complete matching is unattainable in practice.

A detailed study on this has been produced by the Progress in Learning Project. There are two books, *Raising Questions*, which looks at ways of determining a child's level of development, and *Finding Answers*, which looks at the experiences which one could use to match attitudes, skills and concepts for individual children. The material was developed for Inset and though best used in group discussion, it provides valuable information on how to attempt matching (Harlen et al. 1977a, 1977b).

3 Recording children's development

Determining and recording a child's development and progress requires the teacher to monitor and then record the development of each attitude, skill or concept that is felt to be important. To record the twenty-four characteristics listed by the Progress in Learning Project for a class of thirty-two children, will require considerable time and thought and this must be balanced against classroom pressures. However, the method could be used to determine the level of development of several characteristics for one child, or the level of development of one characteristic for all the children in a class. This could be done on a four- or five-point scale. Each school or teacher would need to determine what stage of development each point represented. On a four-point scale it might be:

(A) no understanding;
(B) little understanding;
(C) quite good understanding;
(D) very good understanding.

In *Raising Questions* there are suggestions for ways of recording and a rating scale for each of the twenty-four characteristics (see pp. 52–8; 239–58). Richards et al. (1980) also has a short section which looks at ways of recording and evaluating children's work and development. Using a check-list of attitudes, skills and concepts is also an important way of checking that a child is developing all the attributes, and records will show up those areas where more experience needs to be offered, or where areas of investigation

Name: M. Smith

Attitudes/skills	A	B	C	D
Curiosity	√	√	√	
Open-mindedness	√	√		
Perseverance	√			
Cooperation	√	√		
Observation	√	√	√	
Use of controls	√			
Identifying variables	√			
Recording	√	√	√	

may be deficient in opportunities to develop certain skills. These kinds of records obviously require a teacher to give up valuable time to monitor and then record each child.

We must also use the information we have gathered about children and their experiences to evaluate the effectiveness of our teaching programme. The children's achievement or lack of it may be a reflection of our own performance. Are they failing to develop certain attitudes and skills because we are not offering the right experiences? By keeping records on a class basis we immediately get an overall picture of that group's development. On closer inspection the sorts of questions which might arise could be: Are children of different abilities getting similar opportunities? Are boys and girls making similar progress? Are there any attributes which all the class appear to have not experienced or developed?

Summary

If science is to take its rightful place as an integral part of every primary school's curriculum, the work must be monitored and records made to assist evaluation. The extent to which this is done will vary according to each school or teacher's needs. I have tried to indicate what we should be looking for in terms of attitudes, skills and concepts which ought to be provided. The general skills will need to be developed before blending in the more specifically science-based skills. The point at which the more specific skills are introduced will depend on each child's stage of development. The attitudes, skills and concepts can best be developed by a process approach through topic work. However, there may need to be a compromise between a broad topic approach and a more rigid syllabus in the form of content or areas of investigation guidelines, describing what experiences children should meet in the primary school.

Although simple monitoring of children's attitudes and abilities may need no recording, good evaluation requires evidence. Topic and content areas need to be recorded for future reference to avoid duplication. Monitoring and recording also allows the teacher to ascertain the stage of development which each child has reached, so that a better match of work for the child is achieved. On the other hand, one can become obsessed with the need to record. Be clear about why you want to keep records and about the use to which they are going to be put, and make the methods of recording of value to you or the school within the constraints and pressures of the situation. Any extra work done will bring rewards in being able to enhance the children's development and progress as well as make you a more complete educator in science activities.

Topics for discussion

1. What do we want primary school children to achieve through learning about science?
2. Discuss the choice of a *topic approach* or a *syllabus of specific content* as an appropriate way of learning about science in the primary school years.
3. How can we break the 'vicious circle of primary science' identified by D. Plimmer in *School Science Review*, 1981, and diagrammed below.

The vicious circle of primary science

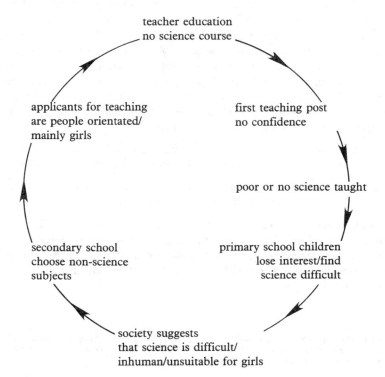

teacher education
no science course

applicants for teaching
are people orientated/
mainly girls

first teaching post
no confidence

poor or no science taught

secondary school
choose non-science
subjects

primary school children
lose interest/find
science difficult

society suggests
that science is difficult/
inhuman/unsuitable for girls

Suggestions for further reading

1. 'Primary School Science' (An 'Education' Digest) *Education*, 1983, 162, 24.
2. Harlen, W. (1977) *Match and Mismatch*. London: Oliver and Boyd.
3. APU (1984) *Science in Schools: Age 11: Report No. 3* London: Department of Education and Science.

READING EIGHTEEN • The growth of language and reading
reading   *D.M.R. Hutchcroft*

It is often difficult to answer the question, 'What is reading?' There are many parents who see 'reading aloud' to the teacher as the only concept of this activity, and a fluent reader who does not read to his teacher during the day or the school week is often thought not to have been actively engaged in reading. In fact, he has probably been engaged in numerous reading activities throughout each day. Reading is, of course, a much more complex activity than just the oral process of reading aloud. Gray's definition of reading (in *Promoting Personal and Social Development Through Reading*) is perhaps useful to recall in this connection:

i   A response to graphic signals in terms of the words they represent;
ii a response to text in terms of the meanings the author intended to set down;
iii plus: a response to the author's meaning in terms of all relevant previous experience and present judgements of the reader.

Gray does strongly emphasize that reading is not just a decoding process but also a thinking skill. It is of the utmost importance, therefore, in the initial stages of reading to use only those words that are within the child's own language register so that he can recognize the relationship of sound to symbol more readily.

'The growth of language and reading', in, D.M.R. Hutchcroft, *Making Language Work: A Practical Approach to Literacy for Teachers of 5 to 13 Year Old Children*. London: McGraw Hill Book Company, 1981, pp 31–50

3.1 The language experience approach to reading

This approach recapitulates the historical development of writing and reading. Communication first developed through touch and signs, followed by spoken sounds developing into language. The recording of events for future descendants was achieved through pictures, and from pictorial representation writing evolved, followed by reading.

If children are involved in worthwhile exciting activity they will *want* to communicate their achievements to others, and it appears logical to use the stages through which written recording developed. So, to begin with, the children will talk about their activities; later a drawing or painting may capture their enthusiasm, followed by a wish to interpret the printed word which tells of a happening that is personally important to them. This is the basis of the language experience approach to reading.

Some teachers may find it difficult to accept an approach to the teaching of reading that is not dependent upon a 'key word'-controlled vocabulary basis. In fact, the 'controlled vocabulary' element is there. The vocabulary content is limited to words already used by the child. The 'key words' approach, which is based upon words that appear most often in written English, does not include the words that are usually most emotive from the child's viewpoint, so possibly loses some impact.

We have considered the transformations:

activity → discussion → questions →investigations →discussion →pictorial recording →verbal interpretation of pictorial record →printed or typed recording of verbal interpretation.

This provides some meaningful reading material for the child, and at the same time provides practice in the uses of language concerned with reporting and logical reasoning. Part of the investigations and discussions may also involve predicting what might happen during an experiment. However, children also need reading material that stimulates the imagination and introduces them to experiences of other people, experiences at secondhand.

Many teachers find that it is possible to produce their own reading schemes or supplementary readers for the classroom library by producing books invented by the children. One class of backward readers, aged seven to eight years, built a village out of cardboard boxes. They each made a house or shop for the village High Street and invented families to live in them. The teacher then provided a tape-recorder so that the children could dictate stories about their 'families'.

Many stories were invented and the children were very proud of the books produced. The texts were typed using a Jumbo typewriter and the upper half of each page was used for an illustration beautifully produced with felt-tip pens. Strong cardboard backs were covered with paste papers and decorated labels were fixed on the front covers.

The gains in reading progress were very impressive, and an unexpected result was that these very anti-social children began to cooperate with each other to produce stories, and became mutually supportive.

The teacher found that she had to struggle with herself when she had to type words such as 'fags' and 'chucked', but she had resolved to use the children's language and carried it out with determination. It was noticed that much of the content was concerned with food, which appears to be of universal interest, yet is not mentioned very much in commercial reading schemes.

Projects of this kind give children a real sense of achievement and provide a purpose for writing. In many classrooms the child's writing is usually read only by his teacher and possibly by his parents on an open evening. Even then his work is probably corrected in red ink by the teacher. The Language Experience Approach makes use of the child's creative ability in language and art and presents his skills in such a way that means that other children can benefit from them and show appreciation. When the child has developed his reading to an appropriate standard and has acquired the necessary manual skill, he can progress to writing his own stories.

Above all, the child should enjoy his involvement in talking, writing, and reading. This can be ensured by making the experience personally interesting to him.

Many children will go from strength to strength in their reading achievements, needing little instruction from the teacher and developing their own strategies for decoding the printed word. Other children, however, will need a careful systematic approach which will ensure that they are ready for each new stage in the reading process.

3.2 Readiness at all levels

The professional judgement of the teacher is crucial in the reading process, and it is vital that the correct 'match' is achieved when selecting reading material for each individual. Reading tests that give a 'reading age' are of little or no help in achieving this match, and teachers are turning to diagnostic tests as an aid to planning individual learning programmes. The booklet produced by the West Sussex Psychological Service (Labon 1972) is a good example of tests that help to plan the next step in the teaching programme. Many teachers develop a system within the classroom that enables them to follow a logical plan for the class as a whole, and this requires a wide variety of materials and approaches and may include the development of an informal reading inventory. One such plan for beginning work with a new class in a new school situation is given here. Teachers who are familiar with their school will already have the general information needed.

The plan is set out as a decision-making flow chart (Fig. 3.1), and a list of references is given as a key for ideas that can be developed by the teacher to suit her own class. This plan could be adapted to include the materials already available within the school, so that the teacher has a wide range of materials and approaches from which to select the most suitable for each child.

Key

1. J.M. Hughes, *Phonics and the Teaching of Reading*, Evans, 1972.
2. *Classroom Index of Phonic Sources*, NARE, 1980.
3. L. Wenden, *Pictogram*, NARE, 1979.
4. D.H. Stott, *Programmed Reading Kit*, Holmes McDougall, 1971.
5. E. Goodacre, *Pictures and Words*, Blackie, 1971.
6. J. Tough, *Listening to Children Talking*, Ward Lock Educational, 1976.
7. J. Tough, *Talking and Learning*, Ward Lock Educational, 1977.
8. *Assessing Reading Ability*, West Sussex Psychological Service, 1972.
9. C.H. Jones, *Left to Write*, Autobates Learning Systems, 1976.
10. Picture Sequence Cards, Learning Development Aids.
11. J.K. Jones, *Colour Story Reading*, Nelson, 1967.
12. *Concepts: 7–9 Listening with Understanding*, Schools Council, 1972.
13. J.M. Hughes, *Aids to Reading*, Evans, 1970.
14. R.I. Brown and G.E. Bookbinder, Clifton Audio Visual, ESA, 1969.
15. B. Hornsby and F. Shear, *Alpha to Omega*, Heinemann, 1974.

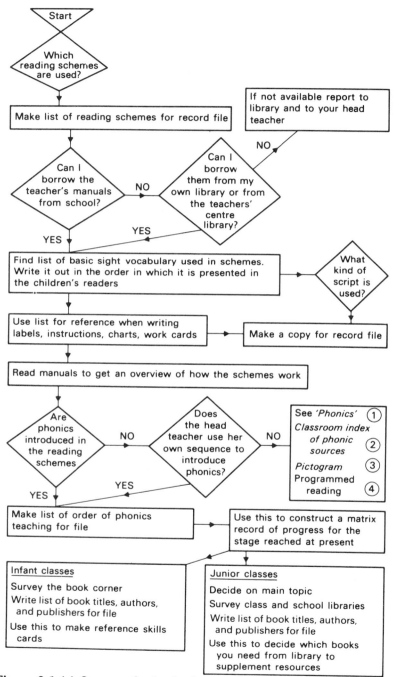

Figure 3.1 (a) Strategy for beginning reading with a new class. General information

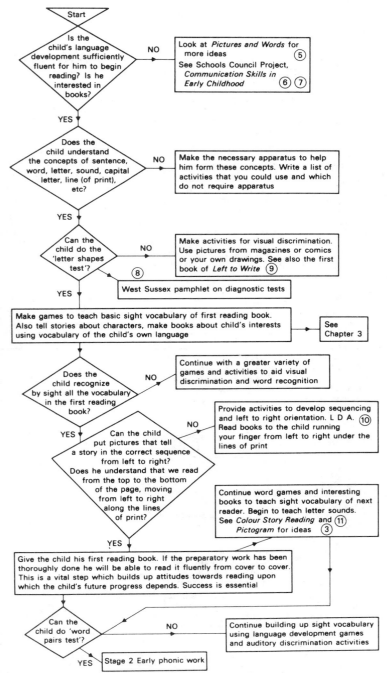

Figure 3.1 (b) Specific information. Stage 1 Introductory

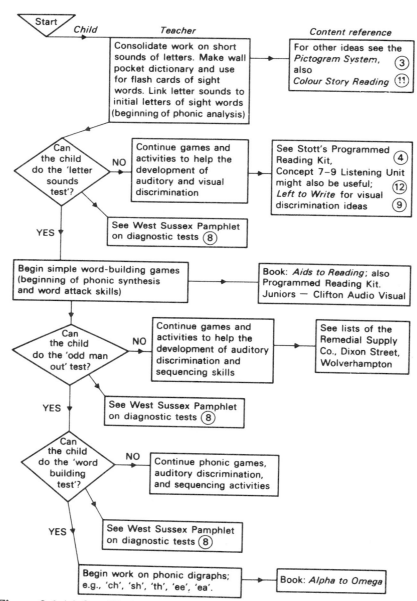

Figure 3.1 (c) Specific information. Stage 2 Early phonic work

3.3 Levels of reading ability

It is useful, not only in the infant years but throughout school life, to categorize a child's reading ability with regard to a particular text as at one of the following three levels.

1. *The independent level.* At this level the child can read a text fluently and with understanding, making not more than one error in any 100 words and comprehending at least 90 per cent of his material. Obviously this gives the teacher the clue to the difficulty of the books that the child ought to be using for his own researches and his own pleasure.

2. *The instructional level.* Word recognition at this level should be 95 per cent with comprehension at least 75 per cent. It is this level of text that the teacher should be using when she hears a child read, for at this stage miscues by the reader help in diagnosis of his problems in the actual decoding of the printed word. So, too, at this level the teacher has the opportunity to develop thinking skills and comprehension abilities in the child.

3. *The frustration level.* As its title implies, this is the level that can do great damage. Word recognition is 90 per cent or less, and this trouble with decoding leads to a failure to comprehend even half the subject matter. It is a level of text at which no teacher ought to ask a child to read, for there is no larger obstacle in the path to fluency than failure.

Occasionally when a child is moved from a text that he can just master at the instructional level to one that the teacher thinks will present only slightly more difficulty, he fails. He has obviously not overcome all the problems at his former level and needs more help.

3.4 The understanding of the heard text

The comprehension of text that is read aloud can also be considered on these levels and judged when skilled questions, using a language similar in difficulty to the text itself, are posed.

All of this should help the teacher to provide reading material for silent reading and for reading aloud at a suitable level, and not to risk the child's frustration in one area, or an abdication of attention caused by inability to follow oral language in the other. Her ultimate aim, of course is for every child to be able to comprehend fully when he reads for himself, so that there will be no necessity for the teacher to translate the printed word into speech.

3.5 Phonic teaching and context cues

In the early stages the child will rely heavily on memory in building up a sight vocabulary through the Language Experience Approach. As his skills in auditory and visual discrimination are refined, he will be able to benefit from phonic teaching which will aid the development of word attack skills.

The key to later success in using flexible reading skills lies in the ability of the teacher to maintain the correct balance in the use of phonic cues and context cues. Too great an emphasis on phonics will result in slow, exact, unimaginative readers. If reading is a thinking activity then children should be encouraged to make sensible guesses by anticipating the text. The opportunity for self-correction will arise if teachers do not correct every word immediately the child makes a mistake, and this will preserve his self-confidence.

3.6 Hearing children read

It is important that every school should have an agreed policy about hearing children read. *Hearing Children Read* by Elizabeth Goodacre (1972) is useful as a discussion document for staff wishing to develop their skills of miscue analysis. This is a method of diagnosing children's reading difficulties so that suitable activities can be provided to overcome them. Some agreement between staff about the frequency of miscue analysis is needed, and the way in which records of this should be kept will ensure consistency of approach within the school.

Another aspect upon which staff agreement is necessary is the phonic progression to be used. Before choosing a phonic programme care should be taken to ensure that there is a progression. Too often children are expected to decode early words containing phonic digraphs that are taught much later in the programme. This can lead to frustration and failure. Readiness is essential at every stage of the reading programme and the teacher must actively prepare this state of readiness to ensure the child's success.

Many necessary reading skills can be developed through the use of various games and activities and the teacher will need to use professional judgement to decide on the value of particular activities in terms of the needs of individual children.

3.7 The development of reading skills through classroom activities

Classroom activities can be evaluated only within the context of the whole reading development programme. A particular activity may have great value in developing reading skills at one particular point in the programme, but be quite useless if used at a different time. The value of an activity is dependent upon a number of factors — the context in which an activity takes place, the expertise of the teacher, the needs of the individual child, the level at which the activity is presented, and the objectives of the whole programme.

The context in which the activity takes place plays a decisive part in estimating its effectiveness. The manner in which the school and the class are organized is important, and various questions need to be considered:

1. How formal or free is the school organization?
2. What type of organization does the class teacher use?
3. Do the children choose their activities or is the decision made by the teacher?
4. If the children choose what they *want* to do, is this also what they *need* to do? (Dearden 1967)
5. Does the teacher make the distinction between 'wants' and 'needs'?
6. If so, how does she do this and what effect does this have on the motivation of the children?

The teacher must know the detailed sequence of stages in any content area in order to provide the optimum conditions for effective learning. Gagné (1977) states: 'If learning at any level is to occur with greatest facility, careful attention must be paid to its prerequisites.' In order to know the prerequisites of any task, the teacher's knowledge must be detailed. In addition, her knowledge of the child must be extensive and up to date if she is to provide a suitable programme of activities to ensure steady progress. She needs to know about his background in order to make allowances for his anxieties and to be able to build upon his interests so that he is strongly motivated to develop his abilities. This information needs to be up to date so that she is aware of the stage and level of the child's progress — in Gagné's terms, she knows the prerequisites that have been achieved by the pupil. She can then combine this information with her knowledge of the content of the reading curriculum and decide on the optimum activities for the child's present stage of achievement. The teacher must therefore keep careful records of progress (. . .)

These records of progress will indicate the stage of development of skills and therefore help the teacher to provide the next step. In the early stages the foundations are laid and activities should be provided to ensure that the later development of higher-order skills is facilitated.

Figure 3.2 illustrates the opportunities provided for the development of reference skills through a succession of activities spread throughout the primary school.

Many teachers assume that reference skills are developed after children become fluent readers, and some even think that they should be left until the secondary stage; yet we believe that the foundation for these skills begins in the reception class.

The activities are viewed in terms of the 'spiral curriculum', mentioned earlier, which starts from a particular activity — that of finding a specified book — and is returned to and built upon at each successive stage.

The development of reference skills can be started at the pre-reading stage in an incidental manner; the teacher notices that a group of children is particularly interested in the animals in the classroom and suggests that there is a book in the book corner which she will read to them. Some dust jackets have facsimiles of the actual cover of the book. When books are new, these paper jackets can be removed, trimmed and mounted to provide work-cards for practice in early book identification skills, provided that the library books are displayed with their front covers showing, not simply their spines. The teacher can then select the card for the book and ask an individual child to find it. This can be done by simple picture matching which helps to develop visual skills, discrimination between cover illustrations, and sorting and classifying abilities. It also helps to develop the child's ability to scan book shelves for a particular book.

At a later stage the teacher can do the same type of thing in another situation but expect something more of the child, so that after he has found the book he is asked to find a picture. For example, he could be asked to find a picture of a helicopter during a discussion about 'flight'.

When the child has reached the stage of beginning reading and has the ability to match sentences and words, the task becomes more demanding. He can be given a card with the title of a story on it, as well as an illustrated book cover. He then scans the bookshelves for the book, and scans the book for the story title, developing still further his ability to discriminate.

It is necessary for the teacher to observe how the child goes about his task; she may write out a card for the child indicating the title of the book and the titles of the chapters that he needs to read in order to satisfy his specific

Activity

Activity	Skill development	Scanning bookshelves	Scanning book	Using contents table	Using alphabetical order	Using index	Devising key words	Skimming page	Synthesis of information	Suitability of materials	Using Dewey system	Using card index
Finding own media for information needed	✓	✓	✓	✓	✓	✓	✓	✓	✓	✓	✓	✓
Finding information from two or more suggested books	✓	✓	✓	✓	✓	✓	✓	✓				
Finding information about topic, given book title only	✓	✓	✓	✓	✓	✓	✓					
Finding information about topic, given book title and key words	✓	✓	✓	✓	✓		✓					
Finding chapter in book when given chapter title	✓	✓	✓									
Finding information in book relevant to present interest, given page number	✓	✓						✓				
Finding story in book (a) picture clues (b) story title matching card (c) given page number	✓	✓										
Finding picture in book relevant to present interest	✓	✓										
Finding book by matching cover	✓											

Figure 3.2 The development of reference skills

purpose. The teacher's objective on this particular occasion may be to create the need for the child to use the contents table in the book, though he could find the chapter by operating at an earlier level (scanning the book to match the chapter title) unless she makes the purpose of the activity clear to him. The opportunities for skill development may be provided by activities, but it is up to the teacher to see that these opportunities are used.

Through the use of classroom activities, many of which can take place in an incidental manner and *at the time when they meet the child's needs*, the teacher is able to lay the foundations for higher-order skills which are necessary at a later stage.

> Discovery methods of learning, to be effective, require certain basic skills of which reading is probably the most important, followed closely by the knowledge of how to use an index, simple dictionaries and reference books. While it is true that young children, even before they have started to read and write, can begin to discover, observe, experiment and compare, their progress is necessarily limited by lack of these skills (Southgate 1977).

It is important that the teacher discusses the value of each activity with the child so that he is involved in his own progress in skill development. The value of activities cannot be judged in isolation: the same activity used by different teachers will have different values and effects. These effects depend on different school situations, different children, different levels of achievement, and different stages in the curriculum. For this reason it is preferable that the activities should be devised or adapted by the teacher herself in order to meet the varying demands of her class. If this is done, the objectives of reading skill development will be efficiently achieved. This is a dynamic exercise and test of the teacher's skill in adapting to changing situations.

3.8 The principles of pleasure and choice

Everyone will pursue an activity that gives him pleasure, and children are no exception. Teachers who give children a choice of activity usually find that children are more committed to their choice than to an activity that is imposed upon them. If the activities for reading can be linked with the interests of the children, then commitment can be sustained and the quality of learning improved. In addition, because the children are interested, there is a greater chance of success, and this builds up positive attitudes towards learning. In the early stages the teacher must be sure to teach, by look-and-say games and activities, all the vocabulary in each book *before* giving it to the child to read. It is important to hear him read his first book from cover to cover so that he has a great sense of achievement, and the teacher must be sure that he can do this with 100 per cent success. This is a crucial step, and an adequate amount of time without interruption should be set aside to do this. Discussion between teacher and child about his first book is another vital factor in establishing desirable attitudes towards reading, and if the content of the book has been dictated and illustrated by the child then his personal interest will be assured. From this talk with the teacher, the child will absorb many things such as how enjoyable it can be to understand the meaning of the printed page; and the way in which the teacher gives him her undivided attention will convey to the child that his progress and enjoyment in reading is important to her. Lots of praise and a shared sense of achievement will enhance his desire to read, and this will be reinforced still further if the book has been made of personal interest to him (see Sec. 3.1 above).

3.9 Children's choice

Allowing the child to make choices in a variety of situations has some advantages for the child and also for the teacher. We believe that the use of children's choices is not sufficiently exploited by many teachers. It is fairly common for the children to be allowed a choice of activities and equipment during a 'free-activity' session, but unusual for this to happen in the context of mathematical activities or reading books.

This is probably because teachers feel that they must ensure progression in easy stages in the basic skills, and the most usual way to do this is to adopt set mathematics and reading schemes for a whole school. In this way continuity from class to class is ensured as well as a gradual progression for each individual child. However, this frequently means that when a child has completed one reading book he is presented with the next one by the teacher without having the opportunity to express his own wishes. As adults we would probably feel rather aggrieved if the local librarian chose our books for us, yet we see no reason why we should not choose for children. If only we gave them five or six books to choose from in the early stages many children might develop a strong affinity for books. Engineering this choice would present teachers with the task of grading books at many different levels and ensuring that the child knew the vocabulary necessary for each group of books before asking him to choose from them.

The advantages would be that, because the child *chose* the book, he would be better motivated to read it. The activity of choosing would also help to train his powers of judgement and discrimination. In addition, the child could read six or more books at the same stage if he wished to, thus building up confidence. The teacher could also ensure that children whose progress is slower could stay at the same level until fluency was achieved.

A school policy for children's choice in reading could be organized in stages as follows:

1. Staff meeting to draw up a list of books (i.e., reading schemes and other early books) that members of staff have found popular with children.
2. Ordering of not more than six copies of each book in a large school, less for a small rural school.
3. Rough sorting into stages using any reading scheme books as a framework for grading non-reading scheme books.
4. Setting up a central store with numbered cupboards, e.g., sets of locker cubes in entrance hall or library arranged to form work bays for individuals or groups to use; cupboard number 1 should contain lots of picture books with no written words so that pre-reading skills can be developed from the child's own choice of picture book.
5. Final sorting of vocabulary analysis so that a list of the vocabulary and phonic blends needed for each cupboard can be provided for each member of staff.
6. Each teacher to ensure that the child is taught through games and activities the vocabulary and phonic blends listed *before* he is allowed to choose from a particular cupboard.

The organization of such a method of working is a time-consuming task in the early stages, but it is very easily built upon once the main framework is established.

The initial stage could be spread over two years if necessary or speeded up if interested parents help by listing the vocabulary content of books. One school found that, because no two children had to use the same progression of books, an unexpected bonus was the elimination of competition among parents by comparing one child with another. Progress was seen not only in the difficulty level of books but also by the number of books listed on the child's reading record.

It is important that children are not expected to progress at too fast a pace, and this type of book organization makes it possible for the teacher to say to a child, 'Today you can choose from cupboard number 5 or 6.' If the child chooses a book from cupboard number 5, he will be extending his interest in books and operating at the independent level of reading, thus consolidating skills already learnt and developing fluency. All too often these aspects of reading are not developed when one or two reading schemes are followed slavishly.

As children produce their own story books, these can be slotted into the book organization, thus providing further resources as well as a purpose for children's writing.

3.10 Points to consider when choosing a reading scheme

1. The context in which a scheme will be used
   (a) Will it be the main scheme for the school or used in conjunction with other reading schemes?
   (b) If so, will it be compatible with the other schemes in terms of vocabulary content, style of language, type of print, content, phonic progression, and size of print?
   (c) Is it suitable for the type of children and their background of experience?
   (d) Is it near to the children's natural speech rhythms?
   (e) Does the vocabulary match the active and passive vocabulary of the children?
   (f) Are the illustrations meaningful for the children?
   (g) Which age groups will it suit?
   (h) Is the construction of the book suitable; e.g., are the covers strong enough and are the books stitched or stapled?
   (i) Is the paper strength and quality suitable?
   (j) Does the cost fit in sensibly with your budget requirements? Is it value for money in *your* school?
2. Progression
   (a) Does the teacher's manual give clear guidance on progression?
   (b) Is there a suitably planned pre-reading stage?
   (c) At what pace are new words introduced?
   (d) Is there a balanced rate of vocabulary repetition (i.e., frequent enough to consolidate learning but not so frequent as to develop bordeom)?
   (e) Are the illustrations complementary to the text and graded in complexity?

(f) Is there a sensible phonic progression and is it acceptable to you?

(g) At what pace are new sounds or phonic rules introduced?

(h) Does the sentence construction encourage contextual guessing right from the early stages? Is this structure for the use of context cues developed gradually to ensure the use of complex context cues at later stages?

(i) Is there a suitable progression in the length of stories and in the development of story plots?

(j) Does the record card indicate clear progression in reading skills?

3. Content

(a) Do the illustrations attract interest?

(b) Do the stories appeal to you?

(c) If there are supplementary readers are they also attractive and interesting?

(d) Is there sufficient variety of content?

(e) What bias do you detect in the content (e.g., is there a sex bias or a bias towards middle class or working class experience)? If so what do you feel about this?

(f) Are there work books? If so, do they help the development of reading skills, or merely test memory at a literal level, or just provide a time filler? Are they varied in format and content? If so, will this be an advantage or a disadvantage?

4. Format

(a) Is there a varied approach? If so does it create interest through different sizes and shapes of books and different styles of illustration or is it likely to develop insecurity through lack of consistency?

(b) Is the print large for early readers and reducing sensibly for readers at later stages of development?

(c) Are the words and lines of print suitably spaced to aid vision?

(d) Are the breaks at the end of a line of print made at points where this is an aid to comprehension?

It should be remembered that structure comes from the teacher's knowledge of the process of reading which leads to alternative pathways to success. This develops from the sensible sequencing of activities and materials, combined with the effective use of records of progress to diagnose weaknesses in reading skill development. Structure does not come from the narrow limits of a reading scheme, although this may provide a rough guideline in the initial stages of development of the comprehensive resources for reading.

3.11 The use of play

The importance of activity has already been stressed, and many language and reading opportunities will arise from children's play. From careful observation the teacher will learn when to intervene in order to carry the children's play a stage further, perhaps to develop oral language or to engineer the necessity for the children to write and to read. Guidelines for using children's play in learning situations is provided in *Structuring Play in the Early Years* by K. Manning and A. Sharp (1977). Children choose to play because it gives them pleasure, and many teachers find that using play as a motivating force for learning basic skills facilitates their task. Useful ideas for sand and water play can be found in E.J. Arnold's 'Sand and Water' (Jackson et al. 1978), and one box can provide resource material for a whole school. Other useful material can be found in *Language for Learning* (1976), which is produced by the Inner London Media Resources Centre.

Young children learn a great deal through their senses, and for this reason it is wise to use real objects in learning situations rather than substitutes. For example, if plastic fruit is used in the home corner or the classroom shop this will not provide the right experiences for the development of concepts related to weight and texture. The quality of provision for children's play is very important, and skilful teachers will ensure that high-quality materials are provided so that a multi-sensory approach can be used. Descriptive language will arise from questions such as 'What does it feel like?' and 'What does it taste like?' It is the development of oral language concerned with personal sensory experience that will release the flow of written language at a later stage.

Topics for discussion

1. '*At the time when they meet the child's needs*, the teacher is able to lay the foundations for higher-order skills which are necessary at a later stage' (Hutchcroft, page 244).
    'If a basic level of literacy and articulateness is not attained by the age of 7, it becomes very difficult to achieve competence in other learning' (DES *English From 5 to 16*, 1984).
    Discuss the apparent conflict of views in these two recent pronouncements on language work with young children.

2. 'If learning at any level is to occur with greatest facility, careful attention must be paid to its prerequisites.'
   What are the implications of Gagné's statement for the teacher of reading?
3. On what grounds does the author argue for a greater use of children's choices in the selection of reading materials?

Suggestions for further reading

1. Perera, K. (1984) *Children's Writing and Reading: Analysing Classroom Language.* Oxford: Basil Blackwell.
2. DES (1984) *Language Performance in Schools.* 1982 Primary Survey Report, London: HMSO.
3. DES (1984) *English From 5 to 16.* Curriculum Matters I. An HMI Series. London: HMSO.

READING NINETEEN • Aesthetic development
Assessment of Performance Unit

Introduction

An important characteristic of the concept of the aesthetic is that, unlike so many aspects of the curriculum, it is not concerned with means to ends. When one makes an aesthetic judgement, by the use of terms such as 'beautiful', 'elegant', 'attractive', one is not appraising the phenomenon in question in terms of its possible success in attaining some purpose outside itself. For instance, one appreciates the elegant design of a Bill Gibb garment or a Charles Rennie Mackintosh chair as a beautiful object in its own right which, as such, can enhance the lives of those who see and live with it. For this reason, we believe that a growing awareness of the aesthetic is an important aspect of education. Serious educational loss would be incurred if aesthetic elements were excluded from the curriculum by an over-emphasis on subjects whose concern was exclusively or predominantly with means to ends. It is reasonably claimed that frequently the most

A.P.U. *Aesthetic Development.* London: Department of Education and Science. 1983. pp 2–6

effective and obvious way of encouraging a developing interest in aesthetic aspects of life is through the arts. A clear example of this is the way in which the visual arts or poetry can help to develop an increasingly vivid, discriminating and sensitive perception of the beauty of natural phenomena.

We regard it as an important aspect of education that children should develop the capacity to make informed judgements about and respond appropriately to the aesthetic quality of natural and man-made environments. For the whole of their lives they will be faced with the need to make judgements of quality and significance in relation, for instance, to their dress, personal adornment and appearance and the personal and living environments they create. Much social interaction involves aesthetic choices such as these and the quality of the environment depends very largely upon general levels of informed judgement. Arts teaching in schools inevitably incurs a considerable responsibility in this sphere, as do other areas of the curriculum such as Craft, Design and Technology and Home Economics. Assessment might help to reveal the extent to which these related subjects, referred to collectively as the arts, contribute to this capacity.

Our decision to concentrate predominantly on the arts rather than the aesthetic is mainly in the interests of manageability since the latter raises issues which may confuse this enquiry. We also recognize that whereas art embraces the aesthetic the reverse may not necessarily be so.

In its examination of the implications for assessment, the Group* isolated and examined the most important issues with respect to education in and through the arts. The proposed framework for criteria of achievement is offered for discussion to both individual teachers, and to advisers.

Objective assessment: Philosophical foundations

In any genuinely educational activity, there must always be objective criteria for what counts as achievement, and therefore for what the teacher is trying to offer. Although such criteria may be, or may be assumed to be, more immediately obvious in subjects such as mathematics, the sciences, history and geography, they inevitably, if less obviously, underlie education in the arts. In arts subjects it is frequently the case that the criteria for

* Following the formation of the APU in 1975, the Exploratory Group on Aesthetic Development was set up in 1977.

achievement are implicit in what the teacher is doing, rather than explicitly formulated. For example, a teacher who wants his or her pupils to play an instrument more expressively, dance more confidently, or paint more sensitively, clearly must have some at least implicit notion of what counts as expressive playing, confident dancing, or sensitive painting. Too often, and for too long, those concerned with arts education have been, albeit understandably, reluctant to attempt to clarify their criteria. However, in order to achieve fruitful assessment procedures, helpful debate and clear guidelines for progress in the arts in education, it is necessary to tackle the difficult tasks of making such implicit criteria explicit. The Group is convinced that this applies at least as much to the arts as to any other aspect of education. Indeed, the existence of some confusion and uncertainty in this aspect enhances the need for attempting to provide clear guidelines, and for these to be debated openly.

Artistic experience is not simply a matter of pleasure or entertainment, from which there is nothing of significance to be learned. This indicates a crucial difference between the aesthetic and the artistic, and is one of the most important educational reasons for the Group's decision to concentrate centrally on the arts. (There is a very common misunderstanding of the concept of art in this respect — a misunderstanding which often underlies the prevalent and serious undervaluing of the contribution of the arts to society generally.) Involvement with the arts can extend and deepen the capacity to learn about oneself; it can give increasing perceptiveness and insight about almost every aspect of life and the world around us.

It can be argued that the arts can achieve this in ways which could not be achieved otherwise. At the very least it is certainly true that such issues can be illuminated through the arts in ways which could not even remotely be achieved by other subjects in the curriculum. This point can be most clearly illustrated by reference to the literary arts. Poetry, short stories, novels and plays are not only aesthetically satisfying verbal forms, but they frequently make incisive comments about the human condition, or make us aware of aspects of nature to which we might otherwise remain blind, or at least relatively indifferent. In these arts such criteria are the most important, whether we are concerned with creation or appreciation. Similarly, Picasso's Guernica can be considered as impressive from a purely aesthetic or formal point of view, but it also gives powerful expression to a certain vision of war and violence. A song like Gershwin's Summer Time is not only a pleasing musical progression but also conveys an attitude to life, a sense of indolence, a feeling of life in the heat of a Southern summer. There are innumerable such examples, from all the arts. It is this central characteristic of the concept of art which the Group believes to be perhaps the most important educational contribution which can be made by the arts. It can be encouraged not only through the appreciation of the arts, but also in the creative work of children, who can thus be encouraged increasingly to express and develop their own individual imaginative perceptions and insights about an indefinitely wide range of aspects of life.

This raises a fundamental yet commonly misunderstood issue. We would emphasize the encouragement of individual creativity, imagination, perceptiveness and insight, but this is almost universally assumed to be incompatible with the objectivity which is a necessary condition for any clear statement of criteria for assessment and monitoring. Many arts educators are reluctant to try to make explicit the implicit criteria on which they inevitably depend. They tend to feel that to state objective criteria — that is criteria which is explicitly tangible for all to see — is to state general criteria which would restrict the individual's creativity, insight, and response to the particular which are the lifeblood of the arts. The Group, however, would argue that:

(a) artistic development certainly can be objectively assessed, and
(b) this does not imply any restriction of individuality and creativity. Indeed, on the contrary, it is only when there are objective criteria that the student or his teacher can make sense of the notion of individual development.

In practice good arts teachers engage in such assessment every day. It is only because of a common confusion about the concept of objective assessment that they tend to deny it theoretically.

In order to illuminate this issue we shall briefly compare the arts with the sciences. The sciences are generally, and rightly, regarded as a paradigm of objectivity, so, by showing that artistic experience is the same in the relevant respects, it can be shown that artistic experience is equally open to objective assessment. This is a complex issue, but it is necessary to offer an outline of the foundations on which the Group bases its case. There are six major interrelated aspects of the objectivity issue which are most relevant to our enquiry. The first three reveal that objective assessment is as possible in the arts as in the sciences: the last three indicate important differences in the character of the two equally objective kinds of activity.

(i) *First*, contrary to what is commonly assumed, a judgement, to be genuinely objective, does not have to be absolutely true, in the sense that its validity could never be seriously questioned — it merely has to be as accurate or precise as possible and generally agreed at the time.

No one doubts the objectivity of scientific judgements despite the fact that there are fundamental conflicts of opinion among leading scientists about the character of the facts with which they are concerned. Such radical differences of opinion among experts in every branch of pure and applied science are very common, and indeed normal. The indefinite possibility of differences and changes of opinion is part of the concept of objectivity, and of the objectivity of the sciences. As Sir Karl Popper, the eminent philosopher of science, has pointed out, it is a mark of a genuine scientific theory, not that it should be accepted as true for all time, but that it should be in principle falsifiable. Moreover, there have been fundamental changes of underlying theory in the history of science, for example from the Ptolemaic to the Copernican conception of the universe, and from Newtonian physics to Einstein. Such changes of conception inevitably change the character even of what can count as a fact, observation, or conclusion. It is true that there are more differences of underlying conception or framework in the arts than in the sciences. For instance, scientists, more often than artists, work within a conception which is commonly accepted. Nevertheless, in a good deal of creative art there is a close parallel in that an artist usually works within one particular paradigm — for instance Impressionism. However, unlike the sciences, there are audiences or spectators for the arts. As a spectator it is possible to respond to a range of different conceptions of art. The importance of this point for this enquiry is, first, that artistic appraisal requires a knowledge of the relevant context, and second, that assessment requires knowledge of and sensitivity to different conceptions.

Within the ambit of a theoretical framework a genuinely scientific statement has to be in principle falsifiable, and the framework, and therefore what can count as true or false, can change.

Hence it says nothing whatsoever against the possibility of objective assessment of the arts that there have been and still are radical changes of approach and opinion. On the contrary, such variety, with its indefinite scope for individual imaginative and creative potential, is as vital for the advance of the sciences as it is for the arts. Of course there are limits. Not anything can count as a valid and fruitful judgement or conception, whether in the arts or in the sciences. From that point of view artistic experience is no more subjective than the sciences. Nevertheless, within those limits, in the sciences as in the arts, there is indefinite scope for individual differences, creativity and imagination. An artistic judgement, in the same way as a scientific judgement, has to be justified by reference to what is objectively there. Nevertheless, there can be radical differences of opinion, in both fields, about the character of what is objectively there, and there is always scope for imaginative individual insight which will give a fresh and more fruitful conception of what is objectively there. Advances in science come from new conceptions. The Group believes that one important contribution of the arts in education is that they can help to foster the open-minded, creative approach to life which is vital in all aspects of the curriculum.

(ii) *Second*, scientific facts depend on theories. It is a consequence of (i) that a scientific fact is inevitably given its sense or meaning by an underlying theory or conception. That theory or conception cannot be achieved by empirical methods, since it is presupposed by and directs the empirical tests and observations, and gives sense to the conclusions. That is, scientific facts are objectively established, but inevitably in the light of a particular theory or conception which is always open to modification, and differences of interpretation and opinion. Similarly, there are different conceptions or schools of thought in the arts, such as Fauvism, Impressionism, Cubism, Surrealism, Abstract Expressionism, High Realism, which gives sense to judgements or created works within them.

(iii) *Third*, it is false to assume that there cannot be objectivity where judgement and interpretation are required. This assumption is closely related to the tendency to equate objective assessment with quantifiability. As we have seen, human judgement, and interpretation, are inevitable in both the sciences and the arts. Moreover, the misconception is contradicted in numerous ways every day. For instance, the ability to understand ourselves and other people, the ability to engage in meaningful personal relationships, and moral and emotional development, cannot be measured, although they can certainly be objectively assessed. One can be objectively certain that someone is sad, angry, afraid or elated, but one cannot reach such a conclusion by quantification procedures. Even more obviously, perhaps, the validity of a reasoned argument can be objectively assessed, but not by quantification. A self-contradiction is not revealed by measurement. Moreover, no quantification has any sense without interpretation. A series of figures, by itself, is meaningless. It is the failure to recognize this point which leads to the fallacy that since interpretation and judgement, not quantification, are the methods of assessment in the arts, therefore the arts cannot be objectively assessable. What matters most, in the arts as in the sciences, is that the judgement and interpretation should be informed with

considerable consensus about the criteria to be applied when determining quality.

(iv) *Fourth*, it is false to assume that artistic development can be assessed only to the extent that it is open to justification by means of scientific methodology.

This is a complex issue, but what is most important for our purposes is to emphasize that although methods of assessment in the two areas may be different in important ways, those methods are equally objective. Most obviously, the empirical methods of experiment and quantification, which are characteristically employed to establish and refute scientific conclusions, are inapplicable in the sphere of the arts. Assessment in the arts always requires sensitive, informed objective judgement.

(v) *Fifth*, it is necessary to recognize the importance of the character of the relation between feelings and the arts. This is related to the common misconception that reason is quite distinct from, or even inimical to, feeling. There can, of course, be excitement, despair and many other feelings in relation to scientific as much as artistic or any other work. But the distinctive feature of the arts is that feelings can be, and characteristically often are, expressed and evoked by means of artistic media. That is, emotional meaning can be intrinsic to a work of art. There is no parallel in the sciences. But this characteristic of the arts is commonly overemphasized, for much creation and appreciation of art, and the meaning of many works of art, do not, at least in any clear sense, involve feeling in this way. More importantly, even where this characteristic is present, it does not in the least imply that the work of art cannot be objectively assessed. Judgements about the emotional meaning of a work of art are equally open to rational justification by reference to objective criteria. The feelings expressed in and evoked by the work are intrinsic to it, and are assessable by references to objective features of it. Moreover, there can be no separation of knowledge or understanding, and artistic feeling or experience. Not just *any* feeling could intelligibly be regarded either as appropriate in response to, or as what is expressed in, a particular work of art. In order to be able to respond appropriately one needs to have understood it, to have grasped the objective criteria in the concept of art. There are several important educational issues here. For example, these considerations reveal how damaging is the fallacy that the arts are a matter of feeling, not reason.

It is necessary to outline the two major aspects of this complex issue which are most directly relevant to our enquiry:

a.   It is a common experience that reasons can be given for seeing a
     situation differently which, if accepted, can change our feelings about
     it. For example, in Romeo and Juliet, Romeo is so dismayed when he
     hears that he has been banished from Verona that he feels suicidal, but
     the Friar gives him good reasons for recognizing how much better his
     situation is than it could have been. Romeo's feelings change with his
     changed view of his situation. The effect of such reasoning on feelings,
     both by others and to oneself, is by no means uncommon. Moreover, it
     has crucial relevance for the way in which feelings can be educated in
     the arts, as a consequence of the reasons a teacher can give for
     understanding or creating an art object in a different way.
b.   There is a logical relationship between the feeling and the character of
     the object or situation. That is, feelings are normally appropriate to
     their objects, including works of art. A very important part of educa-
     tion in the arts is to give reasons for recognizing and developing feelings
     which are appropriate both to particular works of art, and to life-
     situations of which they are expressing a certain connection.

   In short, arts grow out of both emotion and reason but are evocative
of appropriate feelings only when there is rational understanding.

(vi) *Sixth*, and finally, there is an important difference between scientific
and artistic knowledge. In the sciences it is usual to accept conclusions
without working one's way through the empirical enquiry which produced
them. For instance, scientific research frequently proceeds by simply
assuming the validity of the work of other scientists. Similarly, we all accept
numerous scientific conclusions and act upon them, for example with
respect to motor cars, electrical apparatus, and, perhaps the effects of
tobacco smoking, without even being aware of, still less having worked
through, the empirical research which produced them. Such is not the case
in the arts, where it is always necessary to experience and learn from the
work of art for oneself. There is very little to be gained from hearing even an
expert's opinions about a work unless, of course, one tries to see their
significance for oneself as a contribution to one's own revised experience of
it. Again, this is too complex an issue to be considered adequately here. It is
part of the distinction which is often drawn between what is sometimes
called cumulative and non-cumulative knowledge. What is important for
our purposes is to emphasize that the knowledge gained from the arts
requires one's own direct experience in a way which is not so often the case
in the sciences. It should, perhaps, also be emphasized that non-cumulative

knowledge is no less important, on this count, than cumulative. On the contrary, some of the most important aspects of human life, such as moral and emotional development, learning about oneself, personal and social relationships, and religious belief, are all examples of non-cumulative knowledge. It is also significant that artistic experience can encompass and contribute to all these.

It becomes clear why arts educators are reluctant to make explicit the implicit, objective criteria of assessment which they inevitably employ. For what underlies that reluctance is the fear that declared objective criteria would restrict individual creativity. In fact, the opposite is true. Unless the student has learned the objective criteria of an art form, of language, of the sciences, or of any other discipline or activity, he will be unable to develop his own creative potential. That is, the student himself needs a conception of what counts as achievement, or there is no sense in the notion of individual development. If there are no declared, objective criteria the notion of individual development is meaningless. Thus it is the lack of such objective criteria which will be restrictive. Nevertheless, there is an important warning which underlies this fear. For, even with the best intentions, it is dangerously easy, and again not only in the arts, for particular and perhaps narrow criteria to be imposed on students' work to the exclusion of other equally fruitful possibilities. It is this, we think, which underlies the anxiety of those who are worried about objective assessment in arts education. It is not, we suggest, the notion of objective criteria *per se* which should worry them, but the danger that particular, limited criteria may be imposed which might well restrict individual creativity, to which other criteria would be more appropriate. This is why we deemed it important to point out that a difference between the arts and the sciences which is of some consequence for our enquiry is that in the arts there is a greater range and variety of fruitful conceptions. What this implies is not that there should not be objective assessment, but rather that those doing the assessing should be as widely knowledgeable, sensitive and open-minded as possible to the different criteria which may be appropriate to different approaches to the arts. This is not in the least to weaken the Group's conviction that there should be objective standards, and preferably progressively improving standards, in arts education. It is to emphasize that assessment requires a breadth of knowledge and sensitivity, and respect for different but equally valid approaches. It is worth emphasizing again that the arts are not autonomous activities. *They draw from and contribute to the concerns of society in ways which are unique.* It is this characteristic which is perhaps the most important single justification for the arts in education, and gives sense to the notion not only of education in the arts, but also of education through the arts. For through the arts it is possible to give expression to, and to come to understand, fresh, incisive and imaginative conceptions of nature, personal relationships, feelings of various kinds, moral problems, political issues — indeed almost, if not quite, every aspect of life, including the sciences. It is for this reason that the Group feels that the arts have a particularly important contribution to make to the encouragement of the creative attitudes which are so crucial to society — and one worthy of objective assessment for all to see.

Topics for discussion

1. What is meant by the assertion that unlike many aspects of the curriculum, the aesthetic is not concerned with means to ends?
2. Recall personal experiences in support of the statement that involvement with arts extends and deepens the capacity to learn about oneself.
3. What, essentially, are the differences between scientific and artistic knowledge?

Suggestions for further reading

1. Cohen, L. and Manion, L. (1980) *Research Methods in Education.* London: Croom Helm. Chapter 1. 'The Nature of Inquiry'. In particular, see pp. 15–22, 'the nature of science'.
2. Calouste Gulbenkian Foundation (1982) *The Arts in Schools: Principles, Practice and Provision.* London: Calouste Gulbenkian Foundation.
3. Lowenfeld, V. and Brittain, W.I. (1982) *Creative and Mental Growth.* New York: Macmillan.

READING TWENTY • Assessing children with learning difficulties
G. Lowden

Introduction

Assessing children with learning difficulties is an activity undertaken by a variety of interested professionals for a variety of reasons. It is argued here that the main purpose of assessment is *stimulating and extending children's classroom learning* and the main emphasis of this chapter, therefore is placed on assessment by teachers, although the contribution of others such as educational psychologists, speech therapists, and medical practitioners will not be ignored. Some examination of the ethics of assessment will be made and some examination of the value of assessment. The place of assessment in the education of minority community children will be considered in relation to the purposes of such education. Some examples of appropriate practices will be given and the questions '*Why* should we assess?', '*What* should be assessed?', '*for whose information* should it be assessed?', and '*When* should we assess?' will be raised. Reference will be made to the issues of validity and reliability, to the argument about whether norm- or criterion-referenced assessment is better, and to the differences between so-called 'objective' and 'subjective' marking.

The effect of culture pattern

One problem facing the teacher in a minority community — whether indigenous or immigrant — is that instruments for specific use in assessment in that community may not be available. Any competent teacher, however, should be able to devise his or her own approach for general assessment, and should do so rather than attempt to use instruments designed for another community. One factor which would influence the use of tests would be the aim of the educational process, i.e. whether it be to

G. Lowden, 'Assessing children with learning difficulties', in, P. Williams (ed), *Special Education in Minority Communities*, Milton Keynes: Open University Press 1984. pp 95–108

enable the minority to merge fully into the majority community (to the point of eventual disappearance of the minority group) or to ensure the preservation of its cultural identity. In the latter case — especially where an indigenous community is concerned — teachers ought to produce assessment procedures and instruments in the minority culture and resources would have to be made available perhaps by the majority community for this purpose. (As, for example, *Profion Bangor*, Schools Council Committee for Wales, Welsh Tests and Materials Projects. Publication pending.)

Before discussing assessment in minority communities there are a few general points on teacher assessment to consider.

Levels of teacher assessment

There are various kinds of teacher assessment activities and for our purposes four levels are outlined.

1. Day-to-day evaluation by the teacher of a pupil's general progress. This will usually provide an answer to the question 'Is the child coping reasonably well in relation to the class norm?', and concerns step-by-step progress. Most assessment under this heading would be undertaken by the teacher as part of the teaching process, and its results would be used as 'feedback' with almost immediate effect through the modification of the next teaching stage. A mental record of this level would probably be kept, although a brief summary statement might be made in general terms when the teacher reviewed the work of the day. As Dean (1972) puts it:

    Good teachers have always kept records. Sometimes these have been written down, but often the important parts of the process have happened inside the teacher's head. A good teacher is constantly weighing up the situation, constantly looking for clues which tell her whether or not she is succeeding in what she is trying to do. She watches children's behaviour and draws conclusions from what she sees. . . . She takes soundings, by testing and questioning and observing in order to find out more fully where a child is and what he can do.

    The ability to assess at this level appears to be almost intuitive with some teachers, whilst others have to learn what and how to observe. Monitoring, or 'on-going assessment' is an essential element of the teaching process.
2. Assessment of longer term progress, e.g. at weekly, monthly, or even

longer intervals. This level will usually provide an answer to the question 'Is the child understanding the development of the work in question?', and it relates to conceptual progress. The record of this level is likely to be written and the data will usually be collected through two media: the result of 'tests' set by the teacher on an *ad hoc* basis, and the observations of behaviour made more or less systematically over the period. (See Lovell 1973, pp. 77–79.) The form of record is likely to be marks (probably out of the magical 'ten' — with the occasional appended remark) in the case of the former, and evaluation on some form of a five-point scale ('very positive', 'positive', 'neutral', 'negative', 'very negative'), in the case of the latter. Note that this, and the preceding level both relate to the work of the class.

3. Age-groups and ability-group comparison: in other words, 'Is the level of attainment reasonably commensurate with what would be expected from a child of that age and ability?' The first and second levels outlined above can, of course, produce results used to judge conformity with expected levels of performance, but at the third level the teacher would probably make use of published tests in addition to, if not entirely in place of, his or her own material. The form of record is likely to be either 'ages' or standard scores or possibly quotients, again preferably with appended remarks. Assessment at this level could be applicable to a whole school, in which case comparisons could be made between classes of chronological peers, or between successive classes of a specified age group, using previous records.

4. Diagnostic assessment. This will provide answers to the question 'What specific problem prevents this child from successfully performing tasks a, b, or c?' Instruments used here will probably be published tests covering a very wide range of aspects of learning. Some tests might be administered by educational psychologists or specially trained teachers. The form of record is likely to be varied: 'ages', 'quotients', 'scores', 'profiles', graphs and written reports all have a place.

Validity, reliability and standardization

Although observations and subjective evaluations both have their place in assessment, it is unlikely that systematic assessment can take place without the use of tests produced for the purpose; indeed the traditional school examination is one example of these. With any measuring instrument, the two concepts of validity and reliability are of major importance. These relate to the two questions that one must always ask about a test — and obtain satisfactory answers before using it. To check validity we should ask: 'Does it actually measure what it is claimed to measure?' To check reliability: 'Will it give more or less the same result each time it is used?' (It would be unrealistic to ask for identical results since there will be minor personal and environmental variations affecting test performances at different times.) For a detailed examination of these two concepts see Satterly (1981).

Authors of tests should publish details of validation and reliability procedures. They should also publish details of the size and nature of sample upon which the test has been standardized, and an analysis of results. It is important that the standardization population reflects the make-up of the minority community. It cannot be stressed too strongly that the inflexible use of the norms of an inappropriate test amounts, in the writer's opinion, to professional malpractice, although that is not to say that there might not well be some benefit from the use of the test itself (or parts of it) for diagnostic purposes.

It is this point which has led to much controversy over the assessment of children from minority immigrant groups in the UK. English language, western culture tests, standardized in Britain (or in North America) give quite inappropriate assessments when used with children from, for example, Asian cultures, with perhaps limited English. The scores obtained, whether intelligence quotients, reading ages, or other measures, tell us only how the child has fared in relation to the group of children who comprise the standardization sample, in this example culturally very distinct and with no linguistic handicap. In this situation even gifted children from minority cultures will have problems — but these problems are not in any way similar to the learning difficulties of the indigenous British child, with a similarly poor score on the test. One possible solution to this difficulty is to seek to construct 'culture-fair' tests, that is tests which measure intellectual qualities independent of the culture of the person being assessed.

Culture-fair testing

The point has already been strongly made that tests should be set within the culture of the population to be tested. Since comparisons of results of tests set in different culture patterns are largely invalid, much time and effort have been devoted to attempts to produce tests which are equally valid across cultures. Such attempts, however, have not met with success although there are test items, in particular mathematical items, which are relatively neutral. The reader interested in this aspect is referred to the useful chapter entitled 'Culture-fairness in assessment' in Hegarty and Lucas (1978).

The extent to which there is a need for culture-fair tests depends upon the reason for testing in the first place. The main justification is probably for use on occasions when comparisons between the minority community performance and that of the host or majority community are necessary. The criteria for deciding upon necessity are subject to a different set of conditions which might well not be mainly educational. As often happens in education, findings which produce 'factors' apparently showing differences between groups are seized upon as evidence of the need to take differential action in the education of such 'different' groups; a study by Jensen (1969), for example, indicated differences between black and white citizens of the USA, and the findings were taken to support segregated education.

It could, of course, be argued that where the purpose of education was to integrate a minority group to the point of total absorption, then the sooner the minority culture disappeared the sooner integration would happen. In other words, the tests of the host or majority community would increasingly become the ones to use. The corollary is that where the intention of education is the preservation, or development of the minority community, then any tests used should be set within that culture. In any case, the need for 'cross-cultural' tests seems doubtful on educational, if not on political, grounds.

Norm- and criterion-referenced tests

This problem of 'cultural loading' in tests can be circumvented if we use tests which are not norm-referenced, as is usual, but criterion-referenced. Norm-referenced tests provide norms, or average, performances of children in the standardization sample and a child's score on such a test is immediately compared with that of his peers in the standardization sample. Thus the Asian immigrant child mentioned above may be assessed on an intelligence test standardized on a Western population and his score may convert to an IQ of 85. All this means is that his performance on this test is well below the average performance of children of his age in the standardization sample. It tells us next to nothing about his performance in relation to children with a similar background to his own, and little about his educational potential.

On the other hand, criterion-referenced tests provide information about a pupil's skills, his strengths and weaknesses, what he has mastered and what has yet to be learnt. A norm-referenced test of driving skills would tell a motorist how well he drives in comparison with others, whereas a criterion-referenced test makes no such comparisons but indicates which driving skills he has mastered and which he has yet to learn: he is measured against the task, not against others. For the learner driver it is fairly clear which is the more useful approach.

The same principle applies in educational assessment: criterion-referenced measures offer information about educational skills, they lead directly into curriculum planning and into learning programmes. For this reason they offer educational advantages which norm-referenced tests do not possess and they reduce any possibility of making inappropriate inferences from test results. They are particularly useful in work with minority children, where norms may be difficult to establish, since populations may be small in size.

Objective and subjective marking

Questions have been raised about the lack of consistency between markers of the same essays, and there is evidence that multiple choice question papers give as valid an evaluation of the quality of a candidate as does the traditional essay. It is claimed that, whilst essays are subjectively marked, multiple choice question papers are objectively marked. Although the latter kind of paper can be marked accurately by any person with the 'key' (or, indeed, by a machine) and to that extent is certainly 'objective', this is no guarantee that there has not been subjectivity in the selection of the 'right answers' in the first place. This is particularly important in the assessment of minority children. Moreover subjectivity in the choice of *questions*, too, plays a very important part in assessing the performance of minority children.

This point was discussed by the Rampton Committee in relation to examinations generally (DES 1981). The committee recommended that all GCE and CSE examination boards should undertake a systematic review of the relevance of their syllabuses to the needs of Britain's multiracial school population. The same consideration applies to psychological and educational tests used in the assessment of minority children with learning difficulties.

It could be argued that there *should* be a subjective element in the marking of material produced by a pupil in a minority community: if this marking is undertaken by a teacher from the same community, there will be insights into the nature of the work which would not otherwise be possible. An assessment by someone from the majority community with merely an academic awareness of the minority culture would lack such insight. Even in objective testing there should at least be an interpretative element of this kind. The Rampton Report bears on this very point since it asked all education authorities, in relation to assessment for ESN schools, 'to take full account of the particular factors, such as cultural differences and the effects of discrimination which may have a bearing on the progress of West Indian pupils' (op.cit.).

Why should we assess?

It is possible for a teacher to spend more time in assessment than in teaching. If any reader doubts this statement, a brief glance at 'Tests in print' (Buros 1972) should serve to justify it; and in all but the most extreme cases — and then only in the short term — such a situation is unacceptable. In normal practice the teacher needs to know not only how well his or her pupils are acquiring skills, but also how effective his or her own methods are in helping them to do so. He or she needs to know how the progress of her minority community pupils compares with that of comparable children in other communities, and needs to have a knowledge of the standard of attainment to be expected at different levels in other communities. More importantly, the teacher needs to know which skills her pupils have mastered and which they have not.

Thus the purpose of assessment is here seen as motivational. If an assessment procedure does not produce action to enhance the child's learning, then it should not have been undertaken, and must not be repeated.

Tests as predictors

One criterion for the efficacy of a test is its usefulness in *predicting* behaviour, as, for example, in selection processes. The now largely discontinued 'eleven-plus' selection procedure is one example of this use. This is not the place for a discussion of the rights and wrongs of that selection process, but the point must be made that the predictive validity of a test is most unlikely to be the same for a minority community as for the community for which the test was developed. Readers are strongly advised never to make use of 'selection' tests other than those which have been devised within the culture pattern of the group with whom they are to be used, unless the tests have been adequately compared with others which have been so devised and found to correlate highly with them. (A correlation of 0.9 still reflects a prediction error of around 20 per cent.) If members of minority communities have to be 'selected' for membership of majority community groups then teachers' estimates of likely performance based even on their 'intuitive' judgements would seem to be better predictors than inappropriate tests.

What can be assessed?

A *full* assessment will only be undertaken for seriously handicapped children, partly because it is a lengthy process and a costly one, and partly because it is rarely necessary. It involves contributions from an educational psychologist, schools medical officer, and a social worker, as well as detailed teacher's reports. It also involves assessing personality, intellectual and physical skills, social adjustment, and attainment levels in a variety of areas. Teachers are more likely to be involved in 'screening' the population in order to identify those children whose performance was markedly deviant from that of the rest of the group in one or more areas. These would then be the subject of more detailed assessment.

Since, in a school setting, some children are likely to be quickly identified by teachers as having problems of work, and others are likely to be identified for anti-social behaviour, many of the children picked out in the screening process will be those already known to teachers. Specific assessment of their difficulties is likely to start with language and reading skills, and will involve investigation of their oral communication skills, auditory or visual handicaps, home-language situation, and language conflict in the bilingual community context, as well as the more common classroom reading problems. *Profion Bangor* (op. cit.) is an example of tests devised specifically for the diagnosis of such difficulties in children learning through the medium of Welsh as their first language.

The next important area in the minds of many teachers is mathematics, and the assessment of a child's level of numeracy has significance for success at school, as well as for social competence in adult life. Tests of computation can be used in translation provided that any 'problem-type' questions are presented in terms familiar to the children — that is using names, places and situations from the minority community's language and culture. Although norms would not be applicable with a different language, the results should provide useful guidance to the teacher.

If the assessment is being carried out by an educational psychologist a measurement of intelligence will be made by use of a standardized test such as the Wechsler Intelligence Scale for Children in the USA (Wechsler 1949) or, the British Abilities Scales, in the UK (Elliot 1979), both of which produce a profile of the performance on different aspects of the test battery. Although these two tests are probably as good examples of their genre as exist, unless standardizations on relevant minority populations exist, the results need interpretation. It is worth keeping an eye on the literature to see if 'versions' of tests are produced for specific communities, and on which population such versions have been tried out or standardized. With older children, tests of ability and aptitude in specific areas of potential work-linked activity are relevant, subject to the qualifications mentioned in the preceding section.

For whom should we assess?

Perhaps the most important person for whom assessment is undertaken, apart from the child, of course, is the teacher, who needs feedback on the child's learning. Other agencies less directly concerned include the following:

1. *The parents*. In the case of 'incomer' minority communities, liaison with parents about the progress of their children is of even greater importance than usual. With indigenous minority communities, too, the importance is high. The teacher has a professional duty to provide adequate information equal in accuracy to that of any medical or legal adviser, and formal tests will help him or her obtain that information.
2. *Other teachers*. To enable appropriate schemes of work to be devised for optimum learning, teachers who are receiving a child need to know details of the incoming child's educational background.
3. *Other institutions*. Records will usually provide information upon

which transfer of a pupil to a later stage of education will be based. Data relating to the child's performance within the minority community must be augmented by whatever evidence is available of his or her ability to cope within the majority community also. In this context comparisons with other pupils who have successfully made such a transfer might be valuable.

4. *Employers*. Basic information about public examination results, school tests, aptitude tests, and personal qualities is relevant here. An indication should be given as to whether the results are culture-linked or likely to be applicable universally.

5. *Teacher research*. Carefully maintained records of assessment might well enable the teacher to draw useful conclusions about his or her techniques and methods over a period of a year or more. Provided testing is not undertaken solely for this purpose (and if a *limited* amount is so undertaken) the collection of data for deferred action is permissible.

When should we assess?

Monitoring children's progress on a long-term basis necessitates systematic assessment, and this must be compatible with the school organization. It is clearly desirable to make an assessment at the beginning of the school year for a new child, but since the start is normally after a long period of holiday, assessment in the first few days of school does not allow for the spontaneous recovery from the effects of the recess shown by most children. Such 'start-of-year' assessment should not take place until the child has been in school for at least three weeks, and would normally be undertaken only once in each child's case. End-of-year assessments should be timed to avoid the exciting activities so often held at this period. It is probably sufficient for most periodic assessing to take place at no more than annual, or at least half-yearly, intervals. If half-yearly intervals are considered desirable, then the use of parallel forms of tests is advised, if possible. It is assumed that teachers are able to accept the assessments by colleagues in previous years as valid.

The pattern of assessment would probably emerge along the lines suggested below.

Informally: A continuous process, which involves 'feedback' for immediate application to current work.

Formally: (i) A first assessment three weeks after start of school year (in England and Wales, the last week of September), in language and reading (phonic knowledge, word recognition, comprehension, fluency, vocabulary, spelling) and in mathematics (concept development, computation processes).

(ii) An annual assessment three weeks before the end of the summer term (in England and Wales, July). This would involve a first assessment, plus attainment tests in various aspects of the curriculum, rating scales for personal qualities, and social adjustment evaluation. In the context of special education it is unlikely that the traditional secondary school examinations would be a part of this assessment, although certain aspects might be appropriate. (If a half-yearly assessment is made, this would be undertaken in England and Wales in early February.)

Conclusion

The assessment of minority children is based on the same conditions, and requires the same care, as the assessment of any children. The brief analyses of levels of assessment, of the typology of tests and of other forms of assessment are applicable to all kinds of assessment, irrespective of the community to which the child belongs. But there are, nevertheless, a number of particular considerations to which this chapter has drawn attention.

The first of these is the difficulty of making a fair evaluation of the educational progress of minority children when the available assessment techniques have usually been devised by and for members of another culture, and are often in a language which may not be very familiar. This point carries with it an implication that assessment must be more informal and must make more use of teachers' observations, and in particular, observations of how well a child learns, rather than of what he knows of another culture. Informal evaluation will rely more on impression than formal, test-based assessment does, and some loss of objectivity has to be compensated for by observation over a period of some length.

One way of extending the value of informal assessment is by seeking impressions from more than one person. Here not only other teachers but parents, too, can be useful. What the child *does* at home is often useful information.

Assessment of minority children requires sensitivity. When norm-referenced tests are used the scores gained must be interpreted. They must be appreciated in the light of a different tradition, and a different cultural experience. This does not necessarily mean that all minority children are very much more able than their test scores suggest. But it does mean that this possibility must be borne in mind and evaluated against other sources of information.

But a better approach than interpreting standard test scores, as this chapter suggests, is to use criterion-referenced assessment procedures. These can be teacher-produced, set in the context of the pupils' own cultural background and, most importantly, lead directly into the curriculum. It is this link between what is tested and what is taught which is the heart of the criterion-referenced procedure, and which is so much more productive than arid comparisons with remote standardization populations. Indeed, teachers in minority communities should regard the production of criterion-referenced tests as part of their job specification.

This brings up the critical question of language, and here one can be entirely dogmatic. Where the teaching is done in the language of the minority, so should the testing. And this requires not only that the material used should be in the appropriate language, but so should the whole test procedure. The one question not posed in the chapter, but to which there is only one answer, is 'Who should assess?'. The answer implied throughout is that it must be a teacher, and a teacher who is a member of the same minority community as the child.

Topics for discussion

1. Distinguish between the concepts of *reliability* and *validity* in relation to assessment tests.
2. In what ways can *criterion-referenced* tests help the teacher circumvent the problem of 'cultural loading'?
3. Discuss the author's contention that 'if an assessment procedure does not produce action to enhance the child's learning, then it should not have been undertaken, and must not be repeated.'

Suggestions for further reading

1. Taylor, M.J. and Hegarty, S. (1985) *The Best of Both Worlds? A Review of Research into the Education of Pupils of South Asian Origin.* NFER-Nelson.
2. Satterly, D. (1981) *Assessment in Schools.* Oxford: Blackwell.

3. 'Assessment and records: progression and continuity' (1983) in, *Primary Practice: a sequel to 'The Practical Curriculum'*. Schools Council Working Paper 75. Methuen Educational, Chap 10, pp. 116–131.

READING TWENTY ONE • Towards more effective record-keeping   *W.R. Porter*

In any consideration of record-keeping, the most fundamental question is often the one which is never asked; that is, what are records for? Are they for the teacher's own use, for other teachers within the school, for other schools, or for parents? The answer to each of these questions will determine the content and type of record used. The proper implication of asking these questions is clearly to determine what it is that those concerned — that is the 'consumer' rather than those writing the records — will consider useful information. If this exercise is carefully thought out, there will be important results. Firstly, it will avoid unnecessary sheaves of unread paper cluttering up the school. Secondly, and more importantly, the fact that records are useful to the recipient will tend to ensure that record-keeping is taken seriously by those completing them. There is nothing that will ensure bad record-keeping more than the knowledge that nobody will find them of any use. Furthermore, it is useful to have three other considerations in mind; that the child himself is a good record — nothing is achieved by recording self-evident information; that samples of work are often more valuable than a commentary on the work; and that teachers do actually talk to each other, and that this is for some purposes a more efficient way of transmitting information. These three points may be stating the obvious, but it is surprising how often they are ignored in favour of writing long screeds.

These basic principles, then, should influence thinking about the structure of records. It is necessary next to consider the following fundamental questions.

1. Is it information I want?
2. Is it sufficient — or too much?

W. Roy Porter, 'Towards more effective record-keeping', *School Organization*, **3**, 1, 1983, pp 85–95

3. Is it clear and in convenient form?
4. Is it easy to extract relevant parts (e.g. for use by subject teachers in secondary schools)?

A recent Schools Council/NFER project 'Record Keeping in Primary Schools' found there was agreement among teachers on the following general principles of record-keeping. Records should:

1. be easy to fill in
2. be easy to understand
3. have a clear purpose
4. should not be too lengthy or a waste of time
5. should not be full of jargon
6. should not be used to judge the work of a teacher
7. should not be used to transmit prejudices and ill-founded opinions.

I imagine, incidentally, that parents would subscribe to these principles. This is an important factor when one comes to consider confidentiality.

The same piece of research went on to ascertain the priorities teachers gave to different types of information. No surprises here! Following the formal items (e.g. identification, medical and personal facts, persons to contact in emergency, physical handicaps) came particular learning difficulties, referral to psychologist or child guidance and resultant recommendations, attainment in basic skills, and results of standardized tests. Of lower priority were detailed categories on language, mathematics and personal development. At the bottom came information on such things as physical education and games skills, drama and movement ability, and use of study skills. Less experienced teachers required a higher degree of structure than their more experienced colleagues.

There are clearly lessons to be learned here regarding the construction of children's records. A number of those items which are accorded low priority by practising teachers have traditionally been included on many a record sheet. They are, on the whole, difficult to complete, time-consuming and, therefore, often badly done. Perhaps, however, they are badly done because it is recognized as information of little practical use to another teacher.

In addition to the school records, often laid down by the Authority, the individual teacher will keep cumulative records. In order to achieve consistency through the school, it is essential that some of these, particularly in the basic subjects, should be developed by the school rather than by individual teachers. By using the principles already enunciated, a cumulative record of reading skills, written language skills and maths checkpoints can dovetail with the annual record sheet, and be included in the record folder with samples of work. The important point here is to ensure that the cumulative record does lead easily to the completion of school records. It will also ensure that the next teacher will be able to continue the child's progress uninterrupted by a lengthy period of testing and assessment before making further headway.

A constantly recurring problem is the criteria by which teachers assess children. When externally validated tests are used, this is no problem. But to use such tests for much of school work is neither practical nor desirable. One is then faced with the problem of subjectivity. Within the school, one teacher's 'well above average' might be another teacher's 'slightly above average.' This teacher's 'very imaginative' creative writing might be that teacher's 'more interested in ideas than construction.' This can be overcome only partly by posing specific questions (e.g. creative ability) and requiring, say, a tick in the appropriate box, accompanied by a comment only if necessary. It does not, however, solve the problem of the norm against which the judgement is made. Is it a class, a school, the authority or a national criterion? The first of these is obviously the simplest. In spite of the obvious ramifications, could it in the long run be the best? Whatever decision is made, it is of fundamental importance that teachers are abundantly clear about the policy to be adopted.

Another fundamental issue has already been touched on — that of confidentiality. A decision on this is crucial to any formulation of a successful record-keeping policy. It would be useful to rehearse the arguments on both sides of this issue. In a survey by *Where*, the mouthpiece of the Advisory Centre for Education, it was found that only thirteen authorities allowed parents access to records, and twelve of these only at the discretion of the head. Needless to say, ACE is in favour of parents having access to records, and many teachers (but fewer headteachers) support this view. Those opposing confidentiality would cite the following reasons:

1. Parents should have access to records since they contain nothing that isn't already known to them.
2. The records contain only factual information. They should contain nothing that is not absolutely true.
3. Teachers should be frank with parents, and be prepared to discuss the records.
4. Even if parents do not understand what is written, teachers should be

prepared to explain. (No doubt such teachers were among those mentioned earlier, who felt that records should be easy to understand and free of jargon.)

5. Parents have a right to see what is written about their own children.
6. The more frankness in relationships between teacher and parents, the less likely are disagreements. Relationships are improved by open discussion of factual records.

Some teachers prefer a middle course. They disagree with confidentiality in principle, but have reservations in specific areas. Their views are expressed thus:

1. The personality record should not be revealed.
2. Social background should not be revealed. (It is difficult to believe that parents don't already know any factual information under both these headings.)
3. Records should only be revealed at the express request of a parent, and then only in the presence of the head teachers. (Where records are not confidential, heads told Schools Council investigators that few parents asked to see them. One wonders, however, if the parents knew that the records could be seen.)
4. Social development should be written in pencil, so that it can be erased after a fixed period. (Interestingly, this fits in quite well with one of the Younger committee's principles — HMSO 6353, Dec. 1975 'Computers and Privacy' — which says, 'In the design of information systems, periods should be specified beyond which the information should not be retained.')

Those favouring confidentiality advance similarly powerful reasons:

1. Records are solely concerned with passing information from one professional to another, and are therefore not the concern of parents.
2. Parents can discuss their children with teachers, and there is no need for them to see records.
3. Useful information will be excluded from records if they are 'open'.
4. Use of proper professional terminology will have to be dropped in favour of statements made in lay terms.
5. When records are not confidential, information is transmitted verbally. This cannot always be carried out systematically or factually.
6. Facts to which the parent might object would be either omitted or softened, to the detriment of the record. Proper conclusions would be

excluded, since they would be subjective, and therefore open to challenge.

There are, undoubtedly, cogent arguments on both sides. Often the decision is taken in any case by our political masters, who are moved by considerations which are not always in the best interests of children. The Schools Council survey found that, where records had become open to parents, the amount of information written had been greatly reduced, according to the headteachers questioned. We are not told what information was omitted, and one is left to conjecture about its relevance and objectivity.

My own view is that there is little to be lost, and a great deal to be gained by showing records to parents. They are reassured by the knowledge that no secret documents about their children exist. The record sheet is also a useful starting point for a discussion with the parent about the child. In any event, it seems to me consistent with current attitudes on democracy and open government that hostility to confidentiality will increase, and that the teaching profession will be forced to alter its hitherto inviolable attitudes to the passing on of information. It can take heart from those who have accepted open records for some time, and have discovered that their fears have not materialized.

It would be useful to examine the development of records within the ILEA in recent years, to establish how they relate to the general comments made so far.

For many years, the annual record sheet consisted simply of five headings, with a large space under each. The headings were:

General Personality Sketch
Particular Abilities and Interests
Special Needs
Language (a) Reading (b) Oral and Written Expression
Mathematics.

The quality of completion varied enormously, as one would expect from such an imprecise format. Some teachers felt obliged to fill the available space with general comments, which were of little help to another teacher, e.g. 'Has worked hard this year, and made good progress'. On the other hand, many listed the stages reached, for example, in maths and reading. Often no comments were made under the second and third headings — perhaps because there was less space devoted to this and they were thus felt to be less important. What was clear was that there was a great deal of inconsistency, which considerably diminished the value of these documents as aids to the next teacher, whether within the school or outside.

In the early 1970s there began to be rumblings of discontent, and I can identify two reasons for this. Firstly, more and more teachers, including heads, had taken part in Primary Management courses run by the Authority. One of the important ingredients of this course was a consideration of records. The tutors' notes for these courses contain some interesting suggestions for discussion. Some of them have been covered in the earlier parts of this article, but one or two quotes are particularly relevant in examining the record sheet just referred to. 'Records should contain sufficient detail for a balanced judgement to be made by another teacher'. 'They should require the minimum of a teacher's time to maintain them'. 'In some fields one might well limit one's record keeping to simply the unusual'. The Notes also include three golden rules.

1. Keep as few records as possible.
2. Be constantly on the lookout for reducing those already in existence.
3. Regularly revise those in constant use.

The second factor which stimulated fresh consideration of records was referred to in an Assessment of Performance Unit document, which said,

> Recent changes at the DES have been accompanied by a series of critical pronouncements on the system. Formerly statements about the education system from the DES have filtered through the profession via HMIs, LEA district officers, advisers, to the teachers in the schools. More recently opinions have been voiced directly through parliament and political speech-making, e.g. the launching of the 'Education Debate'.

I believe the opening up of the whole debate, with an emphasis on accountability, on assessment, and thus on accuracy and objectivity, was a profound background factor in the ILEA (as in other places, of course), and that these two influences were brought to bear on a detailed examination of records.

A Working Party was set up, consisting of authority officers and representatives of the teachers' associations, and the new records *Mark 1* were adopted. These consisted of three documents.

1. PERSONAL PARTICULARS
In addition to formal information, headings, with appropriate spaces were:

FIRST LANGUAGE OF CHILD
FIRST LANGUAGE OF PARENTS   } If not English
LANGUAGE SPOKEN AT HOME
PHYSICAL DISABILITIES
SOCIAL ADJUSTMENT TO SCHOOL

This document is updated and initialled as the child progresses through the school.

2. NURSERY RECORD SUMMARY
Following the formal information, the headings were:

REGULARITY OF ATTENDANCE — if irregular due to
  (a) ill health
  (b) casual attitude
  (c) crisis at home

PLEASE NOTE ANY POSITIVE INDICATION OF PARENTS' INTEREST IN THE CHILD'S ADJUSTMENT TO SCHOOL AND SUBSEQUENT DEVELOPMENT.

PHYSICAL DISABILITIES IF ANY
  Serious illnesses
  Physical handicaps

ATTITUDE TO OTHERS (Here there were boxes to be ticked and dated)

DEGREE OF INDEPENDENCE (with similar boxes)

LANGUAGE SKILLS including development of oracy
(Four sub-headings, each with five levels of ability to be ticked and dated)

APPARENT READINESS FOR MORE FORMAL LEARNING
(Five sub-headings, to be ticked as above)

SPECIAL NEEDS

SPECIAL INTERESTS AND PREFERRED ACTIVITIES

ADDITIONAL COMMENTS

3. PRIMARY YEARLY RECORD SUMMARY
(All sub-headings to be ticked in the appropriate box on a five-point scale. Ample room for comments in addition.)

LANGUAGE
  ORAL
    Use
    Understanding
  RATE OF PROGRESS
    Use
    Understanding
  WRITTEN
    Ability
    Interest
  RATE OF PROGRESS

READING — Ability
          Interest

RATE OF PROGRESS

CREATIVE ACTIVITIES
  Ability
    Painting, drawing, writing, etc. — descriptive
    Modelling, building, craftwork, etc. — constructive
    Dance, music, drama, etc. — participatory
  Level of interest (Sub-headings as above)
  Rate of progress (Sub-headings as above)

PHYSICAL SKILLS
  Ability
    Body skills — sport, dance, gymnastics, etc.
    Hand skills — tools, instruments, scissors, pens, etc.
  Level of interest (Sub-headings as above)
  Rate of progress (Sub-headings as above)

ATTENDANCE (tick appropriate boxes; room for comments)
  Regular
  Irregular
    If irregular, caused by minor ailments, major illness, accident, other
    reasons, unexplained circumstances.

GENERAL COMMENTS

These three documents were accompanied by a four-page booklet of
explanatory notes for teachers. The scheme was introduced in the school

year 1976–7 with infants and first year juniors, and was also voluntary for other juniors. Just prior to the introduction of these new records, a bombshell was dropped by the Education Committee, which decided that the records should not be confidential. (They were all, incidentally, headed 'Confidential'). The teachers' associations were indignant, mainly because it was felt that such a decision should have been made *before* the new records were designed, since it would have been an important factor in the working party's thinking. However, the Education Committee was adamant, and the scheme went ahead.

It was evident after only one year's experience that there was considerable dissatisfaction with the new records. The working party was recalled, and asked the Authority's Research and Statistics branch to carry out a survey of teachers' opinions. Some of the findings were of great importance in establishing the practical application of the principles suggested at the beginning of this article. Though the general view was that this more structured approach was an improvement, there were a number of specific objections, the most important of which are detailed, together with the changes that resulted.

The *five-point scale* came under fire. It was not felt to fit in with modern primary philosophy. Teachers had no guidance on the standards by which judgements were made (a point mentioned earlier) or how many children there should be in each group. There was no guidance in the booklet on this. Furthermore it did not conform with the three-point scale used on transfer to secondary schools (25 per cent, 50 per cent, 25 per cent) and was therefore confusing to teachers and even more confusing to parents. Infants teachers particularly objected to grading children, and most felt that the emphasis should be on the stage reached by a child, rather than a grading in comparison with others.

The eventual effect of the criticisms was to alter the whole style of the new records *Mark 2*. In READING, a series of ten stages of development were listed, to be ticked when reached, with a space for comments. Further headings followed concerning (a) books read, including reading schemes (b) general enthusiasm and interest (c) special provision in case of difficulty (d) reading test score and date (if any), and (e) other relevant information. Comments only were called for under these five headings.

In WRITING there were four headings:

Personal statements
Factual statements

Imaginatively
Using information from various sources of reference.

Each of these has ample space for comments, and, notably, two boxes available under each heading; one for 'marked ability', and one for 'serious and persistent difficulty'. The change from five ability groups will be noted, as will the fact that most children will attract a comment but no tick.

In MATHEMATICS the assessment system is different. Against each item there are three boxes marked 'First stage,' 'Second stage,' and 'Third stage.' These refer to the ILEA Mathematics Guidelines, but the use of this is *not* compulsory. If not used, there is room for a comment. The headings are:

Sets
Numbers
    Whole numbers
    Operations with whole numbers
    Fractional numbers
Measures
    Length
    Time
    Cost
    Capacity and Volume
    Weight
    Area
    Angle
Geometry
General enthusiasm and interest (with two boxes — again, 'marked ability' *and* 'serious and persistent difficulty')

The CREATIVE ABILITIES section has four headings:

Two-dimensional work
Three-dimensional work
Dance and drama
Music

PHYSICAL SKILLS is subdivided into:

Manual dexterity
Physical education

There is a separate section for HANDWRITING.

All of these have the two boxes previously described.

Readers will again note the dropping of the five boxes, and the drastic reduction in the number of headings.

Penultimately, there are two large spaces for

1. TOPICS/PROJECTS. Note any topics/projects worked on during the year and any noteworthy attitude shown by the child.

2. Any GENERAL COMMENTS on the child, including where appropriate any special educational needs and aptitudes and reference to any action taken. Finally, the section on ATTENDANCE asks for matters which have significantly affected the child's schooling.

So much, then, for the fate of the five-point scale. The next major criticism was the assessment of RATE OF PROGRESS. This was thought to be difficult to ascertain, and in practice was usually marked 3 (average). It has been dropped on the new form, but a reference to a markedly low or high rate of progress could be made in the comments spaces.

A further comment arising from the Research and Statistics report concerned the PLACING OF THE BOXES relative to the spaces for comments. On the old records, the boxes were immediately next to the headings, i.e. towards the left hand side of the sheet, and the space for comments was on the right, thus:

LANGUAGE   Comments

Oral	1	2	3	4	5
Use					
Understanding					

. This was felt to discourage comments. On the new sheets, the boxes are on the right, with the comment space between them and the headings. Since most children will not be markedly above or below average, the comments assume more importance than the boxes.

Most teachers felt that the sections on CREATIVE ACTIVITIES AND PHYSICAL SKILLS were too tightly structured, extremely difficult to complete, and of minimal use to the next teacher. The reader will note the drastic reduction in the number of headings in this section, and, of course, the elimination of the five ability boxes in favour of the two extreme boxes.

The section on ATTENDANCE is also much less structured than before. There is a new section on TOPIC/PROJECTS, which was a notable omission from the old record, whilst the GENERAL COMMENTS section has more space, and an explanatory note of advice.

These are the major changes to the main record which were agreed by the working party, and subsequently implemented. Readers will recall that there were two other record sheets referred to. The Personal Particulars form remained unaltered. There were, however, major changes in the records for lower primary children. It was felt appropriate to extend the NURSERY RECORD SUMMARY to include first year infants, and to expand the records considerably. The major changes were as follows:

1. ATTITUDE TO OTHERS was deleted, and came under a general paragraph headed SOCIAL DEVELOPMENT.
2. The five ability groups were dropped in the LANGUAGE SKILLS and READING READINESS sections, and replaced by checklists headed LANGUAGE SKILLS and EARLY READING SKILLS.
3. New headings were PHYSICAL SKILLS (with two sub-sections on large muscle control and small muscle control); and ATTITUDE TO LEARNING.
4. An eight-stage checklist on EARLY MATHEMATICAL EXPERI-ENCE was added.
5. The section on PARENTS' INTEREST was deleted.

The last of these was clearly a reaction to the lifting of confidentiality.

It would be appropriate to make a brief comment on this latter question, because it is relevant to note that the new records were designed *after* the decision on open records, whereas the old ones were not. It is interesting to note that the only change which took place as a result of this is the one mentioned in (5) above. There is no doubt that many previously held fears were allayed in the light of experience, and that teachers were encouraged to be more objective in their comments, and to be prepared to justify what was written down. Significantly, research showed that there was less apprehension amongst teachers than heads about open records.

Curiously enough, the new records are still headed 'Confidential'!

The new records came out in the autumn of 1979 for use at the end of the school year 1979–80. It is generally agreed that they are more acceptable, more useful and easier to complete. They also lend themselves to use in conjunction with internal cumulative records. Though there would always be individual criticism of any type of record, the current ILEA series seems to meet general approval. Provided each school is prepared to formulate its own policy, and adapt the Authority records when appropriate, I believe that these types of record sheet meet teachers' aspirations as expressed in the criteria enunciated at the beginning of this article.

Topics for discussion

1. The formulation of records should always be a collaborative exercise involving all the teachers within the primary school. Discuss.
2. How far do you agree with the view that record-keeping should be seen as part of the process of teaching rather than as an end of the day or weekly activity?
3. Critically evaluate the arguments for and against the confidentiality of pupil records as they relate to parental access to these documents.

Suggestions for further reading

1. Clift, P., Weiner, G. and Wilson, E. (1981) *Record Keeping in Primary Schools*. Schools Council Research Studies, Macmillan Education.
2. Kay, B.W. (1975) 'Monitoring pupils' performance' (in section entitled 'Educational standards today') *Trends in Education*, 2, pp 11–18.
3. Frith, D.S. and Macintosh, H.G. (1984) *A Teacher's Guide To Assessment*. London: Stanley Thornes.

READING TWENTY TWO • The primary school and the microcomputer: some policy issues   *R. Garland*

Introduction

A decade and a half ago I was a first generation Warden of a Teachers' Centre very much involved in introducing the 'new' mathematics into the curricula of local primary schools. During a visit to one such school I had a cup of tea in the staffroom at break. Sitting in a well-worn armchair in a dark corner of the room was an elderly member of staff. He viewed me in my enthusiasm and beckoned me over: 'Mr. Garland, we're in a lovely rut in

R. Garland, The Primary School and the Microcomputer: some policy issues. *Education 3–13*, 11, 1, 1983, pp 33–37

this school: why can't you leave us alone?' A characteristic of the past fifteen or so years is that schools have not been left alone to get on with the job.

Change

The period of critical interest in the work and achievements of primary education that has been described by Richards (1982) as the end of the golden age is unlikely to be a passing phenomenon. It emerged from factors not solely associated with education and is part of a wider scrutiny of our national institutions; it has been accompanied by rapid technological change within society. Schools have had to take cognizance of both of these phenomena: far greater public interest and a desire to influence their work, and changes in technology that are capable of fundamentally altering work patterns and life styles.

A comparatively recent method of coping with the change and the challenge of the many new ideas that are impinging on the professional horizons of primary school teachers is the creation of curriculum policies (Garland 1982). The development of a policy involves a school in a conscientious and collective attempt to examine critically an area of its curriculum with a view to establishing common agreements on priorities and procedures. The movement was given a powerful legitimizing voice in Her Majesty's Inspectorate (HMI) survey of primary schools (DES 1978a). This has been further reinforced in the HMI's illustrative survey of first schools (DES 1982) where it is argued that 'the day is past' when primary and first schools could be operated by teachers working separately and pursuing their own inclinations (p. 60). The practice arising from such an imperative, typically has a senior member of staff assuming particular responsibility for the developments under the general guidance of the headteacher. There is evidence that such an approach is feasible and that teachers welcome and support it. In this article I wish to explore ways in which this important new trend in primary education might relate to another fresh phenomenon: the introduction of microcomputers into the primary school.

Technology

During the last thirty or so years primary schools have adopted a number of technological innovations and incorporated them in the curriculum. Possibly one of the first was the radio but more recently there have been the tape recorder, the television set, the language master and the video-tape recorder. In each case staff training and familiarity with the new teaching aid was involved: why should the adoption of the microcomputer produce issues that are not already familiar to those working in the primary sector? Not only have there been innovations but there will undoubtedly be candidates in the future. Within the next five years for example video disc machines are likely to be in schools with their enormous potential for the storage of textual and graphical information: a disc the size of a gramophone record with three-quarters of a million pages of text on it. What possible adjustments might schools have to make if the microelectronics industry offered every home the possibility of access to a vast multimedia library with individualized teaching programmes? Are we at this moment however able to claim that the microcomputer is any different in kind from other gadgets and hardware that have graced our classrooms and in some cases ended up in dusty store cupboards as part of the archaeology of curriculum development?

Paradoxically the answer would seem to be both 'yes' and 'no'! Staff will need training to learn how to operate the most sophisticated technology that schools have used to date but microcomputers are qualitatively different from the innovations of the past in the enormous range of tasks that they can undertake and in the manner in which they can perform operations that previously were considered to be the sole prerogative of intelligent living organisms. Of educational significance is the fact that their use is highly motivating to children: they are interactive, and pupils can even 'teach' them. If their potential is to be even minutely explored and exploited in schools teachers will need an appreciation of their power and indeed of their current limitations.

Although the potential is considerable, in practice possibilities will be bounded by the amount of knowledge available to schools and located within the educational thinking and values of the practitioners. It may appear to be trite to state that education is essentially concerned with values but it is these that will determine how the machines are to be used.

It is unwise to be definitive regarding the uses of a microcomputer within the school curriculum as the whole movement is so new. Jones (1980) in a national survey of English local education authorities only discovered some thirty-odd primary schools using them.

Tentatively, however, it would appear that there are four main ways in which they might affect a primary school's work:

1. to support, enhance and extend current approaches;
2. to aid administration;
3. to be studied with the theme of computer awareness;
4. to challenge existing practice and thinking.

Supporting current approaches

At present and in the immediate future the most common use of the microcomputer is likely to be the support and extension of existing curriculum work. Computers require programs to run them and these programs contain assumptions regarding what is desirable and justifiable in a primary school. As Howe (1981) has pointed out they can be chalk and talk transposed to another media; they can treat the learner as an inert memorizer of other people's ideas. They can also enhance practice and present old ideas in new and possibly more interesting guises: learning grid references can become an addictive treasure hunt as in *Pirates*, a program developed by the ITMA team in Plymouth. The computer can simulate for example an archaeological investigation as in 'Expedition to Saqqara' a most imaginative program developed by a practising teacher. The children have to research and plan a dig based on a real site in Egypt. The computer will tell them where they are, what they have found and how much the expedition has cost to date! The hypotheses that were generated by their research will be confirmed or confounded. The majority of teachers could find something that matches their own educational philosophy within these or similar programs. They do not require that teachers or schools should change in any fundamental manner or that valued or traditional ways of doing things should disappear. It is the area in which those enterprising teachers who have taught themselves to program have been active. It is significant to note that those who advocate such uses of a computer refer to it as a tool: in no sense is it to be seen subversive or threatening.

Administration

Primary schools do not have the complicated timetabling problems that exist in secondary education and that can be eased by using a computer but there are obvious uses in the keeping of pupil records, printing updated class lists and in ordering equipment. At the moment cost is a barrier to this development: while a primary school aided by the recently announced 50 per cent government grant might be able to afford around two hundred pounds for a basic machine, the cost of adding a disc system to give quick and easy access to the stored data and a printer to provide a permanent record could well quadruple the cost. This use of a computer might be viewed with suspicion if it were thought in any sense to depersonalize relationships and it would need to be demonstrated that its benefits could justify the expense involved.

Computer awareness

This topic may be interpreted from at least two rather different viewpoints. Just as children engage in projects on a whole variety of topics so there could be an examination of computers. This would involve researching about them, discovering how they work and what sort of task they can perform. In one project (Garland 1982) children were alerted to social, cultural and moral issues raised by computers by becoming familiar with one major aspect of their use. Data about the class — names, addresses, hobbies, etc. — were stored in the computer. Once the children had emerged from the complete novelty of being able instantly to discover or confirm a whole variety of information about their classmates the opportunity was taken to raise questions: Who owns these data? Should everyone in the school be able to see it? Is there any information that should not be stored about us? Could incorrect information harm somebody?

Challenging existing thinking

This final category of use is not so comparatively clear-cut as those discussed previously. Those who subscribe to it hold one value in common however: a dissatisfaction with the current status quo whether it is within the field of the predominantly teacher controlled approach to primary education or more fundamentally with the whole assumption of the need for compulsory schooling. It is important not to exaggerate the size or strength of this category or indeed to claim that the romantic liberals and the deschoolers who occupy it are in any sense united by a multitude of common purposes. In one manifestation ideas have been taken from the study of Artificial Intelligence (AI), a discipline which involves the examination of intelligence using the ideas and methods of computation (Abelson and di Sesson 1981). The mainstream primary microcomputer movement however springs from grassroots practice rather than theory: this has resulted in a most commendable enthusiasm and activity at classroom level but inevitably it has been in danger of encapsulation in existing ways of thinking. Ideas from AI challenge present orthodoxy: they arrive cross-fertilized by contact with a variety of disciplines and informed by research. Significantly AI provides a model of the learner that is congruent to that held by the romantic liberals: he or she is seen as an active problem solver. Papert, a former student of Piaget's, in a seminal book (1980), has spoken to the values of progressive primary school teachers. He discusses the use of Logo, a computer language that he argues enables children to gain insights into the nature of mathematical discovery. These ideas have been introduced into our primary schools (Maxwell 1982; Mullan 1982). At the sharp end of this radical continuum of beliefs about the educational potential of the computer is the anticipation that schools as we know them at present might disappear (Chandler 1982). The deschooling movement, little in evidence of late, may have discovered a technology, though it is unlikely however that the majority of practising primary school teachers will be within the ranks of the deschoolers! What is more certain is that they will wish to assimilate the microcomputer within current practice.

The present

At present only the minority of our primary schools that have purchased machines have accumulated experience and expertise in their use. What are the issues that have been discovered to date? How do those yet to purchase view the problems and do views coincide between the two groups? In a preliminary exploration of these questions six headteachers of primary schools who had assisted in another investigation (Garland 1982) were interviewed. The purposes of the interview were twofold: to discover the headteachers' attitudes towards the educational use of a microcomputer; and to learn of their professional judgements on the problems that would arise if they should decide to purchase one for the school.

None of the schools in question owned a micro although two had limited experience of classroom use through the enterprise of members of staff. All were considering purchase. The heads disclaimed detailed knowledge of micros and indeed the interviewer at times became the interviewee as he was probed on his knowledge and judgements. They had however given thought to both the educational and practical classroom issues as the matter was considered important. Their attitudes were all basically favourable although tinged with the realism that practical reasoning evokes. They had further discussed points informally with staff, parents, advisers and advisory teachers and were conscious that the local education authority had a special subcommittee examining issues.

In their judgements a number of issues were of key importance:

1. staff training and attitude;
2. making an informed purchase;
3. the educational justification of the endeavour.

The creation of favourable attitudes on the part of the staff was seen of paramount and crucial importance: if the staff were not interested then the enterprise was doomed. Associated with this was a desire that suitable in-service training should be available: teachers would need to appreciate the advantages and opportunities that the machines might bring.

None had yet considered relationships between curriculum policies and the microcomputer: the knowledge and the experience to make such links was not yet available. The current considerations concerned the smooth introduction of the machines in the school and the building up of that most valued commodity: experience.

There is no strong tradition of teachers writing about or reporting their work: much of what we know of primary education is based on what observers of the system have written. Microcomputers could well prove an exception to this pattern: although they have not been in primary schools for more than a few years there are already accounts of their use written by practising teachers. Those who write are not necessarily typical of the profession. Many for example are in senior positions: they are committed to the new technology and are not the pedagogical losers of this world! A characteristic of their writing is the manner in which educational considerations are interlaced with problems that are peculiar to the micro. There is no sense of a flirtation with novelty for its own sake that emerged as one of the worries of the group who were interviewed. David Ellingham identified in his review (1982) of a number of case studies written by teachers the following points as of concern to schools purchasing a microcomputer:

1. the teacher and the computer;
2. the equipment and its use;
3. the children and the computer;
4. the classroom organization;
5. organizing the programs;
6. the availability of programs.

These items are remarkably similar to those identified by the heads who were interviewed. Hardly surprising, the only significant additional item concerns the attitudes of the children. The evidence is that schools have a real bonus when micros are introduced: the children love them! What also is apparent is that within schools where the machines have been in use for some time there is still a large and commendable degree of experiment and tentative conclusion.

Ways ahead

Although curriculum policies orchestrate and codify the tried and the existing they should be dynamic and capable of accommodating and assimilating the new. Microcomputers are too new and educationally novel to be incorporated instantly into existing policies: Jones (1982) gives implicit recognition of this fact in his brief discussion of a school's philosophy compared with his overwhelming concern with the efficient organization of the machines. It seems likely that there will be a pre-policy stage in a school that adopts a microcomputer. The eventual aim will be for the machine to take its place in the school's educational thinking with guidance to staff on when, how and where it might be used.

Adopting a microcomputer involves acceptance of not only the physical presence of a machine in one's classroom but of ideas. The ideas are that it is legitimate to use the machines in a primary school, that it can be justified educationally, that there are advantages to be gained and that it is compatible with the educational values of those involved. In view of the microcomputer's complexity it is important to establish that its use is feasible: will in-service training be available so that it may be used efficiently? Are programs available? What will happen if it breaks down? What could profitably follow the acquisition of a machine is a period of trial and experimentation with the results and the judgements of the participants being available to their colleagues.

From this experimentation *a knowledge base* will gradually emerge that will enable the school to appreciate appropriate ways in which the machine might be more directly incorporated into the school's policies. A senior member of staff needs to take overall responsibility working in conjunction with the headteacher. Effort will be required: policies and good practice do not emerge by chance but by the conscious and deliberate efforts of those involved. If it is felt that the microcomputer should play a role in a school's life and not merely remain as a fringe activity and the province of the enthusiast then the steps that are the precursors to sound policy making will be required: thought, management, leadership and imagination.

It has been suggested that microcomputers and their associated technology have the potential to make fundamental changes in the school system but that their use will be determined by the dominant value positions. In reality they will be used as an adjunct to existing practice. Currently primary schools are in the process of developing whole curriculum policies. These policies however codify and regulate tried practice. Microcomputers are still new. At present knowledge of their operation and potential use is limited. Schools would be unwise to decide *a priori* how they might be used. A coordinated period of experimentation and evaluation is required eventually merging into the development of policies for their use. At the moment we are in the position where the printing press has been invented before the book!

Topics for discussion

1. Discuss Garland's assertion that microcomputers are *qualitatively different* from any previous technological innovation.
2. Use your knowledge of learning theory to account for the enormous motivational capacity of microcomputers for most children.
3. What have developments in microcomputers to do with the ideas of the *deschooling* movement?

Suggestions for further reading

1. Maddison, A. (1982) *Microcomputers in the Classroom.* London: Hodder and Stoughton.
2. Fairbrother, R. (ed.) (1984) *Primary Contact: Microcomputers in Education Special.* Manchester Polytechnic.

3. O'Shea, T. and Self, J. (1983) *Learning and Teaching with Computers*, Brighton: Harvester Press.

READING TWENTY THREE • The integration of children with special educational needs into ordinary schools   *K. Pocklington*

Special education is highly topical at present owing to the Report of the Committee of Enquiry under Mary Warnock (DES 1978b) and the Education Act 1981 which in part grew out of this enquiry and which was implemented recently. And there can be no doubt that the central issue of concern to those working within the mainstream of education is the likelihood of significant numbers of children with marked physical, sensory or mental handicaps coming their way. Over the past 15 years or so integration has been associated with this handicapped minority — estimated by Warnock at about two per cent of the school population. Integration is talked about as if it was something done to or by the handicapped. Integration is seen as their problem. Progress is conceived of in terms of their assimilation into the mainstream of education and society.

My brief is to look at the assimilation of such children into ordinary schools, and in doing so I will be drawing on research which Seamus Hegarty and I carried out (Hegarty and Pocklington 1981, 1982). I believe though that it would be narrow-minded to focus on this minority alone — for the following reason: Warnock recommended replacing the existing medical definition of handicap with the broader concept of 'special educational need' — a suggestion duly taken up in the new legislation. It has become today's received wisdom that at some stage in their educational careers a much larger proportion of the school population — up to 20 per cent — may exhibit special needs of one kind or another. The overwhelming majority of these children already attend ordinary schools and indeed have always done so. Whether their educational needs are even recognized, let alone suitably met, is questionable however.

This leads me to urge that the concept of integration be reviewed. My

K. Pocklington, 'The integration of children with special educational needs into ordinary schools', *Secondary Education Journal*, 1983, **13**, 2

own preference is for a return to the original usage, as the process of 'making whole', of uniting constituent parts in a totality. In this sense integration is no longer something ascribed to a minority outgroup but may be construed instead as a challenge facing ordinary schools — requiring that they adapt to the differences in the interests and capabilities of their pupils by differentiating the curriculum on offer. Thus instead of teachers bewailing having to deal with children whom they have neither the time for nor the necessary knowledge and expertise, their coming might be viewed more positively as a means of stretching the school system, as a stimulus to examining existing objectives, looking to develop existing provision so as to cater more appropriately for *all* pupils.

Make no mistake: whether we are referring specifically to pupils with notable physical or sensory impairments — historically part of the two per cent — or to those whose educational progress is slow or who manifest specific learning difficulties, the crux of the matter is providing a curriculum which is differentiated according to individual ability and need. This requires an individualized approach and a level of fine-tuning which all too often in the past has been sacrificed on the altar of public examinations, which continue to exert an unreasonable influence upon our secondary schools. It will further require a shift in attitude so that the successful outcome of schooling is conceived in terms other than examination passes for those pupils who are unlikely ever to be successful in examinations. The truly comprehensive school is surely that which provides satisfactorily for all its pupils. Regrettably the ideal rarely is realized, for as Jones (1979) — among others — noted, the 'real problems' of comprehensive schooling are 'the effective teaching of the slow learner and children with learning difficulties'.

Essential requirements for integration

What is entailed in meeting the *educational* needs of children — whether slow learners, partially hearing or suffering from muscular dystrophy and confined to a wheelchair? I suggest that the following are all crucial elements:

1. sufficient staff to allow for the flexible handling of pupils;
2. understanding the many and varied obstacles to learning, and possessing the necessary knowledge to overcome (and ideally avoid) these obstacles;

3. appropriate teaching methods and learning resources;
4. circumstances conducive to more personalized teaching and learning.

It is hard to disagree with the statement by Booth (1983) that 'the current distribution and organization of resources makes small group or individual teaching a nightmare and the classroom a strait-jacket'. I would add that it is not merely a question of resources but also the way in which the curriculum is organized into separate subjects and pupil groupings are conceived. There also needs to be a change of attitude such that the non-academic pupil is no longer of low status, taught by teachers who are not considered up to the demands of examination classes, in over-large groups and with impoverished facilities and resources, but rather is seen in many respects as presenting the ultimate of professional challenges. Schools need to assume full responsibility for such pupils and not merely for their academic peers.

It is possible that what I am advocating will be dismissed as unduly naive or idealistic. At a time of protracted recession remedial provision frequently is the first to be axed by headteachers or LEA officials seeking economies. While acknowledging this fact, I maintain that it is a question of priorities, and determining priorities ultimately comes down to moral conviction. Providing the necessary staff, laying on in-service training, providing teaching and learning materials to meet special needs: all demand extra resources. The question is how these may be made available. Having determined one's priorities, some reallocation of the existing budget may be possible. There is probably little excess remaining in this system after several years of cutting back. There is however considerable unnecessary duplication, arising out of the separate administering of special and mainstream services. It is surely ridiculous to be actively seeking to blur distinctions between children and yet not be striving for a means of rationalizing these parallel systems of personnel, plant, learning materials and so forth.

I propose now to look at the above elements in rather more detail.

Staffing

The starting point to my mind has to be staffing special needs departments in a manner commensurate with the scope and importance of the task they are being asked to take on. (Relatively few secondary schools will lack such departments — though undoubtedly many of them will need developing considerably. Where there is no such department a special school might be looked to and might function as a powerhouse of expertise, specialized techniques and resources.) Staffing levels should be determined less by a headcount of pupils — we should be striving to move away from largely self-contained units wherein pupils receive a restricted and different curriculum from that of the rest of the school — but rather so as to enable a variety of broadly conceived roles to be discharged.

The flexible deployment of personnel is paramount. The more flexibly educators can operate the greater likelihood of personalizing education — and hence of meeting the special needs of the pupils. For instance, a teacher with knowledge of special needs might undertake some individual or small group teaching on a withdrawal basis. Alternatively, it ought to be possible to provide such attention within the regular classroom; this would involve the specialist working with an individual or with a group of pupils, or advising and perhaps assisting the regular teacher, or, better still, working cooperatively, perhaps along team-teaching lines, and with a class of mixed ability.

There is much to be said for those with specialist knowledge and skills operating in a consultative capacity for other members of staff — just as long as the grounds for doing so are spelt out and understood by all concerned. The rationale behind strategies such as these is the pooling of resources in order to facilitate the more flexible management of pupils — not 'bailing out' the inadequate teacher. It is also about enhancing the capabilities of teachers so that they can cope effectively across the full range of ability. One of the most pervasive and damaging of beliefs to my mind is that which holds special education as something mysterious and arcane, and as demanding knowledge and skills which the ordinary educator does not possess. By this means the regular teacher all too often passes the buck. Worse still, this attitude undoubtedly has been encouraged by some special educators who, perhaps out of professional insecurity, overemphasize the uniqueness of what is entailed in teaching the less able. The regular teacher feels unable to cope and looks towards the wings where it is assumed armies of experts lie in waiting. In reality of course there are no such armies; the regular teacher must assume responsibility, must learn to cope. And while he or she should be helped to do so, it should be emphasized that rarely is special education different in kind.

Extending awareness

Teachers in ordinary schools should be provided with certain basic information: for example, about the concept of 'special need', individual differences or the possible educational consequences of different physical or sensory conditions. The continuous interplay between assessment (based in part upon structured observation), devising and implementing an educational programme and subsequently evaluating what has been achieved, perhaps modifying the programme in the light of this, should also be covered. Our research revealed that frequently the closeness of fit between these successive and interrelated stages was lacking; further, that regular teachers tended to settle for less in respect of pupil performance than a good many pupils were actually capable of. While this no doubt reflects in part inexperience in their coping with special needs, and their limited knowledge, it also reflects their failure to assume responsibility for all children who come their way, seeing these pupils as a distinct group for whom principal responsibility is exercised by special education personnel.

Undoubtedly there is need of concerted efforts across LEAs to provide an initial orientation into special needs. One local authority, Oxfordshire, has for some time now been running 'handicap awareness courses' for the staff of primary and secondary schools. The intention is that a teacher from every school will attend such a course which runs in school time for some 12 weeks — reporting back on a regular basis to colleagues. The DES too has been active in convening regional courses on the topic of special educational needs. While not wishing to denigrate such efforts, I would suggest that optimum pay-off may derive from more local (i.e. specific to a given school) and custom-built courses, wherein learning can more easily be concretized around a particular child's learning difficulties or perhaps some aspect of curriculum revision. Active collaboration between a regular teacher and specialist colleague may even be a way of avoiding formalizing the in-service element altogether. Strategies such as these can serve to bring teachers together to discuss professional issues, and may be instrumental in reducing the professional isolation which has prevailed historically, with each teacher being locked into his or her classroom and having internalized the importance of never admitting to having doubts, limitations or failings in a professional context.

Teaching methods and learning resources

Fifthly, there is a need for appropriate teaching methods and learning resources. The difficulty in learning which some pupils experience probably has more to do with the quality of the teaching they are exposed to, or the learning materials deployed, or the relevance of tasks set, than any failings in themselves. Effective teaching depends to a large degree on teachers being able to operate under suitable circumstances and having the necessary understanding and expertise (or, in the absence of the latter, having access to others who do possess expert knowledge and skills). Utilizing learning materials appropriate to a child's current capabilities, while partly contingent upon the teacher being aware of and comprehending the learner's present standing, may have much to do with the way in which resources are organized and distributed. We found that a benefit which basic studies departments commonly brought secondary schools was improved teaching and better quality resources for the less able pupil. Typically such departments not only subsumed the function discharged by the traditional remedial department but extended this in catering for children who elsewhere would be in schools for the educationally subnormal.

Special schools unquestionably could fulfil a more active role in this regard. For example, one of the schemes we studied involved a school for children with learning difficulties feeding out skilled personnel, hardware and learning materials to teachers in neighbouring primary schools who had children who were in danger of failing. Many special schools, however, are unwilling to share expertise and resources, sticking to an isolationist stance and only becoming involved with pupils from the mainstream once they have failed.

Difficulties and opportunities

Although I am convinced that educators from special and ordinary sectors need to work more closely together, I do not disregard the potential difficulty of putting this into practice. It is not a simple matter of reproducing the essence of good specialist education. Meeting special educational needs in the setting of the ordinary school can differ considerably from how this is approached in the special school environment, which is of course geared exclusively to meeting pupils' special needs. In the ordinary school there is a tension to be resolved between giving pupils the same or similar access to the curriculum as their peers while at the same time providing attention appropriate to meeting their special needs. There is a balance to be struck between, say, basic skills work and real — as opposed to token — teaching in other areas of the curriculum, and this will vary from one individual to another. Additional difficulties may stem from the different norms and values of the comprehensive school, or from the pluralism embodied in so many aspects of everyday life in the comprehensive school.

If asked to identify a single outcome of our research into meeting special educational needs in the ordinary school, it would be that neither enhanced educational opportunities nor social assimilation should be assumed. Benefits are there for the taking but realizing these benefits must be worked at. This demands, among other things, the conviction that integration is right educationally and socially; thorough planning in every aspect of school life; application; knowledge, and the understanding that this can bring; generous resourcing; careful monitoring of circumstances as they evolve; and a preparedness to intervene as necessary. The need for a watching brief is the more urgent because of the size and organizational complexity of the secondary school, and because pupils with special needs will probably be receiving inputs from various sources, which carries the danger of their education being uncoordinated, or even fragmented.

In conclusion, I would reiterate that integration can bring to the ordinary school opportunities as well as difficulties. Having to meet special needs from within the ordinary school can serve to trigger school-wide developments and improvements such that the quality of the education provided for all pupils is enhanced. There can be social benefit too, the school being enriched as a social setting. These benefits do not automatically accrue but they can be achieved, and are as much a part of integration as the disadvantages and difficulties which are more commonly espoused.

Topics for discussion

1. 'Integration is a means, not an end in itself' (Hegarty, Pocklington and Lucas 1981). What are the educational implications of this assertion?
2. In what sense is the educating of pupils with special needs in the ordinary school an extension of the comprehensive ideal?
3. What, in your view, is the greatest obstacle to the integration of pupils with special needs in the ordinary school?

Suggestions for further reading

1. DES (1978) *Special Educational Needs* (The Warnock Report). London: HMSO.
2. Hegarty, S., Pocklington, K. and Lucas, D. (1981) *Educating Pupils with Special Needs in the Ordinary School*. Slough: NFER-Nelson, pp. 7–45 'Integration: Theory and Practice'.
3. Swann, W. (1981) *A Special Curriculum?* Milton Keynes: The Open University Press.

BIBLIOGRAPHY

Abelson, H. and di Sesson, A. (1981) *Turtle Geometry*. MIT Press.

Adelman, C. and Walker, B. (1974) 'Open Space — Open Classroom' in *Education 3–13*, 2, 2, October, pp. 103–107.

Allen, I., Donet, K., Gaff, M., Gray, E., Griffiths, C., Ryall, E. and Toone, E. (1975) *Working An Integrated Day*. London: Ward Lock Educational.

Alexander, R.J. (1984) *Primary Teaching*. Holt, Rinehart & Winston.

Archer, J. and Lloyd, B. (1975) 'Sex differences: biological and social interaction' in Lewin, R. (ed.) *Child Alive*. San Francisco: Anchor Press.

Architects' Journal (1980), quoted in Cooper, I. (1981) 'The Politics of Education and Architectural Design; the instructive example of British Primary Education', in *B. Ed. Res. J.* 7, 2, 1981, pp. 125–36.

Arkwright, D. et al. (1975) 'Survey of Open Plan Primary Schools in Derbyshire', quoted in Bennet et al. 1980.

Ashton, P., Kneen, P., Davies, F. and Holley, B.J. (1975) *The Aims of Primary Education*. London: Macmillan Education (for the Schools Council).

Assessment of Performance Unit (1981) *Science in Schools Age 11: Report No. 1*. London: HMSO.

Association for Science Education (1974) *The Head Teacher and Primary Science*, 1, Science and Primary Education Paper No. 2.

Association for Science Education (1976) *A Post of Responsibility*. Science and Primary Education Paper No. 3.

Barker Lunn, J.C. (1967) 'The effects of streaming and other forms of grouping in junior schools — junior schools and their types of school organization'. *New Research in Education*, 1, pp. 4–45.

Barker Lunn, J.C. (1970) *Streaming in the Primary School*. Windsor: NFER.

Barker Lunn, J. (1982) 'Junior Schools and their Organizational Policies' in *Educational Research*, 24, 4.

Bassey, M. (1978) *Nine Hundred Primary School Teachers*. Slough: NFER.

Bealing, D. (1972) 'The Organization of Junior School Classrooms' in *Education Research*, 14, pp. 231–5.

Bennett, S.N. et al. (1975) 'An enquiry into Cumbria's Open Plan Schools', quoted in Bennet et al. 1980.

Bennett, N. et al. (1976) *Journeys into Open Space*. (Interim Report to the Schools Council) Department of Research, University of Lancaster.

Bennett, N. (1976) *Teaching Styles and Pupil Progress*. London: Open Books.

Bennett, N., Andreae, J., Hegarty, P., Wade, B. (1980) *Open Plan Primary Schools*. Windsor: NFER (For the Schools Council).

Bennett, N. and Hyland, T. (1979) 'Open Plan — Open Education?' in *B. Ed. Res. J.* 5, 2, pp. 159–66.

Biggs, E. (1965) *Mathematics in Primary Schools*. Schools Council Curriculum Bulletin No. 1. London: HMSO.

Blackie, J. (1967) *Inside the Primary School*. London: HMSO.

Blackie, J. (1974) *Changing the Primary School: an Integrated Approach*. London: Macmillan.

Blenkin, G.M. and Kelly, A.V. (1981) *The Primary Curriculum*. London: Harper & Row.

Booth, T. (1983) 'Eradicating Handicap' (Unit 14 of Course E241, *Special Needs in Education*). Open University Press.

Bloom, B. et al. (1956) *Taxonomy of Educational Objectives Handbook I*. London: Longmans.

Bloomer, M. and Shaw, K.E. (eds) (1979) *The Challenge of Educational Change: Limitations and Potentialities*. Pergamon Press.

Boydell, D. (1980) 'The organization of junior school classrooms: a follow-up survey' in *Educational Research* 23, pp. 14–19.

Briault, E. (1982) 'The Politics of Primary Contraction' in Richards, C. (ed.).

Bristol Head Teachers (1963)'The Development of Family Grouping'(By a 'Group of Bristol Head Teachers') *New Era* No. 44, Sept/Oct, pp. 194–96.

Brogden, M.C. (1980) *Open Plan Primary Schools and Team Teaching*. Unpublished Dip. Ed. Dissertation, Froebel College, Roehampton Institute of Higher Education.

Broudy, H.S., Smith, B.O. and Burnett, J.R. (1964) *Democracy and Excellence in American Secondary Education*. Chicago: Rand McNally.

Brown, M. and Precious, N. (1968) *The Integrated Day in the Primary School*. London: Ward Lock Ed.

Bruner, J.S. (1960) *Towards a Theory of Instruction*. Camb. Mass: Harvard University Press.

Bryant, P.B. (1974) *Perception and Understanding in Young Children*. London: Methuen.

Buros, O.K. (ed) (1972) *Mental Measurements Yearbook*. 6th edition. New York: Gryphon Press.

Central Advisory Council for Education (England) (1976) *Children and their Primary Schools*. London: HMSO.

Chandler, E. (1982) 'An Alternative Education' in *Microcomputers in the Classroom*. University of Exeter School of Education.

Clegg, A. (1971) 'Revolution in the British Primary School'. National Association of Elementary School Principals. Washington, U.S.A.

Clift, P. et al. (1981) *Record Keeping in Primary Schools*. Macmillan Educational.

Cook, G. (1973) 'Problems of teacher-student organization in open rooms'. *Studies in Open Education* No. 8, Aurora, Ontario: York County Board of Education. (Quoted in Bennet et al. 1980.)

Dean, J. (1982) *Recording Children's Progress*. London: Macmillan.

Dearden, R.F. (1967) *A Philosophy of Primary Education*. University of London Press.

Dearden, R.F. (1976) *Problems in Primary Education*. London: Routledge and Kegan Paul.

Department of Education and Science (1963) *Half Our Future* (The Newsom Report). London: HMSO.

DES (1967) *Eveline Lowe Primary School*. Building Bulletin 36. London: HMSO.

DES (1976) *Guillemont Junior School*. Building Bulletin 53. London: HMSO.

DES (1975) *A Language for Life* (Bullock Report). London: HMSO.

DES (1977) *Education in Schools: a consultative document*. London: HMSO.

DES (1978a) *Primary Education in England: A survey by HM Inspectors of Schools*. London: HMSO.

DES (1978b) *Special Educational Needs* (The Warnock Report) London: HMSO.

DES (1979) *Aspects of Secondary Education in England* (A survey by HMI). London: HMSO.

DES (1980) *A View of the Curriculum*. London: HMSO.

Department of Education and Science with Welsh Office (January 1980) *A Framework for the School Curriculum*. London: DES.

DES (1981) *West Indian Children in our Schools* (The Rampton Report).

DES (1982) *Mathematics Counts* (The Cockcroft Report). London: HMSO.

DES (1982) *Education 5–9: an Illustrative Survey of 80 First Schools in England*. London: HMSO.

DES (1983) *9–13 Middle Schools: An Illustrative Survey*. London: HMSO.

Dewhurst, J. (1967) *Team Teaching in the Primary School*. Unpublished M.A. (Ed) dissertation, University of London.

Donaldson, M. (1979) *Children's Minds*. London: Fontana.

Downing, J. (1970) 'Children's concepts of language in learning to read', in *Educational Research*, **12**, pp. 106–112.

Eisner, E.W. (1980) *The Educational Imagination*. New York: Collier Macmillan.

Eisner, E.W. (1960) 'Instructional and expressive educational objectives: their formulation and use in curriculum 11–18' in Popham, Eisner, Sullivan and Tylor (1969) *Instructional Objectives*. AERA Monograph Series on Curriculum Evaluation 3. Chicago: Rand McNally.

Ellingham, D. (1982) *Managing the Microcomputer in the Classroom*. Council for Educational Technology.

Elliott, D. (1979) *The British Ability Scales*. Slough: NFER-Nelson.

Ennever, L. and Harlen, W. (1972) *With Objectives in Mind*. MacDonald Educational.

Evans, K. (1979) 'The physical form of the school — school design as rhetoric', *B. J. Ed. Studies*, **XXVII**, 1, Feb., pp. 29–41.

Featherstone, J. (1971a) *Schools where children learn*. New York: Liveright.

Featherstone, J. (1971b) 'An Introduction' in the series *British Primary Schools Today*. London: Macmillan Education.

Flerx, V.C., Fidler, D.S. and Rogers, R.W. (1976) 'Sex role stereotypes: developmental aspects and early intervention' in *Child Development* 47, pp. 998–1007.

Fox, B. and Routh, D.K. (1975) 'Analysing spoken language into words, syllables and phonemes: a developmenⁿ al study', *Journal of Psycholinguistic Research*, **4**, pp. 331–42.

Gagné, R.M. (1977) *Conditions of Living*. Holt, Rinehart & Winston.

Galton, M. and Simon, B. (eds) (1980) *Progress and Performance in the Primary Classroom*. London: Routledge and Kegan Paul.

Galton, M., Simon, B. and Croll, P. (1980) *Inside the Primary Classroom*. London: Routledge and Kegan Paul.

Garland, R.G. (1982) *Curriculum Policy making in Primary Schools* in Richards, C. (ed.).

Garland, R.G. (1982) 'Primary Schools, microcomputers and the curriculum' in *Primary Education Review* 14, pp. 3–6.

Gersham, H. (1967) 'The evolution of gender identity' *Bulletin New York Academy of Medicine* 43, pp. 1000–18.

Goodacre, E. (1972) *Hearing Children Read*. University of Reading School of Education.

Gosden, P.H.J.H. and Sharp, P.R. (1978) *The Development of an Education Service: The West Riding 1889–1974*. Oxford: Martin Robertson.

Gray, W.S. *Promoting Personal and Social Development Through Reading.* University of Chicago Press.

Gulbenkian Foundation (1982) *The Arts in Schools: Principles, Practice and Provision.* London.

Haavio-Mannila, E. (1967) 'Sex differentiation in role expectations and performance'. *Journal of Marriage and the Family,* 29, pp. 568–78.

Hegarty, S. and Lucas, D. (1978) *Able to Learn? The Pursuit of Culture-Fair Assessment.* Slough: NFER.

Hegarty, S. and Pocklington, K. (1981) *Educating Pupils with Special Needs in Ordinary Schools.* NFER-Nelson.

Hegarty, S. and Pocklington, K. (1982) *Integration in Action.* NFER-Nelson.

Hadow Report (1931) *The Primary School.* Report of the Consultative Committee. London: HMSO.

Hadow Report (1933) *Infant and Nursery Schools.* Report of the Consultative Committee. London: HMSO.

Hall, L.C. (1975) 'Linguistic and perceptual constraints on scanning strategies: some developmental studies'. Unpublished doctoral dissertation. University of Edinburgh.

Harlen, W. (1981) 'Some gloom, some satisfaction' in *The Times Educational Supplement,* 18 December.

Harlen, W. et al. (1977a) *Finding Answers.* Match and Mismatch. Oliver and Boyd.

Harlen, W. et al. (1977b) *Raising Questions.* Match and Mismatch. Oliver and Boyd.

Hendry, L.B. and Matheson, P.A. (1979) 'Teachers and pupils in open-plan and conventional classrooms', *Scot. Ed. Rev.,* II, 2, Nov. pp. 107–17.

HMI (1977) *Curriculum 11–16.* London: DES.

HMI (1979) *Aspects of Secondary Education in England.* London: HMSO.

Howe, J.A.M. (1981) 'Artificial intelligence and computer-assisted learning: ten years on', in Rushby, N. (ed) *Selected Readings in Computer-Based Learning.* Kogan Page.

Hurlin, A. (1975) 'Open plan schools and inquiry/discovery learning' *Cambridge J. Edn.* 5, 2, pp. 98–103.

Inhelder, B., Sinclair, H. and Bovet, M. (1974) *Apprentissage et Structures de la Connaissance.* Paris: Presses Universitaires de France.

Jackson, S., Mahon, S. and Wheeler, E. (1978) 'Sand and Water'. E.J. Arnold.

Jarman, C. (1978) 'The organization of open plan primary schools' in Bell, S. (ed.) *The Organization of Open Plan Primary Schools.* Publication No. 3. Glasgow, Jordanhill College of Education.

Jensen, A.R. (1969) 'How much can we boost IQ and scholastic achievement'. *Harvard Educational Review*, 39, pp. 1–123.

Jones, H. (1979) 'The development of remedial education in Scotland' in *Remedial Education*, 14, 2, pp. 54–62.

Jones, R. (1980) *Micro-computers: Their Uses in Primary Schools*. Council for Educational Technology.

Jones, R. (1982) in Garland, R.G. (ed.) *Microcomputers and Children in the Primary School*. Falmer Press.

King, R. (1978) *All Things Bright and Beautiful?* Chichester: John Wiley & Sons.

Kogan, M. (1978) *The Politics of Educational Change*. Manchester University Press.

Labon, D. (1972) *Assessing Reading Ability*. West Sussex County Council.

Language for Learning (1976) ILEA Media Resources Centre.

Lawton, D. (1973) *Social change, Educational Theory and Curriculum Planning*. London: Hodder & Stoughton.

Lawton, D. (1975) *Class, Culture and the Curriculum*. London: Routledge and Kegan Paul.

Lav-Ran, A. (1974) 'Gender role differentiation in hermaphrodites'. *Archives of Sexual Behaviour* 3, pp. 391–424.

Lewis, M. (1977) 'The social nexus: the child's entrance into the world'. Paper to the International Society for Behavioural Development, Pavia.

Linfield, E. (1968) 'Vertical grouping in the junior school'. *Forum*, 10, 2, Spring, pp. 51–3.

Lovell, K. (1973) *Educational Psychology and Children*. 11th Edition. University of London Press.

Macrae, A.J. (1976) 'Meaning relations in language development: a study of some converse pairs and directional opposites'. Unpublished doctoral dissertation. University of Edinburgh.

Manning, K. and Sharp, A. (1977) *Structuring Play in the Early Years*. Ward Lock Educational.

Mason, S.C. (1960) *The Leicestershire Experiment and Plan*. London: Councils and Education Press.

Maxwell, B. (1982) 'A Turtle in the School', in *Microscope* 6, pp. 4–5.

McDonald, B. and Walker, R. (1976) *Changing the Curriculum*. London: Open Books.

McGuiness, D. (1976) 'Sex differences in the organization of perception and cognition' in Lloyd, B. and Archer, J. (eds) *Exploring Sex Differences*. New York: Academic Press.

McNicholas, J. (1973) *Open Plan Primary Schools.* Unpublished M.Ed. Thesis, University of Hull.

McNicholas, J. (1974) *The Design of English Elementary and Primary Schools* (A select annotated bibliography). Windsor: NFER Publishing Co.

Midwinter, E. (1972) *Priority Education.* Harmondsworth: Penguin.

Ministry of Education (1958) *Building Bulletin 16, Junior Schools.* Amersham London: HMSO.

Ministry of Education (1959) *Primary Education.* London: HMSO.

Ministry of Education (1961) *Building Bulletin 3, Village Schools.* London: HMSO.

Moran, P.R. (1971) 'The Integrated Day', *Educational Research*, 14, 1, pp. 65–9.

Morrell, D.H. and Pott, A. (1960) *Britain's New Schools.* London: Longmans for The British Council.

Mullan, T. (1982) 'LOGO in the Primary School' in *Microscope*, 6, pp. 6–7.

Murrow, C. and Murrow, L. (1971) *Children Come First: The Inspired Work of English Primary Schools.* New York: American Heritage Press.

Mussen, P., Conger, J.J. and Kagan, J. (1979) *Child Development and Personality.* New York: Harper & Row.

Myers, D.A. and Duke, D.L. (1977) 'Open education as an ideology' in *Ed. Research*, 19, 3, June pp. 227–35.

Papert, S. (1980) *Mindstorms.* Harvester Press.

Peters, R.S. (ed.) (1969) *Perspectives on Plowden.* London: Routledge and Kegan Paul.

Piaget, J. (1977) *The Grasp of Consciousness.* London: Routledge and Kegan Paul.

Plimmer, F. (1974) 'A survey of some junior team teaching organizations' in Taylor, M. (ed.) *Team Teaching Experiments.* Windsor: NFER.

Plowden Report (1967) *Children and their Primary Schools* (2 vols.) Report of the Central Advisory Council for Education in England. London: HMSO.

Postman, N. and Weingartner, C. (1971) *Teaching as a Subversive Activity.* Harmondsworth: Penguin.

Reid, J.F. (1966) 'Learning to think about reading' in *Educational Research*, 9, pp. 56–62.

Richards, C. (1979) 'Primary Education: Belief, Myth and Practice' in Bloomer, M. and Shaw, K.E. (eds).

Richards, C. (ed.) (1982) *New Directions in Primary Education.* Falmer Press.

Richards, R. et al. (1980) *Learning through Science: Formulating a School Policy*. MacDonald Educational.

Ridgway, L. (1976) *The Task of the Teacher in the Primary School*. London: Ward Lock Educational.

Ridgway, L. and Lawton, I. (1965) *Family Grouping in the Infants School*. London: Ward Lock Educational.

Ridley, K. (1979) 'The National Primary Survey: A Head's Response' in *Education*, 7, 2, pp. 3–13.

Rogers, V. (1970) *Teaching in the British Primary School*. London: Collier Macmillan.

Ross, A.M. (1960) *The Education of Childhood*. London: Harrap.

Satterly, D. (1981) *Assessment in Schools*. Oxford: Blackwell.

Saville, C.J. (1970) 'Towards the integrated day' in *Cambridge Inst. Ed. Bulletin*, 3, 12, Dec. pp. 11–14.

Schools Council Committee for Wales, Wesh Tests and Materials Projects *Profion Bangor*. University College of North Wales, Bangor, in conjunction with Normal College, Bangor (publication pending).

Seaborne, M. (1971) *Primary School Design*. London: Routledge and Kegan Paul.

Seaborne, M. and Lowe, R. (1977) *The English School, Its Architecture and Organization* Vol. II 1870–1970. London: Routledge and Kegan Paul.

Seefeldt, C. (1973) 'Open spaces, closed learning' in *Education Leadership*, 30, 4, pp. 355–7. (Quoted in Bennett et al. 1980.)

Selleck, R.J.W. (1972) *English Primary Education and the Progressives: 1914–1939*. London: Routledge and Kegan Paul.

Sharp, R. and Green, A. (1975) *Education and Social Control* (A study in progressive primary education). London: Routledge and Kegan Paul.

Silberman, C.E. (1970) *Crisis in the Classroom: the Remaking of American Education*. New York: Random House.

Silberman, C.E. (ed.) (1973) *The Open Classroom Reader*. New York: Vintage Books.

Simon, B. (1981) 'The primary school revolution: myth or reality?' in Simon, B. and Willcocks, J. (eds).

Simon, B. and Willcocks, J. (eds) (1981) *Research and Practice in the Primary Classroom*. London: Routledge and Kegan Paul.

Simon, B. and Taylor, W. (eds) (1981) *Education in the Eighties: the central issues*. Batsford.

Skilbeck, M. (1980) *A Core Curriculum for Australian Schools*. Canberra: Curriculum Development Centre.

Smith, B.E., Stanley, W.O. and Shores, J.H. (1957) *Fundamentals of Curriculum Development*. New York: Harcourt Brace and World.

Sockett, H. (1976) *Designing the Curriculum*. London: Open Books.

Southgate, V. (1970) 'The importance of structure in beginning reading', in *Reading Skills, Theory and Practice*. UKRA–Ward Lock Educational.

Stein, A.H. and Smithells, J. (1969) 'Age and sex differences in children's sex role standards about achievement' in *Developmental Psychology*, 1, pp. 252–9.

Stenhouse, L. (1985) *An Introduction to Curriculum Research and Development*. London: Heinemann.

Strathclyde Regional Council (1976) *Primary School Building Report*, quoted in Bennett et al. (1980).

Tanner, J.M. (1978) *Foetus Into Man*. London: Open Books.

Tavris, C. and Offir, C. (1977) *The Longest War: Sex Differences in Perspective*. New York: Harcourt Brace Jovanovich Inc.

Taylor, P.H., Reid, W.A., Holley, B.J. and Exon, G. (1974) *Purpose, Power and Constraint in the Primary School Curriculum*. London: Macmillan.

Taylor, W. (1981) 'Contraction in Context' in Simon, B. and Taylor, W. (eds).

Thompson, S.K. (1975) 'Gender labels and early sex-role development' in *Child Development*, 46, pp. 339–47.

Tyler, R. (1949) *Basic Principles of Curriculum and Instruction*. Chicago: University of Chicago Press.

Vigotsky, L.S. (1962) *Thought and Language*. Cambridge Mass: M.I.T. Press.

Walton, J. (ed.) (1971) *The Integrated Day in Theory and Practice*. London: Ward Lock Educational.

Weber, L. (1971) *The English Infant School and Informal Education*. Prentice-Hall: Englewood Cliffs, New Jersey.

Wechsler, D. (1949) *Wechsler Intelligence Scale for Children*. New York: The Psychological Corporation.

Westbury, I. (1973) 'Conventional classrooms, open classrooms and the technology of teaching' in *J. Cur. Studies*, 5, 2, Nov. pp. 99–121.

Whitbread, N. (1972) *The Evolution of the Nursery Infant School*. London: Routledge and Kegan Paul.

Williams, R. (1958) *Culture and Society*. Harmondsworth: Penguin Books.

Williams, R. (1961) *The Long Revolution*. Harmondsworth: Penguin Books.

INDEX

A View of the Curriculum (1980), 152
A Framework for the School Curriculum
  (1980), 150, 153
abnormalities, 39
action schema, 62, 64
action pattern, 61
actions, 32
activities
  in English, 130
  frequency in Junior schools, 129
  in mathematics, 129
  other, 130
'activity' schools, 4
actual incremental task, 137
adaptation to the environment, 61
adolescence, 37, 42
adolescent spurt, 37, 39, 42
advisers, 9
aesthetic development, 250–259
  concept of objective assessment, 253–259
  scientific and artistic knowledge, 257–
    258
Alexander, R., viii, ix, x, xiii
aims of the school, 115
animism, 60
art and craft, 20
artistic development, xii
assessment, xii
Assessment of Performance Unit (APU),
  xii, 5, 154, 223–224
  children with learning difficulties, 260–
    272
  culture – fair testing, 263–264
  decisions, xii

effect of culture pattern, 260–261
level of teacher assessment, 261–262
norm — and criterion — referenced
  tests, 264–265, 271
objective and subjective marking, 265–
  266
procedures, xii
test as predictors, 266–267
validity, reliability and standardization,
  262–263
what can be assessed?, 267–268
when should we assess, 269–270
why should we assess?, 266–267
assigning tasks, 136
assimilation, 24
attitudes
  degree of permissiveness, 16
  to physical punishment, 16
  of teachers in streamed/unstreamed
    schools, 15, 16
  transformation of, 20
average boy, 36
average girl, 37

Barker Lunn J., ix, xi, 118
basic skills, ix
'basics', ix
Bealing, D., 17
becoming aware of language, 86
Bennett, N., xi, 5, 19, 21, 92, 95, 102, 103,
  133
Biggs, E., 10
Black Paper I, 2
Black Paper writers, 4, 5

Blackie, J., 9, 10
Boyle, E., 11
Brierley, J., x
British Empire, 23
Brogden, M., xi
Brown, G. and Desforges, C., xi
Bruner, J., 35
Bryant, P., 79
Bullock Report, 24, 133

Callaghan's Ruskin Speech, 2, 21
Caribbean, 27
categorical generalizations
Central Advisory Council for Education, vii
child-centred ideology, vii, 94, 101
child centred practices, xi, 6, 96
child-centredness, x
child growth and development, x
childhood language and thinking, xi
children,
    assessment of, xii
    in inner city schools, 184
    low attainers, 138
    of immigrants, 23
    with learning difficulties
    whose home language is not English, 184
children's cognitive confusion, 139
children's thought, 59
chromosomes, 33, 34
class inclusion tests, 87
class size, 124
classwork, 124
classes
    average size of, 119
classroom activity, 106
    learning model, 112
    management strategies, 135
    tasks, 135
    practice of existing knowledge, 137
    remedial, 17
classrooms
    organisation of, 17, 19
    seating arrangements, 19
    traditional layout, 17
cleanliness, 36
Clegg, A., 8
clinical interview, 59, 61, 67
cluster analysis, 19
cognitive assimilation, 51
colonialism, 23
comprehensive schools, 4
comprehensive tests, 130

concrete operations, 68
    (see also operational period), 74
conservation tests, 87
continuity theory, 77
control
    measure of, 18
    reimposition of, 21
controlled vocabulary, 233
conventional female roles, 50
coordination and physical capabilities, 42, 43
coordination skills, 42, 43
councillors, 9
Craft, 181
creative writing, 130
cross-sectional technique, 60
cultural, 25
curriculum inertia, 151
common curriculum, 150
core curriculum, 150
curriculum 11–16 (1977), 149–150, 152, 153, 154
    and its arrangement, 127, 142–155
    and balance, 150, 151
    basic skills, 179–181
    behavioural objectives model, xi, 142–145
    children in inner city schools, 184
    cultural analysis model, xi, p145–149
    and common needs, 172–173
    content and concepts, 176–179
    content and control, 135, 142–155
    cultural mapping, 146
    differences amongst children, 183–184
    and differences of programme, 173–174
    and individual differences, 172–173
    and levels of difficulty, 174–175
    organization, 19
    other aspects, 181–182
    and premature specialisation, 150
    priorities, 183
    range of, 182–183
    and skills, 175–176
    and the structure of knowledge, 147
    of the primary school, 93, 172–179, 179–185
    as means of social justice, viii
    as repository of cultural elements, 142–155
    as in analysis of contemporary culture, 149
    planning, 108, 142–155

as set of learning experiences, viii
'whole' curriculum, x, 150
creative and expressive arts, ix

Davis, B., xii
Dearden, R.F., 241
Department of Education and Science, xii,
    27, 93
details of body composition, 41
development age, 45, 46
development
    emotional, 12
    intellectual, 12
    of logical thinking, 60
    physical, 12
    of mental structures, 58
    of sex differences, 53
developmental change, 57
developmental psychologists, 53, 56
Dewey, J., 8
dictation, 130
dictionary work, 130
differences in aptitude, 47
differences among children, xii
discipline
    permissive, 14
    problems, 19
discovery methods, 4, 9, 35, 101
discriminatory practices, 25, 26
division of labour, 48
Donaldson, M., xi, 79
Down's syndrome, 34
Downing, J., 86

early growth of the brain and head, 38
early growth patterns, 36
early-maturing child, 45
education, 7
    control function of, 21
    discovery, 12
    enquiry, 12
    informal, 7
    policy, 9
    revolution, 8, 21
Education Act 1870, vii
educational conservatism, viii
egalitarian attitudes, 53
egocentrism, 60
Eisner, E.W., 144
elementary school tradition, ix
Eleven-Plus Examination, 5, 16
emotions, 32

english
    remedial courses in, 24
environment, 33
environmental influences, 33
epigenetic view, 53
equilibration, 76, 81
ethnic, 23, 25
ethnic minorities, 25
evolution, 39
experimental factors, 56
experiments on conversation, 72
exploratory aptitudes of boys, 52
external reality, 64
extroverted children, 35

factors affecting growth, 39
family grouping, 95
femaleness, 50
fertilized egg (zygote), 34
fertilization, 33
field trips, 131
'fluid timetabling', 95
foreign language, 9
formal deductive inference, 83
formal experiments, 70
formal experimentation, 60
formal grammar, 130
four rules of number, 180
free choice periods, 131
Froebel, 93

Gagne, R.M., 241
gametes, 33
Garland, R., xii
gender, 50
    development, 51
    identification, x
    identity, 51, 53
genes, 34, 36
genetic blueprint, 34
Green Paper (Education in Schools, 1977),
    26
Goodacre, E., 240
good health, 40
grouping, 18
    ability grouping, 15
groupwork, 126
    collaborative, 20, 132
growth curves of boys and girls, 37
growth patterns
    sex differences in, 38, 45
growth of language and reading, 232–250

of the middle years, 40
growth process, 44

Hadow Reports, 3, 93
happiness, 40
headteacher role, 114
heredity/environment, 33
Her Majesty's Inspectorate (HMI), xii, 5, 13, 14, 20, 133
heredity, 33
heredity endowment, 35
heterogeneous grouping, 97
HMI Primary Survey 1978, viii, ix, 17, 24, 95, 108, 118, 138
HMI Secondary School Survey (DES 1979), 149, 150
horizontal grouping, 97
hormonal control, 44
hormonal exposure, 50
hormones, 44
Hutchcroft, D.M.R., xii

ideology, vii–viii
integration
    of children with special educational needs, 293–300
    difficulties and opportunities, 298–299
    essential requirements for, 294–295
    extending awareness of, 297
    staffing, 295–296
    teaching methods of learning resources, 298
immigrant children, 24
immigrants, 13
immunization, 36
imperialism, 23
importance of exercise, 43
improvements in housing, 36
incremental tasks, 137
independent initiative, 20
individual
    aptitudes, xi
    assignments, 125
    needs, xi
    uniqueness of, 35, 45
individuality, 32
individualization, 19, 98, 99, 137
infant mortality, 36
informal 'experiments', 65
Inhelde, B., 84
innate factors, 56

Inner London Education Authority (ILEA), 24, 27
inspectors, 9
in-service training, 102
integrated day, 8, 18, 19, 95
integration, xii
    children with special educational needs, xii
intended incremental task, 137
interpersonal relationships, 50
intelligence, 32, 33, 58
    testing, 58
    scores, 45
introverted children, 35
intuitive period,
    (see also pre-operational period), 66
Islam, 22
Issacs, S., 93

Kogan, M., 9, 11

language, 9, 20, 83, 86
    acquisition, 89
    experience approach to reading, 233, 234
    foreign, 9
language work, xii
    special problems, 24
later-maturing child, 45
Lawton, D., xi, 142–155
learning by discovery, xi, 163–169
    five strategies, 164–166
learning environment, 114
learning experiences, 136
learning general rules and principles, 157
    how to learn and autonomy, 159
    how to get information, 157
    independently, 168
    outcomes, 136
    to read, 175
    to write, 175
'learning to learn', 159
Leicestershire, 8, 9
Leicestershire Plan, 8
liberal pragmatism, viii
    romanticism, viii
life as continuous re-learning, 161
likenesses, 32
likenesses and differences, 32
linguistic, 25
    diversity, 26
    skills, 83
literacy skills, 112

local authority administrators, 9
'logic' of different forms of enquiry, 158
logical operations, 63
logical reasoning and language, 233
Lowden, G., xii

maleness, 50
male sex chromosome, 34
Mason, S., 8
matching level of work, 183
matching task allocation, xi, 139
mathematics, 20
mathematics 5–11, xii
mathematics in the primary school, 203–218
    place of, 203–205
    purpose of teaching, 205–206
    aims, 206–207
    objectives in teaching, 207–210
    extension of concepts and skills, 210
    planning the programme, 211–212
    organization, 212–213
    assessment, 214–216
    Teacher development, 216–217
mathematics teaching
    objectives, xii
McGarrigle and Donaldson, M., 79
McMillans, 93
media, the, 21
mental structures, 58
methodological problems, 78
methods,
    in junior school, 118
microcomputers, 284–293
    administration, 287–288
    awareness, 288
    challenging existing thinking, 288–289
    and change, 285
    and technology, 285–287
    headteachers' attitudes towards, 289–290
    supporting current approaches, 287
    the present scene, 289–291
    ways ahead, 291–292
misdiagnosis of tasks, 137
mismatch, 135–139
modern language, 174
'modern methods', 2, 22
Montessori, 93
moral realism, 67
moral and religious education, ix
morality, 60

Moran, P., 18
multicultural context, 23, 24
    society, x, 22, 25
multiethnic, 23
mutation, 34

naturalistic observation, 61, 65, 69
nature/nurture debate, 57
N.F.E.R. ix, 27
    Mathematics Test E2
    Reading Test NS6
non-linguistic context, 89
normative evaluation, 98
numeracy skills, 112
nutrition, 36

obesity, 42
objectives, 6, 20
    creativity, 6
    self-expression, 6
'open' education, 6
open plan, 92
open plan schools, 92, 96
    strengths of, 104
operational period, 61, 68
ORACLE studies, ix, 100, 101
organization
    flexibility of, 21
organization of learning, 119, 124
    of primary school, 106
organizational strategies, xi

Parliamentary Select Committee on
    Immigration and Race Relations, 24
patterns of growth, 36
PEP Reports, 26
performance in reading, 180
period of formal operations, 61
permissiveness, 16
personal and social development, 188–203
    moral education, 199–203
    personal qualities, 188–189
    relationships with other people, 189–190
    religious education, 190–198
personal autonomy, 162
Peters, R., 12
physical education, 182
Piaget, J., xi, 88, 89
physiology, 40
phonic work, xii
planning,
participant, 115

play and language experience, 39
Plowden Committee, 3, 11, 12, 14, 15
Plowden Report 1967, vii, 4, 7, 9, 11, 13,
    14, 17, 18, 19, 22, 23, 24, 95, 110, 132,
    152
Pocklington, K., xii
policy, 26
    development of, 27
    implications, 26
Porter, W.R., xii
practices, in junior school, 118
practice tasks, 137
pre-adolescent growth, 38
pre-operational period, 61, 66, 67, 68
pre-school child, 84
primary curriculum, vii
primary education, viii
Primary Education in England (1978), 24,
    35, 39, 42
primary education
    paradox, x
primary pedagogy, viii
primary schools buildings, 94
    organizational change in, 10
primary school methods, 4
process of accommodation, 76
    of assimilation, 76
    of cognitive reorganization, 54
    or imitation, 54
    of modelling, 54
    of social learning, 54
    of task allocation, 136
programmes of work
    assessing, xii
    planning, xii
progressive education, 19
progressivism, x, 101
projects
    progressive, 15
project work, 20, 130
puberty, 41
pupil attainment, xi
pupil performance, viii
pupil interaction, 100
pupils
    responsibility, 20

quality of task matching, 139
questionnaire survey, 17

race, 23
Race Relations Act (1976), 26

racism, 23, 25, 26
reading
    beginning, 236–238
    children's choice, 245–247
    choosing a reading scheme, 247–248
    development of reading skills, 241–244
    development of reference skills, 242–244
    growth of language, 232–250
    hearing children read, 240
    levels of reading ability, 239
    phonic teaching and context cues, 240
    principles of pleasure and choice, 244–
        245
    readiness, 234
    schemes, 233
    understanding of the heard text, 239–240
    use of play, 249
record-keeping, 272–284
    basic principles underlying, 272–274
    confidentiality, 274–276
    cumulative records, 273
    criteria by which teachers assess, 274
    mathematics, creative abilities, physical
        skills, 281–282
    nursery record summary, 283
    parents access to records, 274–276
    reading and writing, 280–281
religious education, 177
reproductive cells, 33
reproductive organs, 44
reproductive roles, 48
restructuring of experience, 51
revolution in primary schools, 3, 7, 8, 17,
    20, 21
Ridley, K. and Trembath, D., xi
Rogers, V., 6, 7
rhetoric and reality, vii–xiv, 12, 21
role of the headmaster, 114
rural schools, 93

same-sex clothes, 51
same-sex game, 51
schemes
    (See also mental structures), 59, 68, 74,
        80, 81
    coordinated, 63
schemes of work, 127
school environment, xi, 108
schools
    organization of, 36
    junior school, 14
    junior mixed school, 13

junior mixed and infants school (JMI),
    13, 14
infant school, 13
    climate, 15
    learning, 82
    visits, 131
Schools Council, 27
    Curriculum Bulletin, 1, 10
    Religious Education in Primary Schools
        Project, xii
    Study (1980), 100
    Working Paper, 75, xi
Science in the primary school, 218–231
    monitoring progress, 219
    finding out what children are doing, 219–
        220
    recording, 220
    evaluation, 220
    what are we looking for ?, 221
    guidelines, 221–222
    attitudes and skills, 222
    general and specific skills, 222–223
    concepts, 224
    topic or specific content?, 225–226
    recording areas of work, 226–228
    idea of matching, 228
    recording children's development, 228–
        230
science, ix, 181
    children's progress in, xii
scientific concepts, xii
Seaborlam, 92
seating arrangements, 126
self
    concept of, 52
    self-identity, 26
    awareness, 88
    management of learning, 158
sensory motor period, 61
sex difference, 49
sex role differentiation, 46
    epigenetic view, 50
sex role standards, 46, 47
sex roles, x, 46, 48, 49, 52
sex stereotypes, x, 46, 48
sexual differentiation of labour, 49
sexual maturity, 41, 45
Silberman, C., 6, 7
Simon, B., x, 22
Skilbeck, M., 145–146
skills, 5
    of listening, 177

literacy, 5
    numeracy, 5
    of observation, 177
    of touching, 177
social behaviour, 40
social democracy, viii, 40
social/communicative preferences, 52
social and environmental studies, ix
Social Science Research Council (SSRC),
    27
socially and culturally deprived, 39
socialization, 53
socialization pressures, 48
Sockett, H., 144
spatial superiority of males, 49
sperm, 33
spelling tests, 130
'split day pattern', 99
spoken drama, 130
stage
    concept of, 76
    theory, 77
Stenhouse, L., 144
stereotypes, x, 26, 46
stimulating learning by discovery, 165
stimulus, 39
streaming
    abolition of, 9
    non-streaming, 14
    parents' views, 16
    patterns of, 14, 17
strengths of open plan schools, 105
    for teachers, 105
    for pupils, 105
    for parents, 105–106
Sylva, K. and Lunt, I., xi
symbolic system, 84

Tannu, J.M., 45
task allocation, 136
task design problems, 137
    processes, 136
tasks
    revision, 136–139
teacher
    attitudes in streamed and non-streamed
        schools, 15
    autonomy, 92
    expectations, xii
    expectations for children of Caribbean
        origin, 27

teachers, 9
  assumptions about children's
    capabilities, 184
  attitudes, 20
  opinions about education, 19
  priorities, 128
  task intentions, 138
teaching
  children to learn mathematics, 179
  children to read, 179
  children to write, 179
  choice of method and type of class, 122
  english, 122
  english to immigrants, 24
  method, 119, 120, 121
  mathematics, 122
  of reading, 179
  resources for, 27
  revolution, 97
  basic skills, xii
  team, 96
  using different methods, 120
teaching-learning process, 4, 13
  individualization of, 4
teaching methods, viii, 14, 19
  formal and informal, 2, 5, 7, 19

Teaching Styles and Pupil Progress (1976),
    19, 21
teaching styles, 2, 15, 17, 19
  mixed, 19
tests of mathematics, x
  reading, 22
third world, 22
'three Rs', 100
topic work, 20, 130
traditional methods, 15
training
  in-service, 27
Tyler, R., 143
Tyndale affair, 2, 5, 20

verbal proficiency of females, 52
vertical grouping, 95, 97
village school organization, 93
Vigotsky, L.S., 87

Warnock, M., 293
West Riding, 8

zygote, 33, 34